BUSINESS ASSOCIATIONS

IN A NUTSHELL

Second Edition

By

JOSEPH SHADE
Professor of Law
Texas Wesleyan University—School of Law
Fort Worth, Texas

THOMSON

™

WEST

Mat #40394214

© West, a Thomson business, 2003
© 2006 Thomson/West
   610 Opperman Drive
   P.O. Box 64526
   St. Paul, MN 55164–0526
   1–800–328–9352

Printed in the United States of America

ISBN–13: 978–0–314–16280–9
ISBN–10: 0–314–16280–1

 TEXT IS PRINTED ON 10% POST CONSUMER RECYCLED PAPER

In Memory of
my Mother and Father
Louis and Ethel Shade

*

PREFACE

This book was written for law students taking the first business course offered in law school. Different law schools have different names for the course—"business associations," "business enterprises," "business organizations," "business structures" or "corporations." I use these terms synonymously and sometimes refer to the course as the "basic business course."

The differences in the business background and motivation of the students who take the course are even more diverse than the names given to the course. For some, who aspire to become "corporate lawyers," it is an introductory course which lays the foundation for advanced courses in securities regulation, corporate finance, mergers and acquisitions, etc. For others, who aspire merely to fulfill their law school's required curriculum and pass the bar, it is the first and last business course they will take. Regardless of your reason, I am glad you are taking the course and reading my book.

My goal was to give students taking the basic business course a reliable overview of the major themes and leading cases in the course, arranged in a logical and understandable way, which covers all of the main types of business associations in current use, not just corporations.

I tried to make the book succinct, and to emphasize explanation of basic concepts. When I felt it helped explain concepts or issues I included some business and historical background.

Putting out a Second Edition gave me a chance to correct mistakes, add new material and improve the way in which the material was presented.

I want to thank the Texas Wesleyan Law School for giving me a grant to support the writing of the Second Edition. I also want to thank Valerie Anderko, student assistant, and Anna Teller, research librarian, both at the Texas Wesleyan School of Law as well as Louis Higgins, Roxanne Birkel and the other good people at Thomson–West, who worked on this project, for their valuable help in turning my manuscript into a book. Last, but not least, I want to thank Professor David G. Epstein, my co-author of the First Edition. But for Professor Epstein's help, encouragement and support neither the First nor the Second Edition of this book would have ever seen the light of day.

Joseph Shade

Dallas, Texas
November, 2005

OUTLINE

OUTLINE

TABLE OF CASES

References are to Pages

NOTE REGARDING
STATUTORY CITATIONS

The law of business associations is primarily statutory nonuniform state law. The statutes governing business associations are not identical but are similar (except in the case of LLCs and LLPs, where the uniform acts are not cited). Most state partnership statutes are modeled on either the Uniform Partnership Act or the Revised Uniform Partnership Act. And most state corporation statutes are modeled on the Model Business Corporation Act or on the Delaware General Corporate Law. This book includes statutory references to the various Uniform and Model Acts as well as the Delaware and Federal statutes listed below.

To save space, I have abbreviated the statutory references as indicated below. I often abbreviate references to sections of the various statutes by referring to the section by number (*e.g.*, Del. § 141). Likewise I abbreviate references to rules under the statutes by giving the rule number (*e.g.*, Rule 10b–5).

Uniform and Model Acts

UPA—Uniform Partnership Act (1914), as amended

RUPA—Revised Uniform Partnership Act (1994), as amended

ULPA—Uniform Limited Partnership Act of 1976, as amended

MBCA—Model Business Corporation Act (1984), as amended

Delaware Statutes

Del.—Delaware General Corporation Law, as amended

Del. LLCA—Delaware Limited Liability Company Act, as amended

Federal Statutes

IRC   Internal Revenue Code, as amended

33 Act—Securities Act of 1933, as amended

34 Act—Securities Exchange Act of 1934, as amended

BUSINESS ASSOCIATIONS

IN A NUTSHELL

Second Edition

*

CHAPTER I

WHAT DOES THE BASIC COURSE IN BUSINESS ASSOCIATIONS (AND THIS BOOK) COVER?

What is a business association?

A business association is a device through which individuals or entities conduct business.

If two students set up a stand in the parking lot from which they sell lemonade and agree to split the profits that is a business association.

Most, if not all, of you have probably heard of Enron. You probably think of Enron as a single "evil empire." In reality, Enron was a large number of related different business entities: (1) corporations, (2) partnerships, (3) limited partnerships and (4) limited liability companies. At its peak there were over 3,000 business entities in the Enron family of companies.

The point is the term "business associations" is extremely broad. It encompasses, at one end of the spectrum the lemonade stand and at the other end complex business associations such as Enron. And there is a vast array of business associations in between these two extremes. Like the subject matter it covers, the course in business associations is quite broad.

Different schools use different names for the first course in the law school curriculum that deals with business—*e.g.* business associations, business organizations, business enterprises, business structures or corporations. In this book, we treat all of these as synonymous terms and sometimes refer to the course as "the basic business course." Many students have different names—very different names—for the course.

Whatever your law school or you call the course, you are going to learn about different business associations. Among other things, you are going to learn about what is common to all business associations and what distinguishes one form of business association from another.

What is the course in business associations about?

Although the course is broad based, it is important to realize at the outset that business associations is, at the most basic level, about the same thing that most law school courses are about. It is about **relationships.**

Just as contracts is about relationships among parties to a voluntary agreement, constitutional law is about relationships between the government and individuals, family law is about relationships among members of the family, etc. **business associations is about relationships within the business association**. There are, as you will learn early in the course, various different types of business associations—including general and limited partnerships, corporations and limited liability companies ("LLCs"). **Specific legal rules govern the relationships within the various forms of business associations. This course is about those rules.**

Since the course mainly explores internal relationships within business associations, it is important at the outset to identify the real people involved in the business association. The law views most business associations as persons in the sense that the business association is a separate entity with legal rights and obligations separate and distinct from the owners and/or managers of the business (the real people involved with the business association). But, obviously, the business association can only operate through real people.

Who are the real people involved with the business association?

The main categories of people involved in any business association are:

- **Owners/Investors**—the people who provide the capital and own the business.

- **Managers**—the people who manage the business.

- **Employees**—the people who carry out the tasks necessary to operate the business, from sweeping the floor to serving as chief executive officer. Some employees, usually called "executive employees," manage the business. All employees acting within the scope of their authority are agents of the business association and thus may bind the business association to vicarious liability for their contracts or torts. Employees also owe fiduciary duties to the business association.

In corporations we call the owners SHAREHOLDERS and the managers OFFICERS and DIRECTORS. In a general partnership both the owners and the managers are called PARTNERS. In a limited partnership the owners are the GENERAL and LIMITED PARTNERS, but only the GENERAL PARTNERS are entitled to manage the business. In an LLC the owners are called MEMBERS. The members may manage the business or elect MANAGERS to perform that function.

In many large businesses these categories of persons may be clearly identified. Usually in smaller businesses, the functions overlap. The same human being can be both a shareholder, an officer and a director. Even in a larger business the same person may act in more than one capacity.

Any person who is not an OWNER, MANAGER or EMPLOYEE in the eyes of the law of business associations is simply a THIRD PARTY. Third parties include customers, suppliers, persons injured by the business, persons to whom the business owes money, attorneys, accountants, etc. The law of business associations mainly concerns relationships among the persons involved in the business association with each other and with the business association itself. Relationships between the business association and third parties are mainly governed by other areas of the law—contracts, property, torts, etc.

How is this book organized?

This book is organized along the lines of the life cycle of a business—*i.e.* selecting the best form of business structure for the business, forming the business entity, governing, operating and financing the business, getting money out of the business and ending the business association. Numerous legal issues arise along the way, which this book explores in the context of the various types of business associations.

A. WHAT IS COMMON TO ALL BUSINESS ASSOCIATIONS?

1. BUSINESS ASSOCIATIONS AND SEPARATE "LEGAL" PERSONS

A "business association" is not a real person, not a flesh and blood human being. Bill Gates is not a "business association." Rather, a business association is a device through which real people like Bill Gates conduct business. The entity through which Bill Gates carries on business is called Microsoft.

While a business association is not a flesh and blood human being, legislatures and courts treat business associations as real persons or "entities" for most purposes. For example, Microsoft can own property, make contracts, sue and be sued in its own name wholly separate and apart from Bill Gates and the other owners of Microsoft.

2. BUSINESS ASSOCIATIONS AND STATE AND FEDERAL STATUTES

Most business associations are "creatures" of statute—**state statutes**. Unlike the case in subjects such as property and torts, the subject of business associations is largely governed by statute. And the different types of business associations are governed by different statutes. Each state has statutes governing each of the types of business associations covered in this book: corporations, general partnerships, limited partnerships, limited liability partnerships and limited liability companies.

There are also federal statutes that effect business associations. The federal securities laws and federal tax

laws are the two most obvious examples of federal statutes that have a significant impact on business associations.

The federal tax laws, among other things, significantly
impact both the choice of the appropriate form of business association for a particular business, as discussed in
Chapter II, *infra,* and how much of the money made by
the business the real people who own the business get to
keep, as discussed in Chapter IX, *infra.*

The impact of the federal securities laws on business
associations are many and varied. The most significant
impact of these laws is in the areas of capital raising (see
Chapter VIII), governance of publicly held companies
(see Chapter V), and potential federal remedies for
wrongs in the nature of fraud (see Chapter VII).

However, federal statutes do not govern the creation,
or regulate the internal operation of business associations. This has been left to the states. While similar, the
governing statutes vary from state to state.

As stated earlier, in the main, the corporate, partnership and LLC structures statutes deal with (1) the relationships among the real people who are a part of the
business structure and (2) the relationship between these
real people and the business structure itself. For example, you would look to the relevant state corporate statute to resolve a dispute among Microsoft stockholders as
to who should be on the Microsoft Corporation's board of
directors or a dispute over whether Microsoft should pay
a dividend to its shareholders.

For these Microsoft disputes, you would look to the
State of Washington's corporate code. Bill Gates, and the

other "real people" who formed Microsoft, chose the corporate form of business association and chose to form the corporation in Washington.

The real people who create a business association have a choice not only as to the form of business association but also as to the state in which they form the business association. And, the business association laws of that state then control the disputes among the real people involved in the business and disputes between those people and the business association. Your professor may refer to this important concept as the **"internal affairs doctrine."**

Almost all large businesses are structured as corporations. A majority of them are Delaware corporations. Thus, many of the cases that you study in your basic business course involve Delaware corporations.

Under the internal affairs doctrine, lawyers or law students working on a dispute among the real people involved in a business structured as a Delaware corporation or a dispute between those people and the corporation will look to Delaware corporate law even though the business and all of the real people are in states other than Delaware. Accordingly, this book will explain provisions in the Delaware corporate code.

While no other state has a corporate code exactly like Delaware's, a number of states have borrowed heavily from Delaware. Even more states have adopted statutes modeled on the Model Business Corporations Act ("MBCA"). Accordingly, this book will also explain certain provisions of the MBCA.

If, instead of being a corporation, Microsoft had been formed as a partnership, then the relevant state partnership statute will be based on either the Uniform Partnership Act ("UPA"), a 1914 statute, or the Revised Uniform Partnership Act ("RUPA"). Since almost half the states still have UPA-based statutes, this book covers both. Similarly, there is both a Uniform Limited Partnership Act ("ULPA") and a Revised Uniform Limited Partnership Act ("RULPA"), and a significant number of state statutes based on each.

The limited liability company ("LLC") and the limited liability partnership ("LLP") are comparatively new forms of business associations. All states have statutes governing limited liability companies and limited liability partnerships, but these statutes vary widely.

3.　BUSINESS ASSOCIATIONS AND OTHER LAWS

Obviously, the law of business associations also involves case law. If you read the assigned cases, you will find not only cases that interpret the applicable state corporate, partnership or LLC statute, but also cases that establish concepts and rules independent of any statute. For example, cases such as *Meinhard v. Salmon* (N.Y. 1928) which describes the fiduciary duty owed by one partner to another as follows: "Not honesty alone but the punctilio of honor . . . is the standard of behavior."

Less obvious, but equally important, the law of business associations also involves contract law. The basic concept of having the power to enter into voluntary agreements and having a legal remedy if those agreements are breached is a fundamental principle of business associations. In significant part, state business structures statutes establish "default rules"—rules that govern only if there is no contrary provision in any agreements of the business association. Another way of saying the same thing is to say that the real people who own and/or manage the business association can contract around most of the default rules in the state business association statutes. For example, a provision in the relevant Partnership Agreement that says partner A shall be paid a salary of $100,000 per year for acting as managing partner of the ABC Partnership, Ltd. will prevail over a provision in the governing partnership statute which says a partner is not entitled to compensation for services performed for the partnership.

Some of the basic agreements you will likely encounter in business associations include: Partnership Agreements in the case of partnerships, Articles of Incorporation and By-laws in the case of corporations, and Operating Agreements in the case of LLCs.

4. BUSINESS ASSOCIATIONS AND MONEY

Most people start businesses to make money—both for the business and for the real people, who own the business. Thus, many of the issues that you will encounter in your basic business course will be about money.

There are issues about how to raise money for the business association so that it can operate and grow:

- Should an "interest in" or "share of" the business be sold to investor(s)?

- Should the business borrow?

- Should the business retain and use its earnings?

And, you will see issues about how to get money into the hands of the real people who own the business:

- Should the business pay salaries to its owners who work for the business? To owners who do not work for the business?

- Should the business distribute the money it has earned to its owners?

- Should the owners of the business sell all or part of their ownership interest? Should they go public?

You will also encounter issues about how the tax laws, and the form of business association chosen, impact how much money the business and the owners of the business make and get to keep.

And, of course, you will see issues about who gets to decide the many questions dealing with money.

5.   BUSINESS ASSOCIATIONS AND ACCOUNTING

Because many issues in business associations involve money, you need to know (1) what money a business association has and (2) whether it is making money. This means that you need to know "something" about accounting and financial statements.

We knew that even before Enron. Now, however, after the accounting fiascos at Enron, WorldCom, Tyco, HealthSouth, etc., your professor is even more likely to expect you to know something about accounting and financial statements.

Accounting is the process of recording, classifying, and communicating financial information. Just as lawyers have cases and statutes (and nutshells) to look to, accountants have GAAP—Generally Accepted Accounting Principles. Financial statements are prepared according to GAAP. Under GAAP, just as under the law of business associations, a business association is treated as an entity.

You do not have to have a deep understanding of accounting to pass the basic course in business associations but an understanding of certain basic accounting concepts is essential. Your professor is highly likely to talk about the two most basic financial statements of a business: (a) the **balance sheet** and (b) the **income statement**. Furthermore, the common language of business includes accounting terminology, and some of the cases you will read in the basic business course assume a certain level of understanding of accounting concepts.

The purpose of a balance sheet is to provide information about what a business entity owns and what it owes as of a particular date. Kind of like a photograph. In contrast, an income statement is more like a video. Its purpose is to provide information about a business' revenues and expenses over a particular period of time.

a. Balance Sheet

A balance sheet is called a balance sheet because it is typically one sheet of paper that has a column of numbers on the left hand side of the page and another column of numbers on the right hand side of the page and the total of the numbers on the left hand side and the total of the numbers on the right hand side are the same. They "balance."

The numbers on the left hand side are the values of the stuff that the business owns, its "assets." You don't have to be an accountant for Enron to see opportunities to be "creative" in determining what assets belong to a particular business association and even more opportunities to be creative in determining what values to assign to such assets.

The top numbers on the right hand side are the amounts that the business owes, its liabilities. Less "wiggle room" in determining the appropriate numbers for liabilities, but nevertheless some. For example, by "creative accounting," Enron passed off substantial liabilities to certain so called "special purpose entities." This have the effect of substantially understating Enron's liabilities.

There is no reason for the total number assigned as the value of the company's assets to turn out to be the same as the total number for liabilities. And, usually it isn't. Usually, it is necessary to plug in another number in order for the left and right hand sides of the "balance sheet" to balance.

That "plug number," the difference between the assets and liabilities, is called the owner's "equity." This is analogous to owning a home. The fair market value of the house less the amount owed on the mortgage is the owners equity.

This concept needs to be understood. So, at the risk of sounding a little patronizing I will say it again, in a slightly different way. The assets are the value of what the business owns, and the liabilities are the creditors' claims on that value. If the asset value exceeds the liabilities, then the excess consists of assets the owners have a claim on. We add that number on the right hand side of the balance sheet, as "owners' equity" or "capital," so that the balance sheet balances.

Even if the liabilities are greater than the value of the assets, we still need to add the number reflecting the difference to the right hand side of the balance sheet. However, in that case it is a negative number. The owners have a negative equity—the business owes more than the value of its assets.

The balance sheet reflects the basic accounting formula: **Assets = Liabilities + Equity**. You can turn that formula around to compute the owners' equity on any balance sheet date—Assets − Liabilities = Equity.

You do not have to be a "financial maven" to understand the basic accounting formula or enough about accounting to survive in the basic business course. Once you learn the basics and a little terminology it mostly boils down to common sense.

Two of the three main sections of the balance sheet, assets and liabilities, are basically the same regardless of the form of business association. However, the equity section varies depending on the type of business association.

In a partnership (or other unincorporated business entity) separate equity accounts, which are discussed later, are maintained for each partner.[1]

1. Equity may appear as a single line on the balance sheet, but, at least internally, separate equity (or capital) accounts are maintained for each partner.

Corporations do not maintain a separate equity account for each investor. However the equity section of a corporation's balance sheet usually consists of three separate accounts, which unfortunately sometimes go by different names but have the same meaning: (1) capital stock, common stock or stated capital, (2) paid-in capital or capital surplus and (3) retained earnings or earned surplus.[2]

b. Income Statement

Like a balance sheet, an income statement can be reduced to a formula: **revenue − expenses = income (or loss)**. Revenue is the money received by the business from the sale of its goods or services. Expenses are the costs incurred by the business in generating revenues Unlike a balance sheet, an income statement covers a period of time, not a specific moment in time.

The period of time covered by an income statement is called an accounting period. An accounting period can be any period of time, but one year is the most frequently used accounting period. The excess of revenues over expenses for the accounting period is profit. If expenses exceed revenues, the business has incurred a loss for the accounting period.

There is discretion as to what revenues and, especially, what expenses to assign to a particular accounting period. A business that wants to show potential investors or

2. (1) and (2) reflect the amount the corporation receives when it sells its stock to investors. The allocation of the proceeds from the sale of stock between these two accounts involves a concept called "par value" (which is discussed later). (3) reflects the cumulative earnings of the corporation from the sale of its products or services, less the amount paid as "dividends" (also discussed later).

potential lenders a strong income statement might be creative in attributing revenues to a particular accounting period or in not attributing expenses to that accounting period. For example, creative accountants for World-Com were able to "reclassify" millions of dollars of WorldCom's expenses and thereby meet analysts earnings expectations. Those accountants, along with their former boss, the former CEO of WorldCom, have been criminally convicted of securities fraud.

c. Examples of Income Statement and Balance Sheet

To illustrate the concepts discussed above I have constructed a hypothetical income statement and balance sheet for a small start-up restaurant (the same taco stand described in § II.D.1, *infra*). The financial statements assume that the company receives $100,000 as consideration for 1,000 shares of common stock it issues to its three founders, that it enters into certain transactions and that during its first year of operation the company has sales of $285,000 and net income of $50,000. Based on these assumptions I have, on the two pages that follow, set up a hypothetical income statement and balance sheet.

DAVE'S TACOS, INC.

Income Statement

Year ended December 31, 2004

Net sales	$285,000
Cost of goods sold and operating expenses	
Cost of goods sold	90,000
Rent	60,000
Depreciation	10,000
Selling and administrative expenses	55,000
	$220,000
Operating income	$ 65,000
Interest on long-term note	5,000
Income before income taxes	$ 60,000
Income taxes	10,000
Net income	$ 50,000

DAVE'S TACOS, INC.
Balance Sheet
December 31, 2004

ASSETS		LIABILITIES	
Current Assets		Current Liabilities	
Cash	$102,000	Accounts payable	$ 10,000
Accounts Receivable	20,000	Notes payable	10,000
Supplies	15,000	(current portion of long-term debt)	
Total current assets	$137,000	Income taxes payable	5,000
Fixed assets		Total current liabilities	$ 25,000
Leasehold			
Improvements	$ 30,000	Long Term Liabilities	
Equipment	60,000	5–year note payable	$ 40,000
	$ 90,000		
Less: Accumulated		Total liabilities	$ 65,000
depreciation	12,000		
		SHAREHOLDERS' EQUITY	
Net fixed assets	$ 78,000	Common stock	
		($1.00 par value)	$1,000
		Paid-in capital in excess	
		of par value	99,000
		Retained earnings	50,000
		Total	
		Shareholders' Equity	$150,000
		Total Liabilities &	
Total Assets	$215,000	Shareholders' Equity	$215,000

d. The Sarbanes–Oxley Act

In response to the accounting and management frauds uncovered at Enron, WorldCom and other companies, in July 2002 Congress passed an Act popularly known as the Sarbanes-Oxley Act. Sarbanes–Oxley deals with a number of accounting and corporate governance issues and the details of this Act are outside the scope of this book. However, your professor may discuss this recent statute and you should know that, relative to heightened regulation of accountants, Sarbanes–Oxley does the following:

(1) Creates a self-regulatory body called the Public Company Accounting Oversight Board to regulate the accounting profession, establish more uniform auditing standards and impose discipline on publicly held companies.

(2) Mandates that publicly held companies have audit committees, composed exclusively of outside directors, and strengthens the powers of such committees.

(3) Requires that the chief executive officer and chief financial officer of publicly held companies certify their company's financial statements under penalty of criminal sanctions.

In addition, Sarbanes–Oxley contains a hodgepodge of other provisions aimed at strengthening accounting practices, governance and internal controls of publicly held companies.

6. BUSINESS ASSOCIATIONS AND THE LAW OF AGENCY

While a business association is a "person" in the eyes of the law, no business association can function without real people. A business association needs real people to provide capital so that the business can operate and grow. The capital providers are the owners of the business—called shareholders in a corporation, partners in a partnership, and members in an LLC.

And, a business association needs real people to make decisions for for the business. A cute little girl with pigtails named Wendy does not make decisions for Wendy's International, Inc., nor does a clown named Ronald make decisions for McDonald's Corporation. It is the managers of those companies, who make the business decisions.

A substantial part of your course in business associations will deal with which real people make what decisions for the various types of business associations and how the various categories of decision-makers interact with each other and with the owners of the business. We will deal with those issues later.

For now, we simply need to understand the legal basis for imposing liability on one legal person, a business association, for the acts of other legal persons, the flesh and blood people involved with the business association. In the main, this occurs under **agency principles**.

Agency law dates back centuries to common law England. Thirty or forty years ago (when many of your professors were in law school) a course in agency was part of the first year curriculum in most law schools. But these courses have now mostly disappeared and some students are first exposed to agency principles in business associations.

Agency concepts are important in business associations for a very simple reason—most of the work in this world is performed by agents. Virtually all businesses employ agents to do all or a part of their work. The nature of the agency relationship varies with the type of business association. For example, the UPA provides that, unless otherwise provided, every partner is an agent of the partnership with authority to bind the partnership in transactions with third parties. And corporations, being intangible legal entities, can only function through the efforts of agents.

Today when courts (and law professors) discuss agency law, they typically look to the *Restatement of Agency*. Section 1 of the *Restatement of Agency* provides:

(1) Agency is a **fiduciary** relation which results from the manifestation of **consent** by one person to another that the other shall act on his **behalf** and subject to his **control**, and consent by the other to so act.

(2) The one for whom action is to be taken is the **principal**.

(3) The one who is to act is the **agent**.

In other words, the business entity is the "principal" and the real people acting on its behalf are the "agents."

Many other *Restatement* sections follow that first section of the *Restatement of Agency*. Generally, these provisions incorporate two basic aspects of agency law that often come into play in business associations. First, is the authority issue. Agents are authorized to conduct business for the principal and enter into contracts that bind the principal. Second, is the fiduciary duty issue. Detailed consideration of this issue is deferred until later, but generally the agent has a fiduciary responsibility to the principal, the exact scope of which varies depending upon the type of business association and other factors.

In your business associations course, you will deal primarily with the principal's contract liability. Under agency principles, a business association is liable under a contract made by a real person only if the real person had "authority" to make the contract. **Authority can be either express or apparent.**

The existence of "express authority" (called simply "authority" by the *Restatement of Agency* § 26) depends on statements from the principal to the agent. A common example of such a statement is a provision in the partnership agreement that "The Managing Partner shall have the authority to enter into contracts binding the partnership to pay up to $5,000, without obtaining the approval of the other partners."

Under *Restatement of Agency* § 27, the existence of apparent authority depends on manifestations from the principal to third parties. Assume, for example, that the partnership has regularly paid *T* under contracts for more than $10,000 even though the managing partner did not obtain the approval of the other partners. *T* enters into a new $10,000 contract with the managing partner to supply products to the partnership. The partnership has contract liability. Even though the managing partner did not have actual authority, she had apparent authority and so the partnership would be liable on the contract. Note the focus is on the principal. Apparent authority depends on the manifestations of the principal to the third party, not the agent's manifestations to the principal. We can not create apparent authority to contract for Microsoft Corporation by claiming we have that authority.

B. HOW DO THE DIFFERENT BUSINESS ASSOCIATIONS DIFFER?

The real people who form business associations have choices as to the form of business association they may use. And there are both business and legal differences among the available types of business associations.

1.   THE FIVE MAIN DIFFERENCES

The five main legal differences, all of which will be discussed later, among the various business associations are **(1) tax treatment, (2) owners' liability exposure, (3)** management **(or governance) of the business, (4)** opportunities **to raise funds for the business and (5) exit strategies**—opportunities for investors/owners to sell their ownership interests.

2.   THE DISTINCTION BETWEEN CLOSELY HELD AND PUBLICLY HELD BUSINESSES

In your basic business course (and in the next nine chapters of this book), you will see legal differences not only among the various forms of business associations but within the business associations which depend on whether the business is "closely held" or "publicly held."

As discussed in Chapter II, a closely held business may be any of the business associations covered in this book— *i.e.,* general partnership, limited partnership, limited liability partnership, corporation (either an S corporation or a C corporation) or limited liability company. Almost all publicly held businesses are C corporations.

What distinguishes a "closely held" business from a "publicly held" business?

A **closely held business** usually has the following characteristics: (1) Few owners, most of whom are usually (2) active in the business and often depend on the business for their livelihood (through salaries and to a lesser extent, (dividends)). They are more than capital providers. They are the managers of the business. The owners typically (3) operate the business informally. They tend to cut corners in the formal requirements of governance imposed by the statutes. Shareholders and directors meetings are typically held infrequently, if at all, and notice and quorum requirements are often ignored. The most significant distinction between closely held and publicly held businesses is that there is (4) **no market for the ownership interests** (*e.g.,* shares) of a closely held business. If an owner of a closely held business becomes disenchanted with the way the business is being run or its future prospects, she rarely has the option of selling her interest, unless she acquired such option by a contract such as a buy-sell agreement.

The characteristics of a **publicly held business** are just the opposite. There are many shareholders and the managers of publicly held businesses typically pay attention to corporate formalities. Most are required to do so under the SEC's proxy rules. If a shareholder doesn't like the way things are run, she takes the "Wall Street option" and sells her shares. By law, other than electing directors, shareholders have no power to take an active role in managing the company. As a practical matter, the only important decision a shareholder of a publicly held company has to make is whether to sell her shares.

We will explore the similarities and differences of the various business associations as well as a number of the legal issues that arise during the life cycle of a business (and in the basic business associations course) in the nine chapters that follow.

CHAPTER II

HOW DO YOU SELECT THE BEST BUSINESS ASSOCIATION FOR A PARTICULAR BUSINESS?

Historically, selecting the best form of a business association for a particular business mainly involved consideration of relatively clear-cut issues related to providing **limited liability** for the owners of the business and **avoiding double taxation.** As late as the early 1990s, only three types of business associations were widely used by businesses with more than one owner—the general partnership, the limited partnership and the corporation. The tax rules as well as the rules pertaining to the owners' personal liability for obligations of the business were relatively well-defined.

Today, limited liability is readily available not only to the owners of corporations but also to the owners of many unincorporated business associations such as LLCs and LLPs. In addition, under the "check the box" regulations adopted by the Internal Revenue Service in 1997, the selection of a tax regime for a closely held business is now a matter of elective choice. Thus, the process of choosing the most appropriate form of business association is now more complex.

What choices are available today?

- Partnership
  - General Partnership (GP)
  - Limited Partnership (LP)
  - Limited Liability Partnership (LLP)
- Corporation
  - C Corporation
  - S Corporation
- Limited Liability Company (LLC)

Today, the process of selecting the most appropriate business association for a given business involves analyzing a variety of (1) factual considerations, (2) legal questions and (3) basic attributes of the business associations.

A. FACTUAL CONSIDERATIONS

Obviously, the decision as to what business association to use for a particular enterprise will be driven by the facts surrounding the particular deal. Facts can be infinite, they appear in various combinations and all won't be present or relevant in every situation. Some of the facts which may influence the choice of a business association are as follows:

Nature of business. What is the nature of the proposed business? Is it a business that is capital intensive, labor intensive, etc.?

Name. What will be the name of the business? Does the name have any special importance to the proposed business?

Participants. Is there **unanimity of interest** among the participants as in the case of a "family" corporation?

Or are their **interests diverse** as in the case of a money/talent deal? What will be the functions of the various participants? Who will contribute what to the deal—*i.e.,* money, service, property, patent rights, etc.? Do any of the participants have substantial outside income or a substantial net worth?

Management. Who will manage the business? Who will actively participate? Will some owners be mere passive investors? What salaries are to be paid to any of the participants? What person or group will manage the business?

Funding. How much money will be needed to get the business started? What are the sources of funding? How much money will the business make during its first years of operation? How long will it take for the business to begin showing a profit?

Dividing the attributes of ownership. How will the profits be divided among the participants? If the business fails, how will the assets of the business be divided among the participants in the event of liquidation?

Exit strategy. How do the participants expect to make money from the business—through salaries, distributions, sale of all or part of their interest in the business? Is a buy/sell agreement necessary? Are there plans to go public sometime in the future?

Much of the above and similar data is often incorporated into a business plan, which often incorporates legal considerations. The above will serve as a partial checklist of factual data on which to focus in choice of entity situations.

B. LEGAL CONSIDERATIONS

Central Questions. The three central legal questions considered in selecting a business association for any business enterprise are:

1. Will the participants be personally liable to third parties for the debts of the business?

2. How much will the government take in the form of taxes?

3. What are the rules for internal governance of the various business associations?

Additional Questions. Two additional questions are often factored into the selection process, and may impact the choice:

1. What are the rules for dividing the attributes of ownership—*i.e.,* profits and assets—among the owners?

2. What are the exit rules?

The above questions translate into what, today, are generally considered the five main legal considerations that govern the choice of a business association. These considerations are the foundation for much of what the basic business course is about.

- **Limited Liability**

- **Tax Considerations**

- **Management**

- **Capitalization and Financing**

- **Exit Rules**

Limited Liability means that the owners of the business structure are not personally liable for the debts or obligations of the business structure. The business association, as a separate legal person, is liable for its debts. The real people who own the business may lose their entire investment in the business if the business fails. But, if the assets of the business association are not sufficient to satisfy the business associations's obligations, creditors of the business association cannot reach the personal assets of the owners, such as their homes, cars or personal bank accounts.

Tax Considerations basically involve contrasting so-called "**double taxation**" with so-called "**pass-through taxation**." **Double taxation** means that the business association itself pays taxes on the income it earns and the owners of the business pay taxes on the income they receive as dividends. This tax regime is imposed on most corporations under Subchapter C of the Internal Revenue Code ("IRC"). Under **pass-through taxation** no tax is payable at the business structure level, but only at the personal level on the individual owners' share of income. This tax regime is available to closely held businesses organized as partnerships, LLCs or S corporations, under Subchapters K and S of the IRC.

Management considerations basically mean who decides what as to how the business operates. This is often called "governance." It often involves contrasting centralized management or management by representatives with direct management where each owner participates in management. The basic concept can best be understood by contrasting the management structure of a corporation with that of a general partnership.

In a corporation the owners (*i.e.* shareholders) elect a board of directors. The board sets policy, appoints officers to manage the day-to-day affairs of the business and oversees the officers. Except for electing directors, the shareholders have no authority to manage the business. In contrast, in a general partnership all of the owners have the right to participate directly in the management of the business, absent an agreement that delegates the management function to one or more of the partners.

Capitalization and Financing relate to the process of (1) establishing a financial framework (called a "capital structure") and (2) raising money (called "financing") for the business. Usually corporations provide greater flexibility of capital structure because in a corporation the different aspects of ownership can be divided up among owners, managers, employees and investors in a variety of ways designed to meet the preferences of the marketplace and the desires of the real people involved in the business association. By contrast, in partnerships or LLCs, the owners are more limited in the way they can divide up these attributes of ownership. Whether or not capital structure becomes a consideration usually depends on how the business is financed. In general, corporations offer obvious advantages over the other forms of business associations in this area.

Exit Rules generally refer to the owner's freedom to transfer interests in the business, the duration of the existence of the business association (*i.e.* at will, for a term or perpetual) and the means by which the owners expect to get their money out of the business (*i.e.*, sale, dissolution or dissociation). The owners' practical ability to exit (*i.e.* find a buyer) is a separate but related issue.

All of these matters discussed above will be dealt with in greater depth later in the book.

C. TYPES OF BUSINESS ASSOCIATIONS AND MAJOR ATTRIBUTES OF EACH

The main types of business associations available today and the only business associations covered in this book are:

1. **General Partnerships**

2. **Limited Partnerships**

3. **Limited Liability Partnerships**

4. **Corporations**

5. **Limited Liability Companies**

The main attributes of each of these business associations are discussed below.

1. GENERAL PARTNERSHIP

A General Partnership ("GP") is defined as an association of two or more persons to carry on as co-owners a business for profit.

Each partner has unlimited joint and several personal liability for the debts and obligations of the business— *i.e.,* **unlimited liability**. Legal claimants can pursue all of the assets of partners, not merely the assets used in the business. The partnership files a tax return but it is only an information return. No tax is payable at the partnership level. Taxes are paid only at the personal level on the individual partners' share of partnership's income—*i.e.,* **pass-through taxation**. In the absence of an agreement to the contrary, all of the partners have the right to participate in the management of the business. The partners may agree among themselves to delegate management authority to one or more managing partners. Such delegation is not binding on third parties unaware of the delegation. In essence, as between the partners, the partnership agreement governs, but as to third parties, agency rules generally govern. In addition, all partners have broad-based fiduciary duties to one another.

While general partnerships are today governed by statute, they were originally creatures of common law. At common law, "partnership" was a label for the relationship between the participants when two or more individuals agreed to operate a business for profit as co-owners. By definition, they legally became partners, whether they realized it or not, and certain legal consequences followed. When you realize that the common law courts conceived of partnerships simply as a group of individuals, the rules that govern the relationship, including the important principles of unlimited personal liability, mutual right of management and pass-through taxation, logically follow. This is sometimes referred to in the legal literature and cases as the **aggregate theory**, to conceptually distinguish the theory governing general partnerships from the **entity theory**, which is the concept of governance central to the corporation. Today, general partnerships are considered aggregates for some purposes such as tax and unlimited liability, but entities for other purposes such as owning property and bringing legal actions.

While partnership law does not require that there be a written partnership agreement, partnership agreements are very important. A partnership agreement is a contract and it is enforceable like any other contract. Basically the partnership statutes provide "default rules." The partnership agreement can change many of the default rules in the law such as the rules as to how profits and losses are divided, how the partnership is managed, etc.; however, the partnership agreement cannot change certain basic attributes of a partnership such as unlimited liability and fiduciary duties. In other words, in an artfully drafted partnership agreement the parties can tailor their deal and their relationship to fit their needs and desires up to a point.

2.   LIMITED PARTNERSHIP

A Limited Partnership ("LP") is a partnership in which there are one or more general partners who manage the business and one or more limited partners who have virtually no management authority. A limited partnership is a hybrid business association. It is like a general partnership for tax purposes, providing pass-through taxation for both general and limited partners. It provides limited liability for the limited partners similar to the limited liability a corporation provides its shareholders. The general partner has management responsibility and unlimited liability for the debts and obligations of the business. Limited partners have no voice in management and no liability over and above their capital contribution. Today, the "no participation in management" rule has been slightly relaxed. Most modern limited partnership statutes have safe harbor rules that enable limited partners to participate in management to a limited extent without losing the shield of limited liability.

The conceptual foundation of the limited partnership is found in history. During the industrial revolution of the 19th century, business units became larger and required more capital than the active participants in the business could provide. Passive investors were reluctant to risk unlimited liability by investing as general partners in a business run by someone else. Borrowing a concept from Europe, state legislatures in the United States adopted statutes which came to be known as Limited Partnership Statutes. The central concept in all these statutes is that **passive investors**, who have no control over the debts or operations of the business, **should have no liability over and above their original investment**. These statutes reflect a trade-off to facilitate raising capital from passive investors for the more capital intensive businesses started during the industrial revolution. For example, Andrew Carnegie's original steel company, which ultimately became U.S. Steel, began as a limited partnership.

Today, limited partnerships are primarily used in three specialized areas: (1) tax shelter investments, such as oil and gas and real estate, where pass-through taxation is critical and centralized management is desired; (2) venture capital and leveraged buy out firms; and (3) estate planning tools called family limited partnerships. The need for pass-through taxation and the desire for strong central management in the operator of the business is common to each of these situations. In most modern limited partnerships the general partner is a thinly capitalized corporation, wholly owned by the promoters of the deal. Thus, in effect, modern limited partnerships can be structured to provide limited liability for all participants. General partners have fiduciary duties to all partners similar to the fiduciary duties of partners in a general partnership.

3. LIMITED LIABILITY PARTNERSHIP

A limited liability partnership (LLP) is a type of general partnership in which, by simply filing a certificate with the appropriate state official, stating that the firm is an LLP, adopting a name that includes LLP or similar words in the firm name, and otherwise complying with the requirements of the applicable statute, partners can protect their personal assets from vicarious personal liability for partnership obligations that exceed the assets of the partnership. In modifying the rule of unlimited joint and several personal liability of partners, the LLP statutes fundamentally changed a rule of Anglo–American partnership law that had existed for centuries. The provisions authorizing LLPs are typically part of a state's general partnership statute rather than a separate statute. **LLPs are a subset of general partnerships, which permit general partners to limit their personal liability**. Despite the similarity of names limited liability partnerships have little in common with limited partnerships.

The original LLP statutes were **"partial shield"** statutes, which grew out of the failure of many banks and savings and loan associations in the late 1980s. Many large law firms had to pay large settlements resulting from malpractice suits arising from work done by the firms for defunct banks and savings and loans. In some instances, due to the joint and several liability of partners in a general partnership, partners in the law firms who did no work for the defunct banks and savings and loans, but who had deep pockets were required to pay substantial sums of money to satisfy judgements or settlements arising from acts of their partners. A partial shield LLP statute permits a general partner to limit his liability for the malpractice of his partners, who he does not supervise. In other words a partner in a partial shield LLP is not vicariously liable for the negligence of other partners or employees, who are not under his supervision, but he has unlimited personal liability for his own negligence, for the negligence of those he supervises and for all other partnership obligations, including partnership contracts.

Most states subsequently expanded the scope of protection by providing a broader shield against personal liability of partners than that provided in the original partial shield statutes. These second generation statutes extended the shield of limited liability to provide protection against contract claims as well as malpractice claims against nonnegligent partners or persons not under their supervision. These are called **"full shield"** statutes, even though none of the LLP statutes shield a partner from personal liability for her own malpractice.

There are numerous other variations in the LLP statutes of the several states. The LLP statutes permit LLPs to be used by any type of business. However, to date, the LLP has predominantly been used by professional partnerships, such as law and accounting firms.

4. CORPORATION

The fundamental attributes of a corporation are (1) separate legal entity status, (2) limited liability of shareholders, (3) double taxation, and (4) centralized management. How these key attributes come into play in selecting a business association for a particular business is discussed below.

Separate entity status means that the corporation is a separate person in the eyes of the law. The corporation has a life of its own, separate from that of its owners who can come and go by transferring their ownership interests. The corporation is created, when the state in response to a filing, grants the corporation life by issuing a franchise called a "charter" or "certificate of incorporation." As a creature of statute, the corporation has an existence separate and independent from its owners (shareholders) and those who manage it (directors and officers). This artificial entity may conduct business in its own name in much the same way that a real person can. It has the power to own property, to make contracts, to sue and be sued, to acquire assets and to incur liability in its own name, separate and distinct from its owners.

Limited liability on the part of shareholders flows naturally from the concept of separate entity status of the corporation. It might be thought of as the opposite side of the same coin. The owners are not personally liable for the debts or obligations of the corporation, subject to certain exceptions discussed in § IV.B, *infra*.

Double taxation means that the corporation itself pays taxes on the income it earns and the owners pay taxes on the income they receive as dividends. The income is, in fact, taxed twice. Under "Subchapter S" of the IRC close corporations, which meet certain requirements can elect to be taxed under a separate tax regime which eliminates double taxation. See § IX.B.3.b, *infra*.

Centralized management. The way corporations are managed is totally different from the way any of the unincorporated business associations, such as the various types of partnerships and LLCs, are managed. The owners of the corporation (called shareholders) annually elect a board of directors to set policy for the corporation. The board appoints officers to carry out the day-to-day management of the corporation. Except for electing directors, the shareholders have no authority to manage the business. They do have a veto power over certain fundamental acts of the corporations—such as dissolving the corporation, changing the capital structure or making major acquisitions. Conceptually, management of a corporation is vested in three tiers of the corporate hierarchy— shareholders, the board of directors, and officers. Corporate management requires observation of certain formalities, such as shareholder and director meetings, notices, quorums, etc. In close corporations often all three tiers of the corporate hierarchy consist of the same people.

In addition to these four bedrock attributes, two other attributes of a corporation, mentioned earlier, capitalization and financing and exit rules may also come into play in selecting the best form of business association. The point to keep in mind with respect to these attributes is that free transferability, a corporate attribute, legally and conceptually makes it theoretically easier for the owners to exit from a corporation than from the other types of business associations. However, whether it is in fact easier for the owners to exit from a corporation depends on whether there is a market for the shares. As earlier stated, the absence of a ready market for the shares is the main factor which distinguishes "close corporations" from "public corporations." See § I.B.2., *supra*.

5.   LIMITED LIABILITY COMPANY (LLC)

The LLC is a hybrid business association which combines the tax treatment of a partnership with the limited liability of a corporation and allows more flexibility of management than either a corporation or a partnership. The LLC came into wide use in the 1990s, the decade in which most of the LLC statutes were passed. Today all 50 states have LLC statutes, but there is much more variation in the LLC statutes of the various states than in the states' corporation or partnership statutes.

The LLC statutes are enabling statutes which, in the main, merely establish default rules that govern if there is no contrary provision in the LLC's operating agreement. Thus, the law of LLCs is primarily contract law. The statutory default rules for LLCs are in part drawn from corporate law and in part from partnership law. A filing with the state is required to create an LLC. While there is variation from state to state, in general the document filed to create an LLC is similar to articles of incorporation, the document filed to create a corporation. The owners of an LLC are called "members," rather than shareholders or partners.

Once the LLC is organized the members usually enter into an agreement which is called an **operating agreement** in most states. The operating agreement is a cross between corporate by-laws and a partnership agreement. It provides the members maximum flexibility in creating a business structure tailored to the members' particular needs and desires. As previously stated the LLC statutes mostly provide only the default rules. The operating agreement, which is a contract, largely governs the organization, structure and management of the LLC. It also allows great management flexibility. For example, in most states members are allowed to directly manage the business. This is called a "member managed" LLC. Or the members can elect one or more managers to manage the business. This is called a "manager managed" LLC. The scope of the fiduciary duties owed by the managers of an LLC is not clear at this time, but it is believed to be similar to that found in a corporation.

Almost all LLCs are closely held business associations. While publicly held businesses can legally be LLCs, few have chosen this alternative because, under the internal revenue code if the LLC is publicly traded, the tax rules change. Publicly traded LLCs are taxed as corporations, which greatly diminishes the advantages of using an LLC.

An LLC can be succinctly described as an unincorporated business association which provides its members with limited liability (similar to that traditionally provided by corporations), pass through taxation (similar to that traditionally provided by partnerships) and management flexibility (which exceeds the management flexibility provided by either corporations or partnerships).

A business association which combines all of the above features would predictably have wide appeal and the LLC has become the business association of choice of thousands of closely held businesses in recent years. In this regard, it is noteworthy that, while the scope of protection from personal liability and from double taxation at the Federal level appears to be virtually the same under an LLC and a full shield LLP, LLPs have mainly been used by professional partnerships, such as law and accounting firms, while the business association of choice in the general business community has been the LLC.

D. APPLICATION

The following three hypotheticals illustrate the process involved in selecting the most appropriate business association for a particular business.

1. THE TACO STAND

Facts: David, who manages a Taco Bell restaurant, and Joe, an accountant, who believes in David's business abilities and loves tacos, decide to open a taco stand. Joe prepares a business plan in which he estimates it will take a $100,000 investment to get the restaurant started. David will work full-time managing the restaurant, for which he will receive an annual salary of $35,000. He will also invest $10,000 in the business and receive a 20% ownership interest in the business. Joe will serve as a part-time bookkeeper and will handle tax, administrative and financial matters. He will receive no salary, but after the first year, he may bill the business as a consultant if he spends more than 10 hours a month on the restaurant's business. He will invest $10,000 and likewise receive a 20% ownership interest in the business.

David's sister, Lee, has expressed a willingness to invest $80,000 in the business. She hopes for an annual return of 10%–20% on her investment, but she realizes that there are no guarantees. Lee, a highly successful business woman, is president of a large corporation earning an annual salary in excess of $250,000. She has neither the time nor desire to be involved in day-to-day operations of the taco stand but wants a say in fundamental policy decisions of the business and the power to veto such decisions. She absolutely wants no exposure to personal liability, over and above her $80,000 investment. In return for her investment she will initially receive a 60% ownership interest in the business. David and Joe will have an option to buy an additional 20% (10% each) of the business from Lee during the first three years of operation for $40,000.

What would be the best choice of business association for the Taco Stand?

Three factors will control the choice of a business association for this closely held small business, initially financed through a typical money/talent deal among three individuals, with a preexisting relationship. The talent intends to operate the business for the foreseeable future. And they have a contractual right to increase their equity ownership if the business is successful (sometimes called "sweat equity"). The factors which will clearly control the choice of business association for this business will be: (1) limited liability, (2) pass through taxation and (3) management flexibility.

Lee, the money, obviously wants limited liability, and the talent, David and Joe, would prefer limited liability as well. This eliminates the general partnership. Lee also wants a veto power. This may be more participation in management than the LP statute allows. "Veto power" is not one of the safe harbors allowed under most limited partnership statutes. Since Lee does not want to risk the unlimited liability which would flow if she were deemed a general partner, this eliminates the LP as a viable choice of business association.

Clearly, all the parties would want pass through taxation. This eliminates the C Corporation. However Subchapter S would clearly be available in this situation and would be an acceptable choice. However, flexibility of management probably makes the LLC a better choice.

Conclusion: The LLC, which provides limited liability, pass through taxation and flexible management, would be the best form of business association for the Taco Stand.

2. THE DRILLING DEAL

Facts: Boone is the President and controlling shareholder of Aggressive Oil Company, Inc., a relatively small independent oil company engaged in exploration and development of oil and gas. Aggressive has leased 640 acres of land in West Texas. Geological tests have identified this land as a favorable prospect for exploring for oil and gas. Boone estimates that Aggressive will need between $3 and $4 million to properly test the prospect by drilling. Since Aggressive does not have that kind of money in its corporate coffers, it will need to obtain the necessary capital from investors. Aggressive, which has had some success in the past in finding oil and gas, proposes to raise the money by selling interests in the deal to wealthy investors, who are interested, not only in finding oil, but also in obtaining tax write-offs.

What would be the best choice of business association for the Drilling Deal?

Here pass through taxation and limited liability are critical because the investors in this high-risk drilling deal are wealthy individuals looking for tax write offs to offset against their earnings from other sources. They are unlikely to have the ability or desire to participate in management. And Aggressive, the operator, would not likely want them involved in management.

Conclusion: The LP, which provides limited liability to the limited partners, pass through taxation and centralized management, would likely be the business association of choice. However an LLC or LLP could also be used in this situation and some would prefer to use these newer forms of business associations.

If a traditional limited partnership is chosen, either Aggressive or a subsidiary corporation would probably be the general partner and the investors would be the limited partners of the limited partnership.

3.   THE HIGH–TECH STARTUP

Facts: Mike and Bill (the "founders"), two young computer engineers, have designed a prototype of a new computer program, which their research indicates will enable computers to perform applications for which there is a large market. Their business plan indicates that it will take a minimum of $6 million to get their business up and running. They estimate it will take approximately two years of operation at a "burn rate" of approximately $500,000 per month before operating revenues are sufficient to meet operating expenses.

Value Venture Capital Co ("Value"), agrees to invest $6 million in the business, which they decide to call Wonder Computer Co. ("Wonder"). Value also agrees to use their best efforts to raise between $10 and $20 million more for Wonder in the next couple of years through private or public financing. In return, Value will receive 52% ownership of Wonder. The founders, Mike and Bill, will each retain 24% ownership interests in the business. Both Value and the founders agree that to develop the business, Wonder will need to attract several high level computer people. They recognize that to attract such people, they will need to give them an opportunity to acquire equity interests in the company through a stock option plan.

What would be the best choice of business association for Wonder?

Here there are conflicting considerations. Obviously, this is a risky venture and all parties want limited liability. Since the business is projected to incur large losses in its early years, the participants would prefer pass through taxation, which would allow them to offset these losses against other income. This would be a factor for considering an LLC. However, in this case that factor would probably not control.

The identity of the investors and owners is an important factor that often governs the choice of a business association. So is access to capital. In this case the "money" in this marriage of money and talent, which is frequently seen in new business startups, is a venture capital firm ("VC"). The VC will control the board of the startup company and decide the form of business structure. VCs are usually partnerships and thus not eligible to be shareholders in S Corporations. VCs do not generally like to invest in LLCs. The VC's exit strategy contemplates a public offering. They want to create a capital structure which will enable them to implement this exit strategy. This entails creating securities that can be sold and used as currency to fund an option plan necessary to attract talented employees, make acquisitions, etc. The VC also wants a capital structure that would allow it to possibly exit with something if the deal does not pan out. This would probably involve creation of a class of convertible preferred stock which would be issued to the VC. This gives the VC a preference over the founders, who would likely be issued common stock, if the startup doesn't make it and has to be liquidated.

Conclusion: This business will require substantial cash investments over a relatively long period and the board is controlled by a venture capital firm, whose exit strategy is to harvest the value through a public offering if the business is successful. If the business is not successful, the VC hopes to salvage something through its liquidation preference as a preferred stockholder. Thus, the realities of financing and the need for a flexible capital structure will likely control and a C corporation will likely be the business association chosen in this situation.

E. SUMMARY OF BUSINESS ASSOCIATIONS AVAILABLE TODAY

While the five types of business associations listed above in subsection C, are by no means the only business associations available today, they are the main choices and the only ones considered in this book. Although, as indicated in the above hypotheticals, many factors must be weighed in determining the best form of business association for a particular business, the analysis must start with the most fundamental of factors—the number of owners of the business.

1. SINGLE OWNER BUSINESSES

A business owned by a single owner is called a "sole proprietorship." In the sole proprietorship there is no legal separation between the business and the person who owns and manages the business. Thus, a sole proprietorship does not fall within the definition of a "business association" as that term is used in this book. However, since there are more than twice as many sole proprietorships in the United States as all other types of businesses combined, I would be remiss if I failed to make the point that **there are far more sole proprietorships than there should be**. The owner of a sole proprietorship is subject to the law of agency and she has unlimited liability for obligations of the business. Today it is possible to significantly reduce one's exposure to personal liability by forming either a corporation (which would likely elect Subchapter S tax treatment) or a single member LLC, which is permitted under the LLC statutes of most states.

2.   CLOSELY HELD BUSINESSES

Business with more than one owner, but which do not
have ownership interests which are publicly traded or
readily saleable have a wide variety of choices. They can
choose from any of the business associations listed above,
namely: (1) GP; (2) LP; (3) LLP; (4) LLC; or (5) Corporation—after weighing several factors as discussed in the
above hypothetical.

3.   PUBLICLY HELD BUSINESSES

Businesses whose ownership interests (*i.e.*, shares) are
publicly traded because of tax considerations discussed
above are virtually always C corporations.

It is arguable that the current menu of business associations available to closely held businesses is larger than
it needs to be. This is confusing and there is significant
overlap among many of the currently available business
associations.

Why is this so?

The only explanation I can offer is that the law of
business associations recently went through an evolution,
which occurred mainly in the 1990s. This evolution is
likely part of the ongoing evolution in the law of business
associations which is briefly described in the following
section.

F.   THE EVOLUTION OF
BUSINESS ASSOCIATIONS
(a little history and a short look at the future)

As described in the famous dissent of Justice Brandeis
in *Liggett v. Lee* (1933), in the last half of the 19th

century, in response to the large amounts of capital needed by businesses as a result of the industrial revolution, **modern corporate law evolved from the era of special charters and tight state controls to the era of laws of general incorporation**. Prior to changes in corporate law during this period, it took an act of the state legislature to get a corporate charter. Such charters were typically only granted in connection with special types of projects such as building a railroad or opening a large mine. However, following the industrial revolution, large amounts of capital were needed to finance businesses. The laws governing corporations were changed, and we moved from the era of special charters and tight state controls to laws of general incorporation.

Today, anyone can form a corporation for any lawful purpose. The same corporate statutes apply to all corporations, both close and public, but these statutes were clearly originally written in a way that contemplated large public corporations. Primarily because the corporation offered its owners limited liability, corporations became the dominant form of business association for both public and closely held businesses in the 19th century. It remained the dominant form of business association through the 1980s and it is still the most frequently used form of business association in businesses with more than one owner, although the LLC is gaining market share every year.

The corporation was not always be the best suited business association for closely held businesses. Thus, just as the modern corporation was created in the 19th century in response to the economic needs of that day, several different business associations, the most notable being the LLC, were created in the 1990s for closely held businesses under the laws of all states. These new business associations provide their owners limited liability like a corporation but have tax and management attributes that make them more attractive to many closely held businesses than the corporation.

The proliferation of business associations during the 1990s and beyond has been dramatic. For example, in 1990 only Wyoming and Florida had enabling statutes authorizing the use of LLCs. Today all states have enacted LLC statutes. Texas passed the first LLP enabling statute in 1991 and today all states have statutes authorizing the use of LLPs.

The LLP significantly overlaps the LLC in many respects and, in general, the proliferation of new business associations in recent years is confusing. The LLC may become the dominant form of business association for closely held businesses in the future. Some scholars have suggested that one day there will be only two types of business associations in the United States—the C Corporation for publicly held businesses and the LLC for closely held businesses. Such a degree of logic and tidiness is more likely to remain a scholar's dream rather than a practical reality. As this book is written, state legislatures, in their infinite wisdom, are continuing to invent new types of business associations. Whatever the "new, new thing" in business associations turns out to be, a body of jurisprudence will undoubtedly develop around that business association. As respects LLCs and LLPs such a body of jurisprudence is currently in the process of being developed by courts and legislatures around the country through analogy to both corporate and partnership principles from the past. This process will remain a work in progress for many years to come.

CHAPTER III

HOW ARE BUSINESS ASSOCIATIONS FORMED?

A. PARTNERSHIPS

The action necessary to form a partnership varies depending on the type of partnership being formed.

1. GENERAL PARTNERSHIP (GP)—THE DEFAULT FORM OF BUSINESS ASSOCIATION

While general partnerships are today governed by statute, they were originally creatures of common law. At common law, "partnership" was a label for the relationship between the owners when two or more individuals agreed to operate a business for profit as co-owners. The statutes of all states have incorporated this common law concept. Accordingly, a GP is defined in both the UPA and RUPA **as an association of two or more persons to carry on as co-owners of a business for profit**. While most modern state partnership statutes contain refinements to the general definition, they do not change the basic concept. Thus, the owners of a business may create a general partnership without intending to do so or knowing they have done so. The general partnership is the only type of business association that can be formed without any sort of filing with a governmental authority.

The general partnership is the "default form" of business association in businesses owned by two or more persons. If two or more persons own a business and they do not take the necessary legal action to create a limited partnership, corporation, LLC, or other business association, they may become partners in a general partnership.

a. Inadvertent Formation

Because (1) the general partnership is the default form of business association and (2) no filing of any kind with the state is required to form a GP, co-owners may create a partnership without knowing that they are doing so. And certain consequences may result, including joint and several personal liability for the debts and obligations of the partnership.

The 1927 New York case of *Martin v. Peyton* (N.Y. 1927) is the leading case on "inadvertent partnerships." The test for determining the existence of a partnership, enumerated in that case, is still the test used today.

Partnership results from contract, express or implied. If denied, it may be proved by the production of some written instrument, by testimony as to some conversation, by circumstantial evidence. If nothing else appears, the receipt by the defendant of a share of the profits of the business is enough. . . . Mere words will not blind us to realities. Statements that no partnership is intended are not conclusive. If as a whole a contract contemplates an association of two or more persons to carry on as co-owners of a business for profit, a partnership there is.

The issue of whether a partnership or some other legal relationship was created most often arises in the context of a failed venture, where creditors seek to hold a solvent individual liable as a partner for unpaid business obligations of the alleged partnership. In these cases the alleged partner argues that she was merely a creditor, landlord, employee or the like, whose compensation was, in part, based on profits of the business. These are usually fact-sensitive cases. Most modern partnership statutes contain helpful guidelines as to which facts are important. For example, most state statutes provide that the sharing of "gross revenues" does not give rise to a presumption of partnership, but the sharing of "profits" is prima facie evidence of a partnership. The presumption created by sharing profits can, however, be rebutted when the alleged partner shows her share of the profits was received as payment for debts, wages, rent, etc.

b. The Desirability and Effect of a Written Partnership Agreement

Although many thousands of so-called "handshake partnerships" (partnerships that have no written agreement) are created every year, **written partnership agreements** are highly desirable. If the partnership is to last beyond one year, involves real estate or is otherwise within the statute of frauds, a written partnership agreement is required to enforce the agreement, just like other contracts.

The UPA, RUPA and modern state partnership statutes mainly provide default rules—rules that govern only if the partners have not agreed otherwise. For example, absent a partnership agreement, the default rules under the governing statute may preclude payment of salaries to partners or may provide for an equal division of profits and losses among the partners, even though the respective partners contributed different amounts of capital to the partnership. **Therefore, if the partners want to modify the statutory requirements, they need a partnership agreement.** In other words, if the partners do not make a deal for themselves the state through the default rules in the statute makes a deal for them. Most partners prefer to make their own deals and that can best be done through a written partnership agreement.

Partnership agreements are enforceable in the same way as contracts generally. Thus, much of the law of partnerships is contract law. When legal issues arise concerning internal relationships within a partnership the two most basic questions likely to be asked are: (1) Was there a partnership agreement; and (2) if so, what does the agreement say about the issue in question? Only in the absence of a partnership agreement do we look to the default rules contained in the partnership statutes.

In short, as to questions involving the internal rights and obligations of the partnership and its partners, **the primary source of "partnership law"** is not the statutes or case law. **It is the partnership agreement.**

While a partnership agreement can govern almost every aspect of the partnership, there are a few mandatory rules in the state partnership statutes that can not be trumped by the partnership agreement. These include: (1) varying the partners' rights to information regarding partnership affairs, (2) eliminating the duty of good faith and fair dealing, (3) eliminating the partners' fiduciary duties to one another, (4) varying the principle of joint and several personal liability of the partners and (5) varying a partner's power to dissociate from the partnership.

2.   LIMITED PARTNERSHIP (LP)

Unlike general partnerships, limited partnerships were unknown at common law. The limited partnership is strictly a creature of statute.

In all states, in order to form a limited partnership, the general partners must execute a Certificate of Limited Partnership and file it with the appropriate state official, usually the Secretary of State. In general, the certificate must set out the name of the limited partnership, the address of the registered office and registered agent for service of process, the name and address of each general partner, etc. Once the certificate has been filed and fees paid, the limited partnership is deemed to have been legally formed.

The partners typically enter into a limited partnership agreement, which is executed by all general and limited partners. As is the case with general partnership agreements, limited partnership agreements are governed by contract principles, which are the main source of the "law of the limited partnerships."

The limited partnership agreement may contain provisions governing matters such as the admission of new general and limited partners, procedures for voting, procedures for withdrawal or removal of general and limited partners, remedies for breach of the partnership agreement and the manner and process for dissolution and wind up of the limited partnership. It will also likely contain provisions pertaining to contributions and distributions. In addition, the agreement will likely set out the manner in which the profits and losses of the limited partnership will be allocated among the partners and classes of partners. If the agreement is silent as to allocation, profits and losses (under the statutory default rules) are usually allocated on the basis of the value of the partners' contributions to the limited partnership.

Once created, the limited partnership has two classes of partners—**general partners** who have full management responsibility and unlimited personal liability for the debts and obligations of the partnership, and **limited partners** who have no voice in management and but whose liability is limited to their capital contribution. The original concept of the limited partnership was a trade-off under which the limited partners relinquished all management rights in exchange for the limited liability granted them under the limited partnership statutes. Today that concept has been slightly relaxed. Most modern limited partnership statutes now contain safe harbor rules which enable limited partners to engage in certain acts and practices without being deemed to be "participating in management or control," which results in loss of their shield of limited liability.

3. LIMITED LIABILITY PARTNERSHIP (LLP)

An LLP is a type of general partnership, which for most purposes is governed by the same rules that govern general partnerships. Unlike limited partnerships, which are governed by separate limited partnership statutes,

LLPs are typically authorized and governed by provisions found in a state's general partnership statute, such as § 15–1001 of the Delaware Revised Partnership Act.

The one difference between the LLP and the GP is, however, significant. The LLP enables general partners to protect their personal assets from personal liability for partnership obligations that exceed the assets of the partnership. In modifying the rule of unlimited joint and several personal liability of partners, state legislatures through the LLP statutes fundamentally changed a rule of Anglo–American partnership law that had existed for centuries.

A filing with the Secretary of State, is required to form an LLP. The state statutes vary in the information they require in document filed. In most states, required information, includes: the name of the partnership, the address of the registered office and registered agent, the number of partners in the partnership, a statement that the partnership elects to be a limited liability partnership, and adoption of a name that includes a reference to the partnership being an LLP. Most states also have a minimum capital requirement and/or a requirement for minimum liability insurance coverage.

The LLP statutes of the various states differ in the degree of protection from personal liability which they afford partners. Some states have so-called "**full shield**" statutes and others so-called "**partial shield**" statutes. See § II.C.3, *supra*.

Bottom line: LLPs are simply general partnerships which permit general partners to limit their personal liability by filing a simple document with the

Secretary of State, complying with relatively meager statutory requirements, revising the partnership agreement to provide for limited liability, and paying a prescribed fee.

B. CORPORATIONS

While the statutory requirements for forming a corporation differs slightly from state to state, the general pattern is similar in all states. The procedure for forming a corporation has become rote.

1. HOW TO INCORPORATE

a. Formation

Formation of a corporation requires the filing of a document, called articles of incorporation, in most states with the appropriate state official, usually the Secretary of State. The articles must be signed by an "incorporator" and accompanied by the prescribed fee. Any person can serve as an incorporator, whose main function is to sign the articles.

The articles of incorporation **must** include the following: the name of the corporation, which in most states must include words such as "corporation," "company," "incorporated," or abbreviations thereof; the address of the corporation's registered office and registered agent for service of process, and the nature of the business of the newly formed corporation. The nature of the business is set forth in the so called "purpose clause." While historically the purpose clause was detailed, today, standard practice is to simply say that the purpose of the corporation is to engage in "any lawful act or activity for which corporations may be organized."

The articles **must** also set forth the aggregate number of shares the corporation is authorized to issue and a description of those shares, including par value. If more than one class of shares is authorized the articles must so state. "Authorized shares" is a word of art under the corporate statutes. It means the maximum number of shares the corporation can issue as set forth in the articles.

The articles of incorporation may also contain: provisions that create, define, limit or regulate the powers of the corporation, directors, and shareholders; provisions that regulate the voting rights of shareholders (such as straight voting or cumulative voting), provisions that give shareholders of the corporation preemptive rights, and a provision that indemnifies directors from liability. In some states, the articles still include a statement as to "minimum capital."

When the state accepts the articles of incorporation for filing it issues a form of receipt typically called a certificate of incorporation. The date on the certificate of incorporation evidences the corporation's beginning the same way that a birth certificate evidences the birth date of a real person.

b. Organization

In addition to the steps necessary to form the corporation, additional steps are required to complete the organization of the corporation. First, bylaws must be prepared and adopted. Bylaws regulate the internal affairs of the corporation and provide a structure for governance. Among other things the bylaws set forth the procedures for calling and conducting meetings of both the board of directors and shareholders, including notice and quorum requirements. The bylaws also provide the basic rules for governance of the corporation and define the duties and authority of the various corporate officers. Unlike the articles, the bylaws are not filed with any governmental authority.

Second, organizational meetings of directors and shareholders must be held.[1] Unless the first board of directors is named in the articles, the shareholders must elect directors to serve until the first annual meeting of shareholders. The directors must adopt bylaws, appoint officers and perform any other acts necessary to complete the organization of the corporation.

Additional steps, which should also be taken to complete the organization of the corporation, include: opening of a corporate bank account, obtaining a minute book, duly issuing the shares acquired by the initial shareholders, obtaining the necessary tax identification numbers and determining whether an S corporation tax election should be made. While all of the above "steps" are important to the operation of the corporation, they are not conditions to the creation of the corporation.

2. WHERE TO INCORPORATE
(herein the Internal Affairs Doctrine)

Formation of a corporation merely requires compliance with the applicable provisions of the corporate statute of any one of the fifty states. The incorporator(s) can choose

---

1. Or in the alternative adopt a unanimous written consent.

any state. It does not have to be the state where the corporation will have its principal office and the corporation does not even have to do business in its state of incorporation. For example, a corporation, whose entire business is in California, can incorporate under the law of any of the fifty states.

This brings into play the concepts of "foreign" and "domestic" corporations. A corporation formed in any state in the United States is a domestic corporation in its state of incorporation and nowhere else. Thus, if a corporation is incorporated in Delaware but does all of its business in California, that corporation would be considered a foreign corporation in California. That corporation would have to qualify to do business in California, as well as in every state, other than Delaware, in which it does business.

Qualifying to do business is a simple statutory procedure, which generally entails: filing certified copies of the articles, filling out a simple form provided by the state, paying a filing fee and appointing a local agent for process. Qualifying in multiple states increases the filing fees and franchise taxes that corporations must pay. A corporation that does the bulk of its business in one or two states will usually incorporate locally—simply because of considerations related to costs and convenience. On the other hand, a corporation which does business in multiple states may choose to incorporate in a particular state and qualify to do business in the other states. In these situations Delaware is by far the most popular choice. More than one-half of the companies on both the Fortune 500 list and the New York stock exchange are incorporated in Delaware.

The most important legal consequence of the choice of the state of incorporation is the **"Internal Affairs Doctrine,"** a conflict of laws rule which provides that the law of the state of incorporation, called the corporate domicile, determines the rights and duties of shareholders, directors and officers. The Restatement of Conflict of Laws states that foreign courts should apply the law of the state of incorporation to issues relating to the internal affairs of a corporation. Thus, when a matter related to the inner workings of a corporation is before a court in any state, the court will likely apply the laws of the state of incorporation to resolve the dispute. This does not mean that the law of the state of incorporation will govern all legal issues involving the corporation. Disputes involving transactions with third parties would likely be governed by the law of the state in which the transaction occurred.

3. SUBCHAPTER S ELECTION

Recall that many closely held corporations may avoid double taxation by filing an election to be taxed as a Subchapter S corporation. If the corporation meets the requirements for subchapter S taxation, it may file an election with the IRS. Once the election is made the corporation is taxed similar to a partnership. See § IX.A.3, *infra*.

Subchapter S status only affects the way in which the corporation is taxed. For all other purposes, including limited liability and management, there is no difference in the way S corporations and C corporations are treated under the law.

4. ULTRA VIRES

You should be aware of "ultra vires," both the word and the legal doctrine. While the doctrine is a relic of the past and essentially a dead letter in the law, the word is still frequently seen in judicial opinions. In the case of ultra vires, understanding the word and the doctrine will reflect the insignificance, rather than the significance, of the doctrine in modern times.

The word "ultra vires" literally means "**beyond the power**." The word is seen in judicial opinions where it is usually used to characterize illegal acts performed by the corporation such as bribes, political contributions, charitable donations, etc.

The term ultra vires also serves as an icon for a common law legal doctrine, which bears its name. That doctrine, which had its heyday in the 19th century in the era of "special charters," described in § II.F, *supra,* relates to the consequences of a corporation doing an act that exceeded the corporation's purpose, as stated in the "purpose clause" of its articles.

During the era of special charters, the purpose clauses in corporate articles used to be specific and verbose. For example, a corporation might have been organized to build a railroad and its specific purpose was so reflected in its purpose clause. If that corporation also engaged in general construction work, it might be characterized as performing an ultra vires act—*i.e.*, an act beyond the purpose for which the corporation was organized.

The main use of the ultra vires doctrine was to disaffirm contracts. It was used for this purpose both by the party who contracted with the corporation and by the corporation itself to weasel out of contractual commitments on the grounds that the contract was ultra vires, beyond the purpose for which the corporation was created.

Ultra vires is no longer a viable legal doctrine for that purpose because: (1) today corporations have broad purpose clauses (*e.g.*, "to engage in any lawful activity ... ") and (2) modern corporate statutes have provisions, similar to § 3.04 of MBCA, that state "no contract or conveyance shall be invalid because it was beyond the scope of a corporation's power...." These provisions typically do give the state power to enjoin ultra vires acts, but such actions are rare.

The result is that the state can enjoin ultra vires acts, but private parties can no longer use ultra vires as an excuse for nonperformance of their contracts.

The ultra vires doctrine and its decline does reflect historical policy concerns—the fear that corporations might get too big and powerful. That fear still exists, but the primary legal safeguard used today to prevent this from happening is the antitrust laws, not the ultra vires doctrine.

5. DEFECTIVE INCORPORATION

Recall, we learned earlier that when the state accepts the articles of incorporation for filing, corporate existence begins, even if the steps necessary to complete the organization—*i.e.*, adopting bylaws, issuing stock, holding organization meetings, etc.—are never completed and even if there is some minor defect in the articles of incorporation. In plain English, the corporation is born. In the jargon of corporate law the resulting business association is a **de jure corporation**—a legal entity recognized by law for all purposes.

Despite the simplicity of the modern process of incorporation, people sometimes do not get it right. For example, the party whose job it is to file the articles may simply forget to do so. In this situation, the persons who own or purport to act for the corporation, which was not formed, can be held personally liable for debts incurred by the business under agency principles or under specific provisions contained in some, but not all, of the governing corporate statutes.

More likely such persons may be held liable under a partnership theory. If two or more parties are carrying on a business for profit as co-owners and that business is not a corporation, what is it? As we learned in Chapter II, it is a general partnership—the default form of business association, for businesses with more than one owner. One of the main consequences of partnership status is, of course, joint and several personal liability.

There are two defenses to personal liability for the debts of a business that was defectively incorporated: (1) **de facto corporation** and (2) **corporation by estoppel**.

De facto corporation. A de facto corporation is a partially-formed corporation that provides a shield against personal liability of shareholders for corporate obligations. When a court invokes the de facto corporation doctrine, the court is saying it will treat the business as if it was a corporation for purposes of adjudicating the rights and duties of private parties, even though all of the statutory formalities for formation were not met.

Three elements must be established to invoke the defense of de facto corporation: (1) **colorable compliance:** the organizers of the corporation attempted to comply with the applicable statutes, but failed to do so; (2) **good faith:** the organizers were unaware of the defect that kept the corporation from being formed; and (3) **use of corporate power:** the company carried on as though they believed the corporation existed (they issued stock, held meetings, entered contracts, etc.). In most states, if all three elements are met, the alleged shareholders of the defectively formed corporation will be shielded against personal liability to the same extent as if they formed a de jure corporation.

Corporation by estoppel. If the owners of the business cannot prove one or more of the three elements necessary to sustain the defense of de facto corporation, they may still avoid personal liability for the debts of the business under the common law doctrine of corporation by estoppel. The concept behind corporation by estoppel is different from that behind de facto corporation. The general idea is so simple it sometimes trips up students. A third party who has dealt with an entity as though it were a corporation and without any expectation that the shareholders will be personally liable for the corporation's debt will be estopped from holding the shareholders liable when it is subsequently discovered that the corporation was not properly formed. Corporation by estoppel is an equitable defense. Therefore the party asserting the defense must have acted in good faith and not affirmatively misled the other party.

The classic illustration of the application of corporation by estoppel, is a 1964 Maryland case called *Cranson v. IBM* (Md. 1964), which is in most law school casebooks. In *Cranson,* IBM sold eight typewriters on credit to Real Estate Service Bureau (the "company"), which was purportedly a corporation owned by Mr. Cranson. It turned out that the Company was not incorporated on the date it bought the typewriters. Unknown to Mr. Cranson, his lawyer forgot to file the articles and did not get around to filing the articles for seven months. However, the attorney advised Cranson that the corporation had been formed and showed him the corporate seal and minute book. Thereafter, the company carried on business as if it were a corporation (Cranson was elected President, he opened a corporate bank account, etc.). When the company failed to pay for the typewriters, IBM sued Mr. Cranson personally on the unpaid debt. The court refused to hold Cranson personally liable, reasoning that since the plaintiff IBM had relied solely on the credit of the supposed corporation when it entered into the transaction, it was estopped from using its later discovery of the defective incorporation as the basis for holding Cranson personally liable.

It is interesting how far the court carried the concept of estoppel in this case. A famous contracts professor, Grant Gilmore, once defined "estoppel" as a word courts use when they want to hold a particular way and don't want to tell us exactly why. Usually estoppel is invoked against a party who makes a misrepresentation in favor of a party who relies on the misrepresentation. But in *Cranson* the party who made the misrepresentation was permitted to escape liability, while the party who relied on the misrepresentation was estopped from disputing the misrepresentation.

Both de facto corporation and corporation by estoppel are common law defenses. Some modern corporate statutes impose specific statutory conditions for liability.

6. PROMOTERS LIABILITY FOR PREINCORPORATION TRANSACTIONS

Recall that modern corporate statutes provide that a corporation's legal existence begins on the date the secretary of state issues a certificate of incorporation. The corollary to that rule is the corporation does not legally exist and thus has no capacity to make contracts prior to that date.

However, often before the certificate of incorporation is issued a lot of preliminary work must be done. Often the person planning the business to be carried on by the corporation makes contracts on behalf of the corporation he plans to form. For example, he might sign a lease for office space, hire employees, buy goods or services from third parties, etc.

These contracts are called **"promoters' contracts"** and the people who make them are called "**promoters**." In the vocabulary of corporate law, the word "promoter" has a more neutral and less negative meaning than in ordinary speech. Not some unsavory, fast talking character with "big hair," just a guy with plans for a new business to be operated by a corporation not yet formed.

Two issues often arise in connection with promoters' contracts: (1) the extent to which the promoters are personally liable under these contracts and (2) the extent to which the corporation is liable under such contracts after it is formed.

Promoters' liability. In dealing with cases involving promoters' liability to third parties on contracts made on behalf of corporations to be formed, most courts recite what has come to be the well-established general rule— the promoter is personally liable on such contracts. Most courts then go on to state the exception to the general rule, which is as well established as the general rule itself. Under the exception, if the other party to the contract, at the time she makes the contract, knows the corporation is not in existence but nevertheless agrees to look solely to the corporation, and not to the promoter for payment, the promoter is not personally liable under the contract.

This general rule and the exception (which is broad enough to swallow the general rule) are good examples of what sometimes happens when courts attempt to reduce factual distinctions to broad-based rules of law. Often we wind up with rules that confuse more than they clarify.

In his *Hornbook on Corporation Law*, Professor Gevurtz explains that the traditional recitation of the rule on promoters' liability is really upside down. The so-called exception, which basically tells us that this is a matter of intent, is really the general rule. And the so called general rule, which tells us that the promoter is liable, is really the default rule. The above analysis applies only to cases in which both the promoter and other party to the contract knew that the corporation did not exist. If the promoter misrepresents the status of the corporation yet to be formed and contracts on its behalf, the promoter can be held liable under a variety of contract or agency principles.

Obviously, the best way to avoid the problem discussed in this subsection is to first form the corporation and then have the corporation enter into the contract. If for some reason this is not possible, the attorney should recognize the difficulty courts have in applying tests based on the parties' presumed intent and spell out what is intended as clearly as possible in the contract.

Liability of the corporation. The corporation is not automatically liable on contracts made by the promoter on the corporation's behalf before the corporation was formed. The reason is grounded on the well-settled principle of agency law that one can not be an agent for an entity which is not in existence. Once the corporation is formed, the corporation may "adopt" the contract. Courts sometimes use the word "ratify." The terms "adopt" and "ratify" are often used interchangeably in this situation. Whatever term is used, the effect is that the corporation assumes the obligation.

Sometimes there is an issue as to whether the corporation has adopted a pre-incorporation contract. Obviously, there can be an express adoption (*i.e.*, the board of directors passes a resolution adopting the contract) as well as a clear and immediate rejection. A corporation can also adopt a contract by implication. For example, in *McArthur v. Times Printing Co.* (Minn. 1892) the promoter made a one year employment contract with the plaintiff to work for a newspaper corporation. The contract was made prior to incorporation but the corporation's shareholders, directors and officers were aware of the contract. After it was formed the corporation did not expressly adopt the contract, but it allowed the plaintiff to continue working for six months. The court held that this inaction amounted to adoption of the one-year employment contract by implication.

C. LIMITED LIABILITY COMPANIES (LLC)

The LLC is a relatively new business association, which came into widespread use in the 1990s. It is neither a corporation nor a partnership, but has attributes drawn from both of the older business associations. Today all states have enabling statutes which authorize the creation and use of LLCs. The LLC statutes of the several states contain much greater variations than the states' corporate or partnership statutes. Despite these statutory variations, there are two important similarities in the state LLC statutes. **First, in all states the law of LLCs is primarily contract law**. **And second, most LLC enabling statutes give maximum effect to freedom on contract.** In other words, they broadly enforce contracts among members, such as LLC operating agreements.

1. FORMATION

Formation of an LLC requires a filing with the state, but the states vary as to specifics required in the filing. In some states, formation of an LLC requires filing a **certificate of formation**. In others, the filing required is called **articles of organization**. Both are rote self explanatory documents. In all states, if there has been substantial compliance with the statute, the LLC is formed when the certificate of formation or the articles of formation is filed.

2. THE OPERATING AGREEMENT

Regardless of whether the relevant state law uses the term "certificate of formation" or "articles of organization" to describe the document necessary to create an LLC, that document is not the most important document relative to the LLC. The state LLC statutes merely establish "default rules" that govern, if but only if there are no controlling provisions in the operating agreement. The operating agreement can be described as essentially an amalgamation of corporate bylaws and a partnership agreement.

The operating agreement governs the internal operation of the LLC and defines the relationships among the members of the LLC as well as the relationship between the members and the LLC itself. More specifically, it may establish the process for the admission of new members, set forth the required contribution, define classes of members or managers, govern voting rights, provide for the allocation of profits and losses as well as distribution and set forth the remedies for breach of the agreement. It can govern all of the above and more in any manner that the members choose.

An artfully drafted operating agreement can be used to structure the LLC in accordance with the owners' desires. There are no statutory requirements for a corporate-like hierarchy of shareholders, directors and officers. The LLC statutes of most states give the members the option of electing to manage the business themselves—in which case the LLC is called a "member managed LLC" or to have one or more managers manage the business—in which case it is called a "manager managed LLC." In short, the LLC provides more management flexibility than any other form of business association.

3. FREEDOM OF CONTRACT

Most LLC statutes incorporate a policy of giving maximum effect to freedom of contract. For example, § 18–1101(b) of the Delaware LLC statute clearly enunciates this policy as follows:

It is the policy of this chapter to give maximum effect to the principle of freedom of contract and to the enforcement of limited liability company agreements.

In *Elf Atochem North America, Inc. v. Jaffari and Malek LLC* (Del. 1999), the Delaware supreme court, after carefully reviewing the basic nature of the business association known LLC and the Delaware LLC statute, concluded that under the policy of "giving maximum effect to freedom of contract," it would uphold the provisions of the LLC operating agreement being litigated.

Flexibility of management (an LLC can be managed like either a partnership or a corporation), coupled with pass-through taxation (like the partnership) and limited liability of members (like the corporation), in the words of the *Elf Atochem* court, combines "the best of both worlds." In recent years the LLC has become the business association of choice for thousands of closely held businesses[2] in the United States.

2. The state LLC enabling statutes do not preclude publicly held businesses from being LLCs, but under the internal revenue code publicly traded LLCs are taxed as corporations.

CHAPTER IV

WHAT ARE THE LIMITS OF LIMITED LIABILITY?

Limited liability, one of the main factors considered in selecting a business association, also plays a key role in operating, financing and managing the business. Today, limited liability is readily available not only to owners of corporations, but also to the owners of certain forms of unincorporated business associations such as LLCs and LLPs. However, the shield of limited liability, though broad, is not absolute. This chapter focuses on two questions:

(1) What do we mean by limited liability; and

(2) What is the scope of the limited liability protection afforded by the various business associations?

A. THE CONCEPT OF LIMITED LIABILITY AND POLICY UNDERLYING THE CONCEPT

While relatively simple, the concept of limited liability is sometimes misunderstood, particularly by students without a background in business. Limited liability in no way limits the liability of the entity which incurs the legal obligation. For example, a corporation, as a separate legal entity, is fully liable for its obligations to the extent of its assets.

A partnership is likewise liable for its obligations to the extent of the assets in the partnership. But, unlike shareholders of a corporation, partners in a normal general partnership, are jointly and severally liable for partnership obligations to the extent that they (the obligations) exceed the partnership's assets.

"Limited liability" as used herein only refers to the liability of the owners of the entity. Anyone who invests in a corporation risks losing all or part of their investment. However, to the extent that the concept of limited liability is recognized and enforced, creditors of the corporation may not reach the personal assets of the shareholders who own the corporation to satisfy corporate debts.

The policy behind the notion of limited liability is clear and if fully understood is helpful in defining the scope of the limitation. If the courts routinely looked behind the separate entity status of the corporation (or other business association offering protection from unlimited personal liability) and routinely held shareholders personally liable for obligations of the corporation, the free enterprise, capitalistic system as we know it, would not exist. Business associations with limited liability are critical to capital raising, risk-taking, diversification and other aspects of our economic system. For example, how many people would buy stock in companies such as Microsoft, IBM or General Electric (much less the start-ups, which might be the Microsofts of tomorrow), if they knew that they might face liability in excess of their investment (*i.e.*, if, not just their investment in a particular company, but their home, bank account, and other personal savings were at risk). Thus, the concept of limited liability is not only critical to capital formation but also encourages business risk taking, savings, investment and diversification.

On the other hand, there are situations in which individual shareholders or in the case of subsidiary corporations, a parent corporation, have used the corporation as an instrument to defraud creditors. A consequence of limited liability is to leave creditors of a failed corporation unpaid. Sometimes equity and basic fairness dictates that the shareholders of the failed corporation, rather than its creditors, should bear the loss. Thus, the courts recognize limitations to the general rule that shareholders are not personally liable for corporate obligations. This chapter explores the scope of those limitations.

B. CORPORATIONS

1.   THE GENERAL RULE—NO PERSONAL LIABILITY

The most fundamental attribute of the corporation, which flows naturally from the Corporation's separate entity status, is that **shareholders of a corporation, whether they are individuals or other corporations, are not personally liable for the debts or other obligations of the corporation**.

2.   EXCEPTION TO THE GENERAL RULE— DIRECT LIABILITY OF SHAREHOLDERS UNDER CONTRACT OR TORT LAW

There are situations in which shareholders are directly liable for corporate obligations under either contract or tort law. First, under contract law, shareholders often assume personal liability for corporate obligations. A lender may refuse to extend credit to a corporation with limited assets unless one or more of that corporation's shareholders agree to personally pay the debt if the corporation does not do so. In this situation, shareholders are personally liable for the corporate debt they guaranteed under general contract principles.

Second, if a shareholder of a corporation commits a tort in the course of the corporation's business, he will be liable under general principles of tort and agency law. For example, if in a closely held incorporated furniture store, the majority shareholder of the corporation injures a pedestrian while making a delivery, he would be liable as a joint tortfeasor. Even if he wasn't driving the truck, a shareholder, who is also an officer, might be liable for negligent failure to supervise.

3.   EXCEPTION TO THE GENERAL RULE— "PIERCING THE CORPORATE VEIL"

The principle limitation to the general rule of limited liability of corporate shareholders is a common law concept that goes by the colorful name of "piercing the corporate veil." If the corporate veil is "pierced" the court will hold one or more of the corporation's shareholders liable for a corporate debt. The classic fact pattern is a situation in which liability has been incurred in the name of a corporation, which has become insolvent. Creditors, trying to reach the assets of a solvent defendant, sue some or all of the corporation's shareholders and argue that they should be held liable for the corporation's obligations. This basic fact pattern has arisen in hundreds of reported cases. In many of these cases the "veil" or the "artificial entity" status of the corporation is "pierced" and the corporation's shareholders have been exposed to personal liability. The courts have not, however, been consistent in defining when "the veil should be pierced" or in articulating a rationale for "piercing."

The policy which underlies the law of piercing clearly indicates that the doctrine should be applied as a narrow exception to the general rule of limited personal liability. In 1985 (then) Professors Easterbrook and Fischel observed in an often quoted statement: "Piercing seems to happen freakishly. Like lightning, it is rare, severe and unprincipled."

Many years ago, in a case called *Berkey v. Third Avenue Railway* (N.Y. 1926), Justice Cardozo expressed the same notion as follows:

The whole area [of piercing] is one that is still enveloped in the mists of metaphor. Metaphors in law are to be narrowly watched, for starting as devices to liberate thought, they often end by enslaving it. We say at times that the corporate entity will be ignored when a parent operates a business through a subsidiary characterized as an 'alias' or 'dummy'. All this is well enough if the picturesqueness of the epithets does not lead us to forget that the essential term to be defined is the act of operation. Domination may be so complete, interference so obstructive, that by general rules of agency the parent will be a principal and the subsidiary an agent. Where control is less than this we are remitted to tests of honesty and justice.

As I read his eloquent passage from the *Berkey* case, Cardozo told us more or less the same thing in 1926 that Easterbrook and Fischel told us in 1985, namely: as a general rule, the corporation is a separate entity from its shareholders and that limited liability should be recognized as the general rule. Cardozo went on to say that sometimes, in unusual or compelling circumstances, courts may disregard the corporate entity and hold the shareholders personally liable for corporate obligations when "honesty or justice" requires.

Piercing is an equitable remedy that courts sometimes impose to avoid injustice. This concept seems to rest on the rationale that since doing business as a corporation is a privilege allowed by law, the law can limit that privilege in the interest of fairness, equity or public policy. While both the rule and underlying principle make sense, they are too broad to give much guidance as to what specific facts establish grounds for piercing. The judicial opinions are in conflict, both in their results and reasoning, and they tend to be long on metaphors, but short on meaningful analysis. As suggested by Professor Stephen Presser in his treatise on *Piercing the Corporate Veil*, many courts do not seem to sufficiently understand the economics or policy behind the general rule of limited liability or the exception known as the piercing doctrine.

a. Example: Factors Considered in a Leading Piercing Case

Piercing cases are fact dependent. While no one case can serve as an icon for the hundreds of piercing cases

CORPORATIONS

decided over the years, a good beginning point for analysis is a case that appears in many casebooks—*DeWitt Truck Brokers, Inc. v. W. Ray Fleming Fruit Co.* (4th Cir. 1976).

Fleming Fruit Company (the "corporation"), a close corporation controlled and managed by a single individual, sold fruit for growers on commission. When the fruit was sold, the corporation would pay the fruit growers the sales price less the corporation's commission and transportation costs. The corporation had contracted with Dewitt Truck (the "Plaintiff") to transport the fruit but defaulted on its obligation to pay Plaintiff $15,000 for transportation costs, despite the fact that the corporation had collected the money to pay these costs from the fruit growers.

Plaintiff brought suit to collect the money due from Ray Fleming ("Fleming"), the corporation's president and principal shareholder. Noting that Fleming had orally assured plaintiff he would personally pay the transportation costs if the corporation did not (an oral promise not enforceable because of the statute of frauds), the Court pierced the corporate veil and held Mr. Fleming personally liable for the debt of the corporation. The opinion listed a number of factors that influenced the court's decision to pierce the corporate veil:

(1) Gross "undercapitalization" and "insolvency of the corporation,"

(2) Failure to observe corporate formalities or keep adequate corporate records,

(3) Nonpayment of dividends,

(4) Control or domination of the corporation by Fleming,

(5) Siphoning of corporate funds by Fleming, and

(6) Nonparticipation by officers, directors or shareholders, other than Fleming, in the affairs of the corporation.

While this case was probably decided correctly, the multiple factors cited in this case as the basis for decision confuse the issue and provide little analytical guidance for future cases. First, there are questions as to how many of the factors on the list must be present and in what combination. Second, one can question the relevance of some of the factors listed by the court. For example, how is the unpaid corporate creditor harmed by nonpayment of dividends to its shareholders. Many loan agreements limit dividend payments to protect the creditor. If the corporation was grossly undercapitalized and insolvent, why did the contract creditor fail to require an enforceable personal guarantee from Fleming? Is the creditor really prejudiced by the fact that the corporation failed to keep adequate records or observe corporate formalities?

In short, it is questionable whether the first three factors listed above were relevant to the decision. The remaining three factors are evidentiary facts that bear on the more basic question: **Was Mr. Fleming in control of the corporation and, if so, did he do a "fast shuffle" with the intent of defrauding the corporation's creditors?** That was the real issue in this case. And on analysis, this seems to be the bottom line issue in many piercing cases (particularly cases involving contract

claims). Scholars have labeled this the **"abuse test."**
Has there been abuse by using the corporate form of
business association to unreasonably favor the controlling shareholders at the expense of minority shareholders, creditors, the government or third parties?

What constitutes such abuse is an elusive question
and, over the years, the judicial decisions have been less
than a model of consistency or clarity. For example,
some, like the *Fleming* case, discussed above, provide
extensive laundry lists to support their decisions. Others
resort to rhetoric and highly charged conclusionary language such as "fraud," "bad faith," "alter ego," "mere
instrumentality," etc. to support their decisions. This
seems even less helpful than the partially relevant laundry lists. This is, I suspect, what Cardoza had in mind
years ago when he spoke of the "mists of metaphor."

b. Analysis of the Factors that Drive Decisions in the Piercing Cases

Numerous writers over the years have analyzed the
reported cases and given us a number of factors, which in
some combination, might persuade a court to pierce the
corporate veil in a given case. One such study cited in
most law school casebooks is Professor Robert Thompson's 1991 empirical study of the over 1600 reported
piercing cases (the "Thompson Study"). The Thompson
Study and other scholarly works provide valuable insight
into the various factors which may influence decisions in
piercing cases.

Piercing only occurs in close corporations. The
Thompson Study showed that piercing only occurs in
close corporations or corporate groups. It does not occur

in publicly held corporations. Professor Thompson's database showed that piercing did not occur in any case in which the corporation pierced had more than nine shareholders.

Tort or contract creditors. Many writers have stated over the years that courts are more likely to pierce the corporate veil in favor of tort claimants than in favor of contract creditors. Their basic reasoning is that contract creditors, such as customers, suppliers and lenders, who voluntary deal with corporations and do not require personal guarantees, assume the risk of the consequences of limited liability. By contrast, involuntary creditors, such as tort victims, did not voluntarily choose to assume that risk and could not protect themselves contractually. While logic supports this reasoning, the case law does not. The Thompson Study found that courts pierced a greater percentage of the time in contract cases than in tort cases.

Professor Thompson's findings notwithstanding, the insights of the scholars that it is important to distinguish between contract and tort claims in evaluating piercing claims is correct. Professor Gevurtz explains in his _Hornbook on Corporation Law_, that the question is not whether a tort claimant is a more sympathetic or deserving plaintiff than a contract creditor in a piercing case, but rather what sort of conduct justifies piercing in contract cases as opposed to tort cases. Contract cases usually involve applications of the abuse test—_i.e._ situations where the contract creditor was (1) induced to do business with the corporation through misrepresentation or fraud, or (2) the person in control of the corporation dealt improperly with the corporation's assets. For example, the control person may have taken money out of the corporation's bank account to pay personal debts.

On the other hand, tort cases often boil down to issues of public policy. Is it reasonable for the owners of the corporation to transfer a risk of loss to a third party by conducting business through a marginally financed corporation? In this type of situation liability insurance or the lack thereof should be considered in deciding whether or not to pierce. For example, assume an airline created a separate corporation for each airplane in its fleet and that the airplane-owning subsidiary corporations have inadequate equity capital or liability insurance to cover losses which are foreseeable in the event of an accident. The parent corporation would risk piercing liability in the event of an accident where the liability exceeded the assets and liability insurance of the subsidiary corporation, which owned the airplane involved in the accident.

Undercapitalization. In piercing cases, inadequate capitalization means a capitalization that is very small in relationship to the foreseeable capital needs of the business. Inadequate capitalization alone is not sufficient to cause a court to pierce the corporate veil. On the other hand inadequate capitalization plays a supporting role in many piercing cases, and coupled with other factors such as wrongfully dealing with corporate assets or creditors, is often a factor that has a powerful influence on a court. For example, if assets that could be used to purchase insurance or pay creditors are paid to the controlling shareholder as salary, dividends or similar payments, this might be viewed as purposeful insolvency, rather than mere undercapitalization, and influence a court to pierce.

Fraud or deception. Using the corporation as a device to defraud or deceive creditors can be a powerful factor in piercing cases. Sometimes the undercapitalization cases are more about fraud or deception than about inadequate capitalization. "Fraud" is an imprecise term. In his treatise Professor Presser observes that the language in many piercing opinions suggests that something close to common law fraud is required to support piercing.

Commingling. "Commingling," when done by a person who "dominates" the corporation, is another powerful factor which might influence a court to pierce. "Commingling" includes failure to keep separate bank accounts for the corporation and the controlling shareholder and writing checks to cover personal expenses out of the corporate account. It also includes situations in which the dominant shareholder treats the corporation's bank account as his private "piggy bank." In some cases the personal assets of the dominant shareholder and the assets of the corporation may be so commingled that the third party may think she is dealing with the shareholder rather than the corporation.

Self-dealing. Abusive self-dealing, like commingling, can take many forms and is often a powerful factor in piercing cases.

Control or domination. In piercing cases, courts often speak at length about the degree of control exercised by the defendant over the debtor corporation. They sometimes say that domination is so complete that the corporation has become the "alter ego" or "instrumentality" of the controlling shareholder. Some opinions even seem to suggest that excessive domination or control can itself be a grounds for piercing.

This is not "good law." Real people control all corporations. Since piercing is a close corporation problem, all of the corporations whose veils are pierced are likely to be under the control of one or a few decision makers. If control alone were grounds for piercing, few, if any, close corporations could be counted on to provide limited liability. There must be some kind of misconduct (*i.e.* some kind of abuse—fraud, self-dealing, commingling, etc.), which tells the court **when** to pierce. However, control may be relevant in telling the court **who** has potential piercing liability. Shareholders not in control of the corporation are unlikely to be held personally liable in piercing cases.

Failure to follow corporate formalities. Courts often cite failure to follow corporate formalities, such as holding shareholders' and directors' meetings, issuing stock, keeping corporate minutes, etc., as a factor they consider in piercing cases. This factor has been criticized by many scholars because failure to follow corporate formalities is not a factor that often prejudices the plaintiff seeking to recover a corporate debt from an individual shareholder. At best it may furnish some evidence that the shareholder treats the corporation as an "alter ego" and does not recognize its separate existence.

Most experts agree that unless the complaining plaintiff can show he was harmed by a corporation's failure to follow proper corporate formalities, that factor should

not significantly influence the piercing decision. A few
states have passed statutes which mandate that failure to
follow corporate formalities will not be a ground for
piercing.

———

The factors discussed above appear in an infinite variety of combinations. No one factor controls nor does any
combination of factors. The cases contain highly impres-
sionistic results and many cases are irreconcilable. In the
last analysis piercing is an equitable doctrine, which
should be applied sparingly as an exception to the general rule of limited personal liability. As stated in Professor
Presser's treatise on *Piercing the Corporate Veil:* Limiting liability by doing business as a corporation is perfect-
ly legal. In fact, it is legal to incorporate for the express
purpose of limiting personal liability. But manipulating
the corporate entity to avoid liability at the expense of
creditors, either by fraud or acts clearly contrary to
public policy, crosses the line. As the many cases in this
area indicate, this "line" is a difficult line to draw, but it
is a line that must be drawn by the judge and jury on a
case by case basis factoring in the considerations discussed above.

4. PIERCING CASES INVOLVING
MULTIPLE CORPORATIONS

a. Parent–Subsidiary Cases

In many piercing cases the controlling shareholder is
another corporation rather than an individual. This is

called a parent/subsidiary relationship. In these cases, the plaintiff is seeking to hold the parent corporation liable for the subsidiary corporation's debts.

Some writers have suggested that courts are more willing to pierce when the shareholder seeking to be held personally liable is a corporation rather than an individual, and business assets rather than personal assets are sought by the unpaid creditors. However, the Thompson Study found that courts actually pierced more often when the defendant was an individual than when the defendant was a corporation. Further, courts cite prior cases against corporate and individual defendants interchangeably and without distinction.

Is the standard different when the defendant is a corporation rather than an individual?

Logic suggests that the answer should be no and the Thompson Study confirms that answer. So long as the reasonable expectations of creditors or other third parties are not abused by misrepresentations, fraud or improper dealings with corporate assets or public policy is not violated, it should not make a difference whether the owner of the corporation whose veil is sought to be pierced is an individual or a corporation.

Often, however, cases involving attempts to pierce the corporate veil when the defendant is a parent corporation have a different flavor than cases in which the defendant is an individual shareholder. This is mainly due to differences in the factual patterns involving parent/subsidiary relationships. Examples of some of the fact patterns that have raised issues in parent/subsidiary piercing litigation include the following (1) the relationship is structured so that all profits of the subsidiary inure to the benefit of the parent, (2) there is no clear delineation as to which transactions are the parent's and which are the subsidiary's, (3) the parent does not allow the subsidiary to have adequate capital, or (4) the board of directors of the parent makes decisions for the subsidiary. Thus, while the underlying principles should be the same, the factual context in which the problem arises may be sufficiently different to influence a court in a given case.

b. Sister   Corporations   and   the   "Enterprise Theory"

Either an individual or a corporation may own controlling interests in a number of corporations which are engaged in related activities. These are called sister corporations. Many large corporations own subsidiaries, and usually there is a legitimate business purpose for conducting operations through subsidiary corporations. However, sometimes multiple corporations are used to artificially divide what is essentially one business enterprise into segments in order to unreasonably limit liability or to mislead creditors or customers.

Consider *Walkovszky v. Carlton* (N.Y. 1966), a case in most law school casebooks. Carlton was the controlling and dominant shareholder in each of ten cab companies in New York City. Each of the ten corporations owned two cabs, which reflected a common practice in the New York City taxi cab business. Expensive licenses granted by the city entitled the owner of the license to own and operate two cabs. None of the corporations had much equity capital, and each carried the minimum amount of liability insurance required by law—$10,000. The driver

of a cab owned by one of the ten corporations ran over
Mr. Walkovszky, who sued (1) the corporation which
owned the cab that hit him, (2) the other nine sister
corporations on an enterprise liability theory, and (3)
Carlton, individually, on a theory that he was personally
liable.

In an appeal from the trial court's order granting a
motion to dismiss the case against Carlton, the court
accepted enterprise theory liability on the part of the
nine sister corporations, since what was held out to the
public as a single enterprise was artificially separated
into different corporations. But the court rejected the
theory that Carlton's use of the minimally capitalized
multiple corporations made him personally liable.

In cases involving enterprise liability courts often cite
confusion as a reason for disregarding the separate corporations. Customers may be justifiably confused about
which entity they are dealing with or creditors may be
confused about whose credit is on the line. Mixing assets,
having officers who do not identify in what capacity they
are acting and using the same trade names, stationery or
common facilities are other factors cited in imposing
liability based on the enterprise theory. The motive and
business purpose, or lack thereof, for setting up the
multiple sister corporations may also be relevant to finding enterprise liability.

c. Parent Corporation's Liability for Statutory Violations by a Subsidiary

Another type of piercing case where the issues take on
a different flavor occurs where a plaintiff seeks to impose
liability on a parent corporation for statutory violations

by a subsidiary. A good example of this kind of case is the relatively recent United States Supreme Court case of *United States v. Bestfoods* (1998).

In *Bestfoods* the issue was whether, under the Comprehensive Environmental Response, Compensation, and Liability Act ("CERCLA") a parent corporation that actively participated in, and exercised control over, the operations of a subsidiary may, without more, be held liable as an operator of a polluting facility owned or operated by its subsidiary.

The court held: The parent would be liable for cleanup only (1) if it (the parent) owned the polluted site, (2) the corporate veil of the subsidiary could be pierced because of misuse of the corporate form under traditional piercing tests, or (3) the responsible officers of the parent were actually operating the site. The court also held that if Congress wanted to remove the traditional corporate shield of limited liability protection for the parent, it should have done so by clear and unequivocal language in the statute.

C. LIMITED LIABILITY PROVIDED BY UNINCORPORATED BUSINESS ASSOCIATIONS

Historically, a fundamental attribute that distinguished most unincorporated business associations from corporations was unlimited personal liability by the owners for debts of the business association. However, state legislatures have created three unincorporated business associations which provide full or partial limited liability—the **limited partnership**, the **limited liability**

company and the **limited liability partnership**. In this subsection I will discusses some of the major issues that might arise in determining the scope of the limited liability provided by these unincorporated business associations.

1.   LIMITED PARTNERSHIPS

Recall we learned earlier that a limited partnership (LP) is a partnership in which there are two classes of partners: (1) general partners who manager the business and (2) limited partners who have virtually no power to manage. The original Uniform Limited Partnership Act of 1916 ("ULPA") reflected a policy that limited partners (perceived as passive investors with no power to manage) should not be liable for the debts of the partnership over and above their original investment. The original ULPA prohibited limited partners from participating in management. And it provided that a limited partner who violated the "non-participation rule" would become a general partner and loose her shield of limited liability.

a.   Statutory Safe Harbors

A major problem under the ULPA, as originally written, was that the prohibition against "participation in management or control" gave no clue as to what specific acts violated the broad-based prohibition. The open ended prohibition created uncertainty regarding the scope of the limited partners' shield of limited liability.

That problem was addressed in § 303(b) of the Revised Uniform Limited Partnership Act ("RULPA"), which creates a number of statutory "safe harbors." The governing statute now defines a number of actions limited partners can take without being deemed to be "participating in the management or control" of the business. The list includes:

(1) being a contractor for, or agent or employee of, the limited partnership or a general partner;

(2) being an officer, director or shareholder of a corporation that is a general partner;

(3) acting as a surety, guarantor or endorser for the limited partnership;

(4) serving on a committee of the limited partnership or the general partner; and

(5) participating (usually by voting) in a variety of decisions relating to the limited partnership, including removing a general partner, changing the nature of the business, dissolution, etc.

The above list is not exclusive and the listed safe harbors vary somewhat from state to state. If a limited partner's activity falls within a safe harbor the activity is permitted without risk of exposure to personal liability. If a limited partner takes part in activity not covered by any of the safe harbors, she does not automatically become liable for the debts of the limited partnership. Instead, the courts will consider whether her activity constitutes "participation in management" under the case law defining the scope of the prohibition.

b. Corporate General Partners

Today, it is well settled that a corporation (or other limited liability entity such as an LLC) can be the sole general partner of a limited partnership. Further, one of the safe harbors listed in the preceding subsection permits limited partners of the LP to be officers, directors or shareholders of the LP's corporate general partner. Combining the business associations in this way results in limited liability for all concerned—creditors can only look for payment from the assets of the limited partnership itself and of the corporate general partner, which are usually small in relationship to the enterprise as a whole.

In re USACafes, L.P. (Del. Ch. 1991), the Delaware Chancery Court held that directors of a corporation, whose only business was acting general partner of a limited partnership, owed fiduciary duties to the limited partners as well as to the corporation. Whether a court would pierce the shield of limited liability of a limited partnership with a corporate general partner by analogy to the corporate piercing cases, discussed above, is still an unanswered question.

2.   LLCS AND LLPS

While for many years the only business association that could provide owners of a business who wanted to be active in the management of the business with limited liability was the corporation, today, the state legislatures of all states have created viable alternatives and many closely held businesses are migrating to new unincorporated business associations, which now provide limited liability—primarily the LLC and LLP. This raises the question:

What is the scope of limited liability provided by these unincorporated business associations compared to the scope of limited liability provided by the corporation?

The law regarding the scope of limited liability provided by LLCs and LLPs is largely undeveloped. There are few cases, although there has been a fair amount of scholarly writing on this subject in recent years. Most writers, who have focused on the question, seem to assume that (1) there will be no significant difference in the scope of limited liability afforded by the LLC and LLP and (2) the scope of limited liability afforded by both of these business associations will not significantly differ from that afforded by corporations.

An issue likely to play out in this area in the coming years is:

Can the veil of an LLC be pierced?

What few cases there are suggest that some degree of veil piercing will likely be permitted with respect to LLCs. Despite uncertainties surrounding the piercing doctrine as applied to corporations, most writers assume that generally, the same sort of analysis currently applied to corporations will likely be applied to LLCs, namely: If the the reasonable expectations of the LLC's minority owners, creditors or third parties dealing with the LLC are abused by misrepresentations, fraud or improper dealings with LLC assets or if public policy is violated the courts will "pierce" the veil of an LLC in much the same way as they currently pierce the veil of a corporation.

CHAPTER V

WHO DECIDES WHAT AS TO HOW BUSINESSES OPERATE? (Governance)

Partnerships are governed in a way that differs significantly from the way corporations are governed. Also, the governance issues likely to arise in closely held corporations differ dramatically from those likely to arise in publicly held corporations. And the LLC gives its owners the ability to mix and match between the corporate model of governance and the partnership model of governance. Numerous issues, discussed in this chapter, flow from these basic distinctions.

A. GOVERNANCE OF PARTNERSHIPS

1. GENERAL PARTNERSHIPS

Partnership governance begins with the fundamental concept, rooted deep in the common law, that each partner has equal rights to participate in the governance of the partnership. This concept is carried forward in the default rules under both UPA and RUPA. As to matters in the ordinary course of business, the decision of the majority of the partners controls. See RUPA § 401 (f) & (j) and UPA § 18(e) & (h). However, under both UPA and RUPA, the partners can contract around the basic rule in the partnership agreement and delegate governance authority to one or more partners.

In deciding whether a partner had actual authority to act on behalf of the partnership, look first to the partnership agreement. If the partnership agreement does not answer the question, then and only then, look to the governing partnership statute for an answer.

If there is a partnership agreement, that agreement will usually control the scope of a partner's actual authority in a dispute among partners. If the dispute is between the partnership and a third party, rather than between partners, apparent authority will likely come into play and the outcome will likely be governed by common law agency principles. The following examples illustrate the application of these principles.

EXAMPLES:

1. Assume Dave, Joe and Lee, each contribute $10,000 and agree to start a Taco Stand, which they will own as equal partners. Joe and Dave want to lease a building owned by Robert, but Lee prefers another building owned by Jane. While relations among the partners are generally governed by the partnership agreement (RUPA § 103), in this case the oral partnership agreement does not speak to the question of who can make decisions on behalf of the partnership. Thus, we must look to the default rule under the partnership statute to resolve the issue. RUPA § 401(j) provides that matters related to the ordinary course of the partnership's business may be decided by a majority of partners. Therefore, Joe and Dave can direct the partnership to lease the building from Robert.

2.   Assume the same facts as #1, but also assume that the parties signed a written partnership agreement, which provided that "Lee shall serve as managing partner and have authority to lease property on behalf of the partnership." In this case, the parties contracted around the default rule and Lee would have authority to lease the building on behalf of the partnership.

3.   Assume the same facts as #2, but assume the provision in the partnership agreement reads as follows: "Lee shall serve as managing partner and shall have authority to enter into agreements in the ordinary course of business on behalf of the partnership, provided however, Lee shall not have authority to lease property on behalf of the partnership without the express consent of her partners." In spite of this provision Lee signs a lease on Jane's building, without consulting Dave or Joe. Here, Lee violated the partnership agreement and might be liable for breach of contract to her partners: however the partnership would be bound by the lease with Jane under the agency principle of apparent authority. A partnership agreement can not extinguish apparent authority. See RUPA § 103(b)(10).

————

These examples illustrate that partnerships begin with the basic concept that partners have equal rights in the management of the partnership's business. That basic concept finds value in the default rules that govern disputes among partners. The statutes provide that the partners can contract around most of these default rules in a partnership agreement. However, the partners can not change their basic status as co-principals and co-agents of the partnership and when rights of third parties are involved, the principles of actual and apparent authority often control.

2.   LIMITED PARTNERSHIPS

As previously discussed, limited partnerships consist of two classes of partners (1) general partners, who have the authority to govern and (2) limited partners, who have "**no authority**" to participate in the management or control" of the business. If a limited partner violates the "no participation rule" he becomes a general partner and loses his shield of limited liability.

The ULPA offered no statutory guidance as to what constituted "participation in management or control." However § 303(b) of RULPA provides a number of safe harbors, which are listed in § IV.C.1.a, *supra*. As discussed in that section, the listed safe harbors are not exclusive. If a limited partner takes part in activity not covered by any of the safe harbors, she does not automatically become liable for the debts of the limited partnership. Instead, the courts will consider whether her activity constituted "participation in management" within the scope of the case law interpreting the general prohibition.

The issues and rules relating to a general partner's management of a limited partnership are the same as a general partner's management of a general partnership. Today, the general partner of many limited partnerships is a corporation (or other limited liability entity such as an LLC). The practical effect of combining business associations in this way is provide everyone in the venture with a significant degree of limited liability.

Today, while the use of LLCs is increasing, the use of LPs is declining. The LLC is playing the role once occupied by the LP in many modern business deals. And, the LP is becoming mostly a nitch type business association. LPs, today, are still extensively used in three areas: (1) tax sheltered investments (*i.e.* oil and gas drilling deals and real estate ventures), (2) deals put together by leveraged buy-out firms and venture capital firms, and (3) as an estate planing tool (*i.e.* family limited partnerships).

B. GOVERNANCE OF CORPORATIONS

1. THE STATUTORY SCHEME OF CORPORATE GOVERNANCE

In contrast to the direct democracy scheme of governance followed in partnerships, corporations follow a so-called republican (or representative) scheme of governance. The owners of the corporation (shareholders) elect a group of individuals (called the board of directors) who are in charge of the corporation and set the policy for operating the corporation. The board appoints officers to carry out the policies dictated by the board and monitors the officers' performance.

This republican form of corporate governance is mandated by the corporate statutes of all states, to wit:

All corporate power shall be exercised by or under the authority of, and the business and affairs of the corporation shall be managed by or under the direction of the board of directors. Cf. MBCA § 8.01(b); Del. § 141(a).

Statutory provisions, such as the above, reflect the fundamental idea that **in a corporation ownership of the business is separated from control**. Although the shareholders "own" the corporation they have virtually no decision making power (in their capacity as shareholders) with respect to how the business is run. They only have the right to elect and remove directors and to vote on certain matters proposed by directors.

In broad overview, issues concerning the governance and decision making process in corporations largely revolve around the following questions pertaining to the actions and interactions of three groups within the corporate constituency: (1) shareholders, (2) the board of directors and (3) officers.

You should be able to answer the following questions with respect to these three groups in the corporate hierarchy:

(1) *Which of these groups has authority to decide what?*

(2) *How do the groups go about deciding?*

(3) *How do the three groups interact?*

The **shareholders** elect directors and usually they can remove directors. Their vote is also required to approve certain so called "fundamental" transactions. Otherwise, even though they own the corporation, shareholders do not participate in management, nor do they have any authority to act for, or bind, the corporation.

The **board of directors** is the center of management authority. Under the corporate statutes, all corporate power and authority flows from the board. However, the board does not run the day to day operations of the corporation. It delegates that function to the officers, who it appoints. The board typically meets on a regular basis and monitors performance. The board does not derive its authority from the shareholders, who elect them, but from the corporate statute. The directors have fiduciary duties to the corporation and they are subject to liability if they violate those duties.

The **officers** perform the day to day management of the corporation. This function has been delegated to them by the board of directors and they are answerable to the board not the shareholders. Officers can bind the corporation as to matters within the "ordinary course of business," but must get board approval as to "extraordinary" matters. Officers have fiduciary duties similar to those of directors. See § VI, A, *infra,* regarding the scope of both officers' and directors' fiduciary duties.

Scholars have described the traditional corporate governance model as an inverted triangle. The shareholders, who own the business, elect the board. The board, which is described as the "center of corporate governance," appoints the chief executive officer and other officers, determines corporate policies and monitors the management of the corporation by the officers and rank and file employees.

Numerous governance issues play out within this broad framework. If you understand the basic framework the specific issues and applications are not difficult to resolve.

a. **Authority of the Board of Directors to Make Decisions For and Bind the Corporation**

An artificial entity like a corporation can only act through individuals (*i.e.* "real people"). The individuals, who the corporate statutes vest with the authority to act for and bind the corporation are the board of directors. The same corporate statutes place certain requirements on the manner in which the board must act to bind the corporation.

The board must act as a body. Except in one-person corporations and a few other exceptional situations, the board of directors is a body—more than one person. Some corporate statutes require a minimum size, often three. The size of the board is always set forth in either the articles of incorporation or the by-laws. The key point is **all power vested in the board is vested in the board of directors as a body**. The corporate statutes vest no power on individual directors to act for the corporation in their individual capacity.

Formal requirements for board action. Certain formal requirements that govern board action flow from the concept that the board must act as a body. The board can only validly act at **meetings duly called, pursuant to proper notice, at which a quorum is present.** Usually a majority vote of the directors present is required to pass a resolution, but the bylaws may require more than a mere majority.

Generally, directors, unlike shareholders, must vote **in person**. Most modern corporate statutes permit meetings to be held by conference telephone calls or by **unanimous written consent,** if the corporation's bylaws authorize these procedures. Under the unanimous written consent procedure, resolutions circulated to all directors and unanimously adopted by all directors (not merely a majority) constitute valid board action even though there was no meeting.

If the formal requirements described above are not followed—*e.g.,* lack of a quorum, improper notice, or no meeting, then whatever action the board purported to take is **invalid**. In other words, if the formal requirements are not followed, the action taken is simply the action of a bunch of individuals; it is not the action of the "board" and therefore is of no force and effect.

Ratification, estoppel and waiver. When third parties, whose rights are adversely affected by improper board action, justifiably relied on the improper action, particularly if the board knew the action was improper, a court may uphold the transaction on the basis of estoppel, waiver or ratification, concepts with which all students in the basic business course should be familiar.

A case which effectively illustrates this point is *Mickshaw v. Coca–Cola Bottling Co.* (Pa. Super. 1950). In *Mickshaw* the plaintiff was an employee of Coca–Cola Bottling Co. ("Coke") prior to World War II. Coke had only three directors, one of which, in an interview by a local newspaper, stated that Coke would make up the pay differential between the Coke salary and the military salary of any Coke employee who went into military service. The director's promise was published in the local newspaper and the other directors did not object.

Two years after the article appeared, Mickshaw went into the service. When he returned to work for Coke after the war, Coke refused to pay him the difference between his military salary and his Coke salary. Mickshaw sued and won. The court said even though the action had not been formally approved by the board of directors, the board's inaction under the circumstances was tantamount to a ratification.

b. Authority of Officers to Make Decisions For and Bind the Corporation

Unlike the board of directors, which derives its authority to manage and bind the corporation from the corporate statutes, corporate officers do not have any special status under the corporate statutes. While some corporate statutes contain broad provisions describing the functions of the officers (see, *e.g.*, MBCA § 8.41), **generally, the scope of an officer's authority is determined under the law of agency.** The corporation, acting through its board, is the principal and the officers (as well as other employees) are the agents. Thus, most questions concerning officers' authority to authorize corporate transactions are determined under the agency rules of **actual** and **apparent authority**.

Actual authority. Under agency principles, actual authority can be **express** or **implied**. The clearest example of express actual authority arises when the board, acting in a proper manner (*i.e.*, as a body, at a meeting, etc.) adopts a resolution authorizing an officer to carry out a specific transaction. This sort of authority is frequently granted for major transactions such as a major acquisition or a stock offering.

Bylaw provisions are another common source of actual authority. For example:

The President shall be the principal executive officer of the Corporation and shall . . . make all decisions relating to the ordinary course of the company's business.

Actual authority can be implied. Several techniques—all based on common sense and the common law of agency—are used by the courts. For example, one judicial technique for finding implied authority is to interpret the scope of the express grant broadly. A court might interpret a bylaw provision, like the above, that gives the president authority to "manage the day-to-day affairs of the company," broadly to include various specific acts.

Apparent authority. Even when there is no actual authority, if a third party justifiably relies on action taken by an officer, a court might hold that the corporation is bound under the concept of apparent authority. A court might conclude that by virtue of his office the president of the corporation has the "inherent" power to authorize a particular act. Apparent authority issues often turn on whether a particular transaction is an ordinary course of business transaction or whether it is an "extraordinary" transaction outside the ordinary course of business.

Ratification, estoppel and waiver. Finally, even when an officer exceeds the scope of both his actual authority and apparent authority, the corporation may still become bound by his actions retroactively if the board, having knowledge of a transaction, does not question or reverse the action. In this situation a court might conclude that because of the board's inaction, the corporation ratified the action or that it is estopped or waived its right to question the act.

c.   Uncertainty as to the Scope of the Power of Directors and Officers to Bind the Corporation—the Problem and the Solution

As noted above, there is much uncertainty regarding application of the rules governing the authority of directors and/or officers to bind the corporation. The cases usually turn on factual questions such as: (1) What is "ordinary course of business" as distinguished from an "extraordinary transaction"? (2) Did the particular officer act within the scope of his "actual" or "apparent" authority? (3) Did the board comply with the requisite formalities of "meetings," "notice" and "quorum"? (4) Was the board acting as a "board" rather than as a group of individuals? (5) Do the facts support a "ratification," "estoppel" or "waiver"?

Is there is an effective way to eliminate these questions?

Yes. **Ask for a certified copy of the board resolution authorizing the transaction**.

In re Drive–In Development Corp. (7th Cir. 1966), a case found in many casebooks, illustrates a simple but effective procedure for eliminating the uncertainty. In that case the corporate secretary of Drive–In, signed and delivered to a lending bank, a certified resolution of Drive–In's board of directors. The resolution authorized Drive–In to guarantee a loan from the bank to Drive–In's parent corporation.

Later, in the parent's bankruptcy proceeding, the bank's claim for payment under the guaranty was disallowed by the referee in bankruptcy because Drive–In's minute book did not show that the board of directors had authorized Drive–In to guarantee the loan, despite the secretary's certification to the contrary. Reversing the referee's finding, the court held that even if Drive–In delivered the guarantee without actual board approval, the secretary's certification that the board had approved was conclusive (based on the concept of apparent authority). In other words the bank could justifiably rely on the fact that Drive–In acted pursuant to board authority, regardless of whether or not the authorizing resolution had actually been adopted by the board.

d. The Shareholders' Role in Corporate Governance

Can shareholders participate in management or make decisions that bind the corporation?

The answer is **no**. And the rule is clear: **Shareholders, even a majority of them, though they own the corporation cannot (in their capacity as shareholders) manage the corporation, nor can they act for or bind the corporation**.

The corporate statutes give shareholder authority to vote on certain so called fundamental matters, which include mergers, sales of substantially all the corporation's assets, dissolution and amendments to the articles of incorporation. But even as to these matters the shareholders can not initiate any of the transactions. All the shareholder can do is vote yes or no on transactions proposed by the board. The shareholders' vote is like a power to veto certain transactions proposed by the board.

Do the shareholders, who own the corporation, have any ability to influence the way the corporation is managed?

The answer is **yes**. Shareholders have a right to vote, and through their right to vote indirectly exercise a great deal of influence over the board. In most corporations, shareholders elect directors annually. And under most corporate statutes, shareholders can remove directors.

In general, the law protects shareholders by providing them with three principal rights: (1) the **right to vote**, (2) the **right to information** and (3) the **right to sue both directors and officers for breach of fiduciary duties**. This chapter focuses on the shareholders' right to vote. We will discuss shareholders' rights to information and to sue for breach of fiduciary duties later.

e. Mechanics of Shareholder Voting

General. The broad parameters which govern shareholders voting are set out in all the state corporate statutes. See, *e.g.*, § 7.01–§ 7.25 of MBCA. Except for variations found in so called "Integrated Close Corporation Statutes," a topic discussed later, the statutory rules for shareholder voting are the same for close and public corporations, but the rules were written with public corporations in mind. And, the rules are applied differently in public corporations than in close corporations. This section contains an overview of the mechanics of shareholder voting, which are generally straight forward. Shareholders exercise their voting rights at meetings. State corporate statutes generally specify how meetings are called, notice and quorum requirements, the manner of voting, the vote required to pass a resolution, how votes are counted, etc.

Annual and special meetings. There are two kinds of shareholders meetings: (1) **annual meetings**, held once a year, at which the board of directors is elected and other regular business is conducted and (2) **special meetings**, which are defined in the corporate statutes as any meeting other than the annual meeting. The bylaws typically specify when annual meetings are held and how and by whom special meetings can be called.

Notice, quorum and voting. All state corporate statutes require that shareholders be given written notice of both annual and special meetings. The statutes further require that the board set a **record date**. Only shareholders "of record" as of the record date are entitled to notice and to vote at the meeting. See MBCA § 7.07. The statutes usually specifies a time frame for notice (*i.e.* notice be given no less than 10 days or more than 60 days prior to the meeting).

There must be a quorum and the statutes typically set the quorum as a majority of the shares entitled to vote. This may be altered by provisions in the articles or bylaws in most states. Most modern corporate statutes allow shareholders to act without a meeting by giving their written consent. The statutes vary as to percentage necessary for a valid shareholders' consent.

Voting by proxy. Shareholders can vote either in person or by proxy. A proxy is simply a grant by a shareholder of the power to vote his shares to someone else. See § V.B.4.b *infra* for additional information on voting by proxy and Federal regulation thereof.

Revocation of Proxies. Unless "coupled with an interest," proxies are revocable. "Coupled with an interest" means the proxy holder has some interest in the shares other than the mere right to vote such shares. For example, assume X borrows money from Y and pledges his shares as collateral for the loan. If X gives Y a proxy to vote the shares until the loan is repaid, then Y has a proxy coupled with an interest.

f. Who Decides How a Large Public Corporation Like McDonald's Runs Its Business?

We can illustrate how some of the basic rules of corporate governance play out by considering the following hypothetical questions related to the operation of McDonald's Corporation, a company probably familiar to us all.

First, we should all realize that the question—*Who decides how McDonald's runs its business*—is too broad to be answered. To derive answers, we have to break the question down into a series of more specific questions. *Who decides:*

(1) Where the next store will be located?

(2) Whether a new type of sandwich will be added to the menu?

(3) Whether McDonald's will begin operating in China?

(4) Whether McDonald's will buy Wendy's, a large competitor?

(5) Whether McDonald's will liquidate its business?

Where the next store will be located?

This is clearly an ordinary course of business transaction and an officer, probably the vice president in charge of that particular aspect of McDonald's business, will decide. There will likely be a provision in the bylaws governing this question.

The menu question?

Again, probably an officer decides. Maybe, in the case of a basic menu change, McDonald's, after performing and analyzing test market results, would let the CEO decide. This is a closer question but still likely an ordinary course of business decision, which would not require Board approval. Of course, the answer to this question might be different if the menu change were something much more fundamental then merely adding a new type of sandwich. For example, replacing french fries with refried beans.

Whether McDonald's should begin operations in China?

Expanding into a new market like China is clearly an extraordinary undertaking, which will probably entail spending millions to create the appropriate infrastructure as well as high-level research on Chinese people's tastes in food. This is not ordinary course of business. Thus, board approval would likely be required.

Whether McDonald's will buy its competitor Wendy's?

Obviously the board must authorize a transaction of this magnitude. Further this is the sort of fundamental corporate change that must be submitted to a vote of shareholders for approval. Under a body of law we haven't yet discussed, since both McDonald's and Wendy's are publicly held companies, this matter would fall within the SEC proxy rules, which we will discuss later. See § V.B.4.b, *infra.*

Liquidation of the company?

Obviously, this transaction must be initiated by the board of directors and approved by a vote of shareholders.

2.　GOVERNANCE PROBLEMS DIFFER IN "CLOSE" AND "PUBLIC" CORPORATIONS

A person reading any of the state corporate statutes for the first time would likely conclude that the same statutory scheme of corporate governance applies to all corporations. While that is the way the statutes read, the fact is that close corporations are governed differently from public corporations. And the **statutory scheme does not truly reflect how either close corporations or public corporations are governed in the real world.** Further, the type of governess problems encountered in close corporations differ from those encountered in close corporations.

Understanding the differences in how the governance rules play out begins with understanding the differences between close and public corporations. Recall that a close corporation is owned by a few shareholders who are usually active in the management of the business. There is no market for their shares.[1] By contrast, public corporations are owned by numerous shareholders, the vast majority of whom are passive investors, in no way in-

1.　While legally transferable, the shares of a close corporation are not marketable because few people want to buy them and become minority shareholders of a closely held corporation.

volved in management, whose shares are readily market-able.

The next section, V.B.3, discusses the principal governance issues in close corporations and the succeeding section, V.B.4, discusses the principal governance issues in public corporations.

3. GOVERNANCE OF CLOSE CORPORATIONS

How and why does governance of a close corporation differ from the statutory scheme?

In a close corporation the controlling shareholders typically elect themselves directors of the corporation. And then the shareholder/directors typically appoint themselves as officers. Thus, the same real people usually occupy all three tiers of the corporate governance hierarchy.

The controlling shareholders typically view themselves much the same way as partners in a general partnership view themselves—namely, as running a business they own. They often ignore corporate formalities associated with the three-tier-hierarchy imposed by the statute, and often pay little attention to the role in which they are acting at any given time.

In a close corporation, **the seat of power is in the controlling shareholders**. But under the statutory scheme of corporate governance, controlling shareholders (in their capacity as shareholders) have no power to manage the corporation. That power by statute is vested in the board of directors. This need not be a problem because in the overwhelming majority of cases the controlling shareholder is a director and controls the board.

It can become a problem when persons acting in multiple roles act in the wrong capacity in a given transaction.

The four main governance problems that arise in close corporations are:

(1) Controlling board decisions;

(2) Controlling voting by other shareholders;

(3) Controlling the transfer of shares; and

(4) Abuse of minority shareholders by majority shareholders.

a. Attempts to Control Board Decisions

The typical fact situation. The cases you will read in your casebook illustrating this problem involve variations of the following fact situation. The controlling shareholder of a close corporation (who is a member of and typically controls the board), in his capacity as a shareholder, enters into a contract either with other board members or a third party. Later one of the parties to the contract alleges the contract is not enforceable because it usurps the authority granted to the board of directors under the corporate statute. This fact situation raises the following question:

Should the law allow a person to avoid a contract because the contract was made in a corporate setting, even though that contract could not be avoided if it were made in a partnership or LLC setting?

Both the courts and legislatures have struggled with this question over the years and have proposed certain solutions:

(1) Judicial Solutions

In *McQuade v. Stoneham* (N.Y. 1934), Stoneham, the controlling shareholder of the corporation that owned the New York (now San Francisco) Giants baseball team, McGraw (the hall of fame manager of the Giants) and McQuade entered into a contract. They all agreed to use best efforts to (1) elect each other as directors and (2) elect each other as officers at specified salaries.

Later McQuade had a falling out with Stoneham, and Stoneham caused McQuade to be replaced as a director and officer contrary to the terms of their earlier contract. McQuade sued for breach of contract. The lower court found a breach and awarded McQuade damages. On appeal, the court reversed on the grounds that the contract was void as against public policy because it impinged on the authority of the board of directors to manage the corporation mandated by the New York corporate statute.

While the broad holding of this case probably no longer reflects the law, *McQuade v. Stoneham* appears in most casebooks and effectively makes the point that in a corporation a person can act in several roles simultaneously. **The rule of the case is that the three men, as shareholders, could agree to elect each other directors, but they could not, in advance, agree what they would do as directors.**

Many students are uncomfortable with *McQuade*. They ask who was harmed by this agreement and why should the parties be condemned for doing something in a corporate setting, which would be allowed (and likely applauded as good planning), if done in a partnership setting. The New York court apparently had some misgivings about its holding in *McQuade* because in two subsequent cases with similar facts—*Clark v. Dodge* (N.Y. 1936) and *Long Park v. Trenton–New Brunswick Theatres Co.* (N.Y. 1948)—the New York court narrowed the scope of its holding in *McQuade*.

These three cases established a common law rule relative to the governance of close corporations in New York, namely—slight impingements to the statutory scheme that do not damage anyone who is not a party to the agreement are acceptable.[2] This rule was too vague and uncertain to give corporate counselors sufficient guidance in this area.

Judicial decisions outside of New York have been equally ambivalent and have laid down equally murky rules. *Galler v. Galler* (Ill. 1964), decided by the Supreme Court of Illinois, is the example found in many casebooks.

The *Galler* case, like the *McQuade* case, illustrates the multiple roles individuals often play in closely held corporations. Two brothers, Isadore and Benjamin Galler, each owned 47.5% of the outstanding stock of a successful closely held corporation in the wholesale drug business. A key employee of the company owned the remaining 5% of the outstanding stock. The brothers were also two of the three members of the company's board of directors and both were officers of the company.

The brothers entered into an agreement, which was intended to provide financial security for their respective families if one of the brothers died. The agreement contained several provisions, such as agreements to (1) amend the bylaws, (2) to vote for certain persons as

2. A statute has now changed this common law rule.

directors and (3) restrict the sale of the stock, which were clearly enforceable because they related to actions Isadore and Benjamin could take in their capacity as shareholders. But two of the provisions in the agreement were objectionable. These provisions required the corporation to (1) pay a pension to the widow of either of the contracting shareholders in the event of his death and (2) pay dividends at a specified rate. These provisions were objectionable on the grounds that they impinged on the directors' authority to manage the corporation.

Following Benjamin's death, Isadore's widow and son repudiated the agreement and Benjamin's widow sued to enforce the agreement. The court upheld the agreement and in so doing, announced the following rule: **An arrangement concerning management of a close corporation should be upheld, if the arrangement was agreeable to all of the shareholders and if there was no fraud or injury to creditors or the public**.

The *Galler* opinion discussed the need for special statutes for close corporations. State legislatures have responded in two ways, discussed in the next two subsections.

(2) Legislative Solution #1—Integrated Close Corporation Statutes

The legislatures in 17 states responded to the suggestion made by the *Galler* Court that there should be special statutes for close corporations. Those states adopted special provisions in their general corporate statutes designed specifically for close corporations. These provisions have come to be known as "Integrated Close Corporation Statutes."

The Integrated Close Corporation Statutes vary widely from state to state, but share certain common characteristics. They are all opt-in statutes, which means that eligible close corporations must specifically elect close corporation status. If an eligible corporation opts to be governed by the special rules contained in the state's Integrated Close Corporation Statute, that corporation will be treated as a special subset of corporations and will be allowed to dispense with some of the formalities associated with the shareholder, director and officer hierarchy of corporate governance. In other words, in 17 states, close corporations which meet certain statutory requirements can voluntarily elect to be governed under a separate governance scheme.

Relatively few corporations have to opted for special close corporation treatment in states in which that election is available and the details of such statutes are outside the scope of this book. It is, however, fair to conclude that, in general, the Integrated Close Corporation Statutes never accomplished their desired goal. The Integrated Close Corporation Statutes, which had their heyday in the 1980s, the decade in which most of such statutes were adopted, never received wide-spread acceptance. It is unlikely that more of such statutes will be adopted in the future, due to the advent of the LLC, discussed in the next subsection.

(3) Legislative Solution #2—the LLC Statutes (herein governance of LLCs)

Recall I previously described a new form of business association known as the "LLC," which came into wide spread use in the 1990s. See § II.C.5, *supra*. Among other things, the LLC provides more management flexibility than any other form of business association available today. There are no statutory requirements for a corporate-like three tiered hierarchy of shareholders, directors and officers.

The governance rules of an LLC are incorporated in a document called an "operating agreement" in most states. The LLC statutes merely establish "default rules" that govern, if, but only if, there are no controlling provisions in the operating agreement. The operating agreement is most often described as a combination of corporate bylaws and a partnership agreement. It governs the internal operation of the LLC, defines the relationships among the members of the LLC, provides for the allocation of profits and losses, etc. There are few restrictions on how an LLC can be governed. It is, in the last analysis, governance by contract among its owners. An LLC can be governed like a corporation, a partnership, or something in-between.

The LLC statutes, typically give maximum effect to **freedom of contract** in LLC agreements. See *e.g.* Del. § 18–1101(b). Thus, an artfully drafted operating agreement can structure the management of the LLC in accordance with the members desires. The LLC borrows from both corporate law and partnership law but in reality **LLCs are governed by contract law**. In other words, the governance rules are established by a contract among members called an operating agreement and the terms of their agreement are given maximum effect under the policy of freedom of contract.

State LLC statutes give the members the option of electing to manage the business themselves, more or less, the way partnerships are managed—called "**member managed LLCs**." Alternatively, the LLC statutes of most states give members the option of electing one or more managers to manage the business. These LLCs are managed more like a corporation and are called "**manager managed LLCs**."

For reasons more fully discussed in § IX.C., *infra*, it is important to most LLCs that they be taxed as partnerships, rather than as corporations. While a number of LLCs were formed before 1997, prior to 1997, the IRS had a set of of rules under the internal revenue code called the "Kintner Regulations," which created uncertainty as to whether particular LLCs would be taxed as partnerships. For a time this tax uncertainty inhibited the use of LLCs. However, effective January 1, 1997, the IRS repealed the Kintner Regulations and substituted an elective scheme of taxation called "**check the box**" under which most LLCs, can choose to be taxed either as partnerships or corporations on an elective basis simply by checking the appropriate box.

b. Control of Voting by Shareholders

Recall that in a corporation, ultimate management authority rests with the board of directors. Consequently, **in a corporation having control of management means having control of the board of directors**. Obviously, the most important decisions shareholders make are decisions about directors. Shareholders elect directors (see Del. § 211(b); MBCA § 8.03(c)) and shareholders can remove directors (see Del. § 141(k); MBCA

§ 8.08). Thus, shareholders of close corporations frequently form coalitions and create devices or enter into agreements to control voting. I will discuss the most common of these devices or agreements.

(1) Cumulative Voting

If a single individual (or an allied group) owns a majority of the stock of a corporation, that individual (or group) will be able to elect all the directors unless the corporation has **cumulative voting**. Cumulative voting, which only applies to the election of directors, allows shareholders to accumulate all of their votes and allocate the votes to one or more candidates for the board. Cumulative voting increases the chances that minority shareholder will have representation on the board of directors.

What is the difference between **"straight voting"** *and* **"cumulative voting***?"*

Under straight voting each shareholder is entitled to cast one vote per share owned for each director running for election. For example, assume Dave's Tasty Tacos, Inc. has three directors on its board and has three shareholders—Dave, who owns 60 shares, Joe, who owns 30 shares and Lee, who owns 10 shares. Under straight voting Dave has 60 votes, Joe has 30 votes and Lee has 10 votes for seats 1, 2 and 3 on the board. Thus, a shareholder owning the majority of the stock (like Dave) will be able to elect every director. Minority shareholders (like Joe and Lee) will be unable to elect any members of the board.

With cumulative voting, however, directors are not elected seat-by-seat. Rather, there is one "at large" election, in which the shareholders cast votes. In our example, the top three vote getters would be elected to the board. In casting their votes, the shareholders get to "cumulate" their votes. This means each shareholder gets to multiply the number of shares times the number of directors to be elected. In our example Dave has 180 votes (60 shares times 3 directors), Joe has 90 votes (30 shares times 3 directors) and Lee has 30 votes (10 shares times 3 directors). Each shareholder can allocate her votes, as she sees fit, and the top three recipients are elected.

How would cumulative voting work in our example?

Cumulative voting would allow the minority shareholders to vote all their shares for a single candidate. The following formula can be used in determining the number of shares needed to elect one director:

$$S \div (D + 1) + \text{(some fraction or 1)}$$
$$S = \text{number of shares voting}$$
$$D = \text{number of directors to be elected}$$

In our example, the numerator would be 100 (shares to be voted). The denominator would be 4 (3 directors to be elected plus 1). Thus 26 shares is the minimum needed to elect one director[3] (*i.e.*, $100 \div 4 = 25 + 1 = 26$).

If Joe cumulates his 90 votes for a single candidate there would be no way that Dave could spread his 180

---

3. The part of the equation that says "some fraction or 1" merely requires rounding to the next full number of shares if the answer is a fraction—*i.e.*, if we were electing 5 directors and the answer came out to 16.67, 17 shares would be needed to elect a director.

votes in a way that would defeat Joe's candidate. But Dave has enough votes to elect two directors or a majority of the board. Lee, on the other hand, does not have enough votes to elect even one candidate. This illustrates that cumulative voting does not guarantee minority representation on the board. It simply makes minority representation easier to obtain.

In most states cumulative voting is permitted but not required. In the states where cumulative voting is permitted but not required, whether or not cumulative voting exists is controlled by a provision in the articles of incorporation. In a majority of states, for shareholders to have cumulative voting the articles must contain a provision stating that shareholders may vote cumulatively. These statutes are called **"opt in"** statutes. See, *e.g.,* MBCA § 7.28(b). A significant minority of states, however, allow shareholders to vote cumulatively unless the articles contain a provision denying shareholders the right to vote cumulatively. These statutes are called **"opt out"** statutes.

As shown in our example, cumulative voting requires planning. If a shareholder casts her votes in an inefficient way she may not get the directorships she is entitled to.

The lower the number of directors standing for election, the higher the percentage of stock required to elect a director by cumulative voting. Thus, the majority shareholder may mitigate the effect of cumulative voting by reducing the size of the board, or by creating a staggered board.

A staggered board means that not all of the directors stand for election each year. For example, a board may consist of nine directors, each elected for a staggered term of three years. Thus, only three directors would stand for election in any given year. Staggered boards have been challenged in states in which cumulative voting is mandatory and in most cases the courts have upheld the validity of staggered boards despite the adverse effect of staggering the board on cumulative voting.

(2) Supermajority Requirements

Another means of modifying a corporation's usual control structure to give minority shareholders a greater voice in governance is through so called "supermajority" requirements. Supermajority requirements modify the usual rule that the vote of the majority controls. Typically a majority of the shares entitled to vote is needed for a quorum and a majority of the shares voting is necessary to carry a particular resolution.

The notion behind imposing a supermajority requirement is that instead of a mere majority, a vote of 2/3 or 3/4 is necessary to constitute a quorum or to carry a resolution. This gives a significant minority something akin to a veto power and makes it hard for the corporation to act without the assent of at least a significant portion of the minority. Supermajority requirements can be imposed at the shareholder level, the board level or both. They can be made applicable to all matters or to specific matters such as approving mergers, fixing dividends, etc. And they may alter quorum as well as voting requirements.

Most states permit the imposition of a supermajority requirement. Some state statutes require that the enabling provisions be in the articles of incorporation; others allow the provisions to be in either the articles or the bylaws. Supermajority requirements have generally been upheld by the courts on the basis that while they add to the risk of deadlock, they provide a bargained-for benefit to minority shareholders.

(3) Shareholder Voting Agreements

Shareholder voting agreements, sometimes called vote-pooling agreements, are contracts among shareholders to vote their shares in the manner prescribed in the contract. Today voting agreements are generally controlled by ordinary rules of contract law and are specifically authorized by most state corporate statutes. See, *e.g.,* MBCA § 7.31.

Historically, courts were reluctant to enforce shareholder voting agreements. The 1947 case of *Ringling Bros. Barnum and Bailey Combined Shows, Inc. v. Ringling* (Del. 1947) was a major decision in the development of the jurisprudence of voting agreements. Though now somewhat dated, this case has a great set of facts and tells us a lot about the concept, use and enforcement of voting agreements. The case is in almost all of the casebooks.

At the time the *Ringling* case arose, the original founders of the famous circus had died, and ownership of the closely held corporation, which owned the circus was vested in three sets of heirs: (1) Edith Ringling (and her son Robert) with 315 shares; (2) Aubrey Haley (and her husband) with 315 shares and (3) John North Ringling with 370 shares. The board of the Ringling corporation consisted of 7 directors, who were elected annually by cumulative voting.

For several years, John North Ringling ran the circus, but as often happens in close corporations, sometimes personalities get in the way, factions develop and the factions often vie for power. In 1943 Edith and Aubrey joined forces and signed a voting agreement. Under the terms of their agreement, the two ladies agreed to vote their shares together. By so doing, they were able to elect 5 of the 7 directors and seize control of the corporation from John. Mr. Haley, Aubrey's husband and Robert, Edith's son, took over control of the business from John. However, in 1944 during a performance of the circus in Connecticut the circus tent caught fire. One hundred eighty people died and over 500 were injured. Mr. Haley, who was in Connecticut running the circus, was prosecuted, convicted of manslaughter (failure to have sufficient staff), and forced to spend time in prison. Mr. Haley's, experience in jail embittered him against Edith's son Robert. After his release from prison, Mr. Haley persuaded his wife Audrey to end her alliance with Edith. At the 1946 annual meeting, Aubrey refused to vote with Edith (or per the arbitrator's instructions) and litigation ensued. The two issues on appeal were :

(a) Was the voting agreement a valid agreement the court would enforce?

The Delaware Supreme Court held yes. The agreement was not void as against public policy. The court reasoned it was analogous to a proxy coupled with an interest.

(b) Would the court grant specific performance?

The court refused to grant specific performance. Instead it ordered that the Haley votes be ignored.

As a result of this litigation John regained control of the board. Through control of the board, he controlled the circus, which he managed for several years following the decision until the circus was sold.

The *Ringling* case illustrates a turn around in judicial hostility toward voting agreements. Today, most courts would go further than the *Ringling* Court and enforce the agreement by specific performance. Further, most states, today, have statutes validating shareholders' voting agreements. Most of those statutes provide that such agreements are enforceable by specific performance. See, *e.g.,* Del. § 218(c); MBCA § 7.31.

(4) Voting Trusts

The voting trust is another legal device used to vest control in the hands of a particular person or faction. Its effect is similar to the effect of voting agreement. However, the differences between a voting trust and voting agreement outweigh their similarities. Some law professors like to focus on these differences.

Self-enforcing. Unlike voting agreements, which are not self-enforcing and are grounded on contract principles, voting trusts are self enforcing and they are grounded on trust principles. In a voting trust, shareholders transfer legal title to their shares to one or more voting trustees. The voting trustees, for a defined period, have exclusive power to vote the transferred shares. Other attributes of ownership, such as rights to dividends, remain with the former shareholders, who become bene-

ficiaries of the trust. Typically the beneficiaries are issued voting trust certificates as evidence of their benefi-
cial ownership of the shares transferred to the trust.
Because the voting trustees become the legal owners of
the shares, their right to vote such shares is not dependent upon a court order of specific performance. Rather,
the voting trust is self-executing. The voting trustee does
owe the former shareholder/beneficiaries fiduciary duties.

Creatures of statute; express requirements. Unlike voting agreements, which have common law roots,
voting trusts are strictly creatures of statute. The statutes authorizing voting trusts typically impose a number
of formal requirements, which, in general, must be strictly complied with to insure the validity of the voting trust.
The requirements for creating a voting trust vary from
state to state. MBCA § 7.30 is typical. It requires that:
(1) the trust agreement be in writing, (2) the shares be
specifically transferred to the trustee, (3) the trust be
limited in duration to not more than ten years and (4)
the trust agreement be on file at the corporation's principal office.

Termination. Once a particular shareholder transfers
her shares to a voting trust, the shareholder's are held in
trust in for the duration of the trust. Voting trusts can
only be terminated early if all the beneficiaries of the
trust agree to terminate the voting trust.

Uses of voting trusts. Voting trusts can be used for
the same purpose as voting agreements—*i.e.,* to enable a
coalition of minority shareholders to control the board.
However, voting trusts are used for a variety of other
purposes—in public as well as close corporations. They

are often used in corporate financings, including bankruptcy reorganizations. A voting trust can ensure a management acceptable to creditors for an extended period of time. Similarly, an elderly controlling shareholder, who wants to pass ownership to younger family members, can use a voting trust to permit management free of family rivalry for a period of time.

In sum, voting trusts are consensual. They bind only the parties who agree to participate. But once a shareholder agrees by transferring her shares to the voting trustee, that person is bound for the duration of the trust. The trustee is a fiduciary, who owes the beneficiaries of the voting trust (the former shareholders) fiduciary duties similar to those owed by any trustee to the beneficiaries of an express trust. Voting trusts are devices by which the power to vote is temporally, but formally and irrevocably, separated from the other incidents of stock ownership.

c. Stock Transfer Restrictions and Buy–Sell Agreements

In theory, the shares of all corporations are freely transferable. The concept of free transferability reflects reality in publicly held corporations. A shareholder of a public corporation, whose shares are traded daily in the organized securities markets, can sell her shares by a telephone call to her stockbroker or a mere click of the mouse on her computer. But the reality is different for owners of shares of closely held corporations. By definition there is no active market for these shares.

The practical problem of finding a buyer is particularly acute for minority shareholders. Few people are interested in buying a minority interest in a close corporation. The only likely buyer is the majority shareholder and he is usually only willing to buy at a favorable price. Moreover, shareholders of a close corporation, who are often active in the business, may want to restrict their fellow shareholders from selling their shares to outsiders.

For these reasons, while free transferability of shares is said to be a fundamental attribute of a corporation, it is often not possible for shareholders in close corporations to sell their shares. Furthermore, unlike partners, in a partnership, in a close corporation, absent a buy-sell agreement, there is usually no practical way for a minority shareholder to redeem her interest for fair value.

Transfer restrictions must be reasonable. Free transferability is not an absolute right. The law allows reasonable restrictions on transferability. The types of restrictions allowed by law may serve a dual purpose, namely: (1) provide minority shareholders with a greater degree of liquidity and (2) give shareholders the ability to promote harmony by restricting sales to outsiders. In short, the modern rule is: **stock transfer restrictions are allowed but they must be reasonable under the circumstances.** See, *e.g.,* MBCA § 6.27.

The approach of the courts in applying this rule is to balance the competing considerations of fostering free transferability of ownership, on the one hand, and giving shareholders some power to exit and/or to limit ownership to persons the remaining shareholders know and trust, on the other. Thus, while outright prohibitions against transfer are invalid, restrictions such as: (1)

purchase options, (2) rights of first refusal and (3) buy-sell agreements, have all been upheld by the courts.

Purchase options and rights of first refusal. A purchase option is an agreement which requires a shareholder (or the estate of a deceased shareholder) to offer his shares to the corporation or to the other shareholders of the corporation at a specified price.

A right of first refusal obligates a shareholder to offer her shares to the corporation (or to the other shareholders) at the same price and on the same terms offered by an outsider for such shares, before selling the shares to an outsider. The main difference between a purchase option and a right of first refusal is that in the former the price is set by agreement, while in the latter the price is whatever the outsider offers for the shares. Both are generally valid and enforceable. See, *e.g.,* MBCA § 6.27(d)(1); Del. § 202(c)(4).

Buy-sell agreements. As the name suggests, a "buy-sell agreement" is simply a contract that requires the corporation, the majority shareholder or all remaining shareholders pro rata to purchase the shares of a selling shareholder in specified situations at a specified or ascertainable price. Buy-sell agreements are the most widely used types of stock transfer restrictions. They are valuable and effective tools in closely held corporations. A properly drafted buy-sell agreement should answer the following questions: (1) what triggers an obligation to buy or sell, (2) what the purchase price will be and (3) where the money is to come from. Most of the law pertaining to such agreements comes from the law of contracts and is beyond the scope of this book.

Third parties. Restrictions on the transfer of shares which are valid and enforceable between the parties to the restrictions (*i.e.,* the parties to a buy-sell agreement) may not be binding against third parties. The restrictions are valid and enforceable against a third party only if the third party (1) knows of the restriction or (2) the restriction is "conspicuously noted" on the stock certificate. See MBCA § 6.27(b).

d. Deadlock and Oppression in Close Corporations—Avoidance and Remedies

There is obviously no need for shareholders in public corporations to get along. Shareholders in public corporations have no expectation of participating in management, beyond voting for directors. And, more importantly, shareholders of public corporations know that if they do not like the way the corporation is being run they can "take the Wall Street walk"—sell their shares in the public market.

(1) The Potential for Deadlock and Oppression in Close Corporations

The situation is quite different in a close corporation. In close corporations the shareholders are usually involved in running the business. Often they depend on the business for their livelihood. These shareholders are likely to be linked by family ties or close personal relationships. And the Wall Street walk is not an available option.

What happens if the shareholders of a closely held corporation have a falling out and can no longer agree on how the company should be run?

Generally, the answer to that question depends upon the division of stock ownership among the shareholders. The two problems most likely to result are **deadlock** or **oppression**. These are two key concepts that raise a host of issues.

Deadlock. Assume a corporation has two shareholders each owning 50% of the stock. The two shareholders would normally elect themselves and perhaps one crony each to the board. As board members, the two shareholders would elect themselves officers and would run the company. If the two shareholders have a falling-out and can no longer agree, there is potential for "**deadlock**." Deadlock refers to fundamental disagreements among equal shareholders that can virtually paralyze the corporation's ability to operate by destroying the ability to agree at either the shareholder or the director level. Students (particularly those having professors that emphasize planning) should be able to recognize environments with the potential for deadlock and be aware of the legal tools available to avoid deadlocks.

How can you recognize the potential for deadlock and how can it be avoided?

Anytime two shareholders or two factions have an equal ownership of a corporation's voting shares, particularly if there is an even number of directors on the board, a potential for deadlock exists. In real life, deadlock most frequently occurs when one or more of the founding shareholders of a successful closely held business dies and the deceased shareholder's shares pass to the next generation.

Various mechanisms are available for dealing with deadlocks. These mechanisms include some we have already discussed, such as: (1) pre-dispute arbitration agreements like the one found in the *Ringling* case and (2) buy-sell agreements, structured to resolve deadlocks.

Another effective device for avoiding deadlock is a deadlock-breaking director. An example of how deadlocks arise and how they can be avoided by effective planning is found in the case of *Lehrman v. Cohen* (Del. 1966). In that case Lehrman and Cohen founded a company, Giant Food Stores, Inc., which at the time of this litigation had become the leading grocery store chain in the Washington, D.C. area. The two founders had no trouble getting along (just as the founders of the Ringling Brothers Circus had no trouble getting along) but at the time the case arose, one of the founders had died and the other was elderly and no longer active in management. Giant Foods was equally owned by the Cohen and Lehrman families and a new generation was running the company. Recognizing an environment ripe for deadlock, counsel for the company caused the company to be recapitalized. He created a class of common stock called AL—owned by Lehrman family and a class of common stock called AC—owned by Cohen family. Each of those classes could elect two directors to a five-person board. The counsel created a third class of stock called AD and issued one share of AD stock to himself. The AD stock could elect one director (*i.e.,* a deadlock-breaking director), but it had none of the other attributes of ownership.

The court upheld the deadlock-breaking director arrangement. Today, a deadlock-breaking director, whether chosen by agreement, arbitration, or built into the capital structure of the corporation, is an effective deadlock preventing device.

Oppression. Assume three shareholders A, B and C, each own 33.3% of the voting stock of a company and that A, B and C constitute the entire board of directors. There is a disagreement and A and B remove C from the board. Through control of the board A and B can take action against C. The action, may include terminating C's employment with the company, refusing to pay dividends and siphoning off corporate earnings through high salaries A and B pay themselves. Often these techniques (called "freeze-outs" or "squeeze-outs"), are used individually or in combination to force a minority shareholder such as C to sell her shares to the majority shareholders A and B at an unfairly low price. This kind of action is commonly called "**oppression**."

(2) Remedies for Deadlock or Oppression

What judicial remedies are available if deadlock or oppression occurs?

The principal judicial remedies available to equal shareholders, trapped in a dysfunctional corporate marriage, by deadlock, and oppressed minority shareholders are actions for (1) **involuntary dissolution** and (2) **violation of fiduciary duties.** We will discuss violation of fiduciary duties in the next chapter. See § VI.A and § VI.D *infra.*

Involuntary Dissolution. The principal statutory remedy available to shareholders who want a corporate divorce is "involuntary dissolution." All states have statutes authorizing involuntary dissolution, but the specifics of such statutes and the manner in which they are applied vary significantly from state to state. MBCA § 14.30 is as good an example as any for considering the issues that might arise in a statutory proceeding for involuntary dissolution.

Historically, courts were reluctant to grant involuntary dissolution. The Official Comment to MBCA § 14.30 advises courts to be "cautious" in granting this remedy and some state statutes provide that courts should grant this remedy "only if ... all other remedies available either at law or in equity ... are determined by the court to be inadequate."

In recent years: (1) many courts have become less reluctant to order involuntary dissolution and (2) some courts have ordered majority shareholders to buy out the oppressed minority shareholders, even when the applicable corporate statute does not contain specific language which empowers the court to order a buy-out.

The MBCA was amended in 1991 to permit majority shareholders in a close corporation to elect to buy out the petitioning shareholder in an involuntary dissolution proceeding at fair value. See MBCA § 14.34(a). Obviously, what constitutes "fair value" can be a significant issue when this remedy is elected or ordered by the court. Courts ordering dissolution typically encourage the shareholders to agree on a price, but if the parties fail, the court will set the price.

Grounds for involuntary dissolution. MBCA § 14.30(2) specifies the following grounds for involuntary dissolution:

(a) deadlock at either the board or shareholder level;

  (b) illegal, oppressive or fraudulent conduct by directors or control shareholders; and

  (c) misapplication or waste of corporate assets.

Alternative remedies short of dissolution. Many courts are hesitant to order dissolution, even when dissolution is specifically authorized by the statute. Sometimes courts order remedies, short of dissolution, which include: (1) awarding damages to the oppressed shareholder, (2) ordering a buy-out (based on the court's inherent equity powers), even where the statute does not expressly empower them to do so, and (3) appointing a "receiver" or "custodian." "Receivers" generally liquidate the business, while "custodians" generally preserve the assets and operate the business for an indefinite period. See, *e.g.,* MBCA § 14.32.

4. GOVERNANCE OF PUBLIC CORPORATIONS

Recall the same statutory scheme of corporate governance applies to all corporations, both "public" and "close." But as earlier noted, the statutory scheme does not reflect reality in either close of public corporations. We have discussed how the actual governance of "close" corporations differs from the statutory scheme. The next question is:

a. How Does the Governance of Public Corporations Differ from the Statutory Scheme?

The difference was explained in an irreverent, but understandable way in a management book entitled *Up the Organization*, written by Robert Townsend, former President and CEO of Avis Corporation, in 1971. Mr. Townsend wrote:

The huge, successful company is a dinosaur, but it has one decisive advantage over the middle-sized outfit that is trying to grow.... [M]ost big companies have turned their boards of directors into non-boards.... This achievement has to be understood to be admired. While ostensibly the seat of all power and responsibility, directors are usually friends of the CEO put there to keep him safely in office. They meet once a month, gaze at the financial window dressing, provided them by the managers who run the business, listen to the chief and his team talk superficially about the state of the operation, ask a couple of dutiful questions ... and adjourn until next month.

Over their doodles around the table, alert directors spend their time in silent worry about their personal obligations and liabilities in a business they can't know enough about to understand....

Though perhaps a bit overstated, Mr. Townsend's description of the relationship between the board and the CEO was probably accurate (as to most corporations) when written almost 40 years ago. Today, most boards are more independent then the board described by Mr. Townsend, although, not as independent as most experts on corporate governance think they should be. What movement there has been in recent years toward greater board independence has been brought about by pressure from shareholders and civil litigation against directors for violation of fiduciary duties, as discussed in the next chapter.

In additional revelations in the recent corporate scandals involving Enron, Tyco, WorldCom, etc. and increased governmental regulation through the new Sarbanes–Oxley law, discussed earlier, will likely accelerate the movement toward greater board independence.

In his *Hornbook on Corporation Law*, Professor Gevurtz describes the difference between the statutory model and reality in the governance of public corporations in a more traditional way:

> The divergence between the corporate governance model and reality in a public corporation does not involve the melding of shareholders, directors and officers into the same few people, but instead involves the flow of power between these three groups. The model perceives power will flow from shareholders, who decide who will be the directors, to directors who select the corporate officers. The reality in most publicly held corporations has been almost the reverse. The officers, particularly the CEO, decides who will be the directors and what policies the corporation will pursue.

Governance problems in public corporations resulting from the "inversion" referred to by Professor Gevurtz, have, in the years subsequent to the Enron scandal, emerged as a hotly debated topic in corporate law. Many corporate law professors are currently debating this problem in the legal journals and are likely to discuss the problem in class. Resolving this problem is a work in progress, which is beyond the scope of this book. But, the following discussion might help you understand the problem.

What is the problem?

The best way to understand the problem is to go back to basics—all the way back to basic agency concepts. The principal has the authority to control the agent, and the agent is supposed to act in the principal's best interest. But, in the real world, agents and principals often have different interests. For example, assume the taco stand, we have from time to time used in examples in this book, is owned by Dave, as a sole proprietorship. Dave, the sole owner of the business, has several employees—the people who make the tacos and ring up the sales. These employees are agents of the owner Dave.

Dave, the principal, wants his employees, the agents, to work hard for as little money as possible. The employees prefer the exact opposite. They would like to get paid as much as possible for as little work as possible. This divergence of interest is not a serious problem for Dave since he is personally managing his taco stand—keeping control of his agents' performance and an eye on the purse strings.

In a public corporation the officers and other employees are agents of the corporation. But here the shareholders, who own the corporation, are not physically able to watch what is going on. Moreover, under the statutory scheme of corporate governance, the shareholders have no authority to manage the business.

In the corporate scheme of things, who is supposed to look out for the shareholders' interest?

The obvious answer is the board of directors. The shareholders elect the directors. The directors, like the officers have fiduciary duties to the corporation. One of the main roles of the board of directors, at least in theory, is to keep an eye on the CEO and his team as well as on the cash, much like Dave does in managing the taco stand.

How do situations like Enron occur?

The answer is actually rather obvious. A corporation's agents, its officers, run the corporation, and they are in a position to siphon value from the business. They can do this in a number of ways. They can grant themselves lavish compensation packages (including massive option grants), and expensive executive perks, like corporate jets, company apartments and country club memberships. They can engage in projects that do not benefit the corporation's bottom line, but rather feed the CEO's ego or increase his personal power, such as building a corporate art gallery or giving large amounts of money to the CEO's favorite charity. And in a few cases, they may even steal or engage in self dealing to the detriment of the corporation and its shareholders, as revealed in recent criminal trials of former officers of companies such as Enron, Tyco and World Com.

The board has a legal duty to see that none of this happens and they can be held legally liable for violating their fiduciary duties if it does happen (as we will discuss in detail in the next chapter). But the board's job is not easy. If the board is too intrusive and tries to micro manage or second guess the CEO's every move, this will hurt morale and drive away many good managers and employees. Organizations function best when the various constituencies within the organization operate with a high level of trust and confidence. Too much intrusion and suspicion can damage the enthusiasm, loyalty, and performance of the CEO and his team. So the board has the awkward job of being both the cop and head cheerleader.

Other factors further complicate the board's job. First, officers are in a better position to make important business decisions than the board. Officers work full-time at their job and they usually have years of relevant experience in the company and the industry. Outside directors (board members who are not also officers of the company), while usually experienced business executives (often retired CEOs), ex-public officials, etc. serve only part time. They usually meet only once a month. One recent survey found that the average board member of public companies spends about four or five hours a week on board work.

Second, directors depend to a large extent on the officers for their information. The CEO makes the business decisions and is at the nerve center of the corporation's information network. No one in the company has more access to information than the CEO. And the CEO controls what information is presented to the board.

Third, the board is usually friendly toward the CEO. In many public corporations, most of the board members were selected to serve on the board by the CEO. There is usually a high level of respect among the CEO and the board members. Thus, boards tend to back their CEO. They tend to generously compensate CEOs who perform and they are often reluctant to fire CEOs who do not perform.

So for a variety of reasons, most of the time (though not always), the board finds itself simply trusting the decisions made by the CEO and his team. This is not necessarily bad, if the company has the right CEO in place. But experience has shown that sometimes boards put too much trust in the CEO and find that the corporation was mismanaged (and sometimes even looted). When that happens, the members of the board may find themselves defendants in a shareholders' derivative suit, which we discuss in the next chapter.

This brings us to the ultimate questions: How much board governance is desirable? How independent should the board be?

These questions are currently being debated, not just in academia, but also in the halls of congress, the state legislatures and regulatory agencies, such as the SEC. The current debate was in large part fostered by the loss of confidence which resulted from the recent corporate scandals. While definitive answers are not available at this time, there is a discernable trend toward more independent boards, which better protect shareholder interests and provide greater oversight of corporate officers.

b.   Voting by Shareholders in Publicly Held Corporations and the SEC's Proxy Rules

Shareholders elect directors and, in most states, shareholders can remove directors. As previously noted, a shareholder does not have to be present to vote his shares at either an annual or special meeting. All state corporate statutes provide that the shareholder may vote by "**proxy**." Cf. MBCA § 7.22; Del. § 212(b). In this subsection we will discuss the process by which shareholders vote and how the voting process is regulated under the federal securities laws.

What is a proxy?

A proxy is simply a grant by a shareholder of the power to vote her shares to someone else. The person who grants the power is called a proxy giver. The person who receives the power is called a proxy holder.

A proxy is a form of agency. The proxy giver consents to the proxy holder's voting the shares for her. Under basic agency principles, the proxy holder must vote the shares in accordance with the proxy giver's instructions and the proxy is revocable, unless it is coupled with an interest.

Why do publicly held companies solicit proxies?

All state corporate statutes mandate that shareholders meet regularly and elect a board of directors. Usually, the corporation's bylaws contain the details governing these meetings and the process of electing directors.

Shareholders of publicly held companies are a dispersed, disorganized, and largely disinterested group. Seldom will voting for directors at the company's annual meeting be a matter of high priority for the overwhelming majority of shareholders. For example, assume a company's annual meeting of shareholders is to be held in New York City. It is highly unlikely that a shareholder living in Comfort, Arizona or other shareholders, living outside of New York, would consider taking the time or spending the money to attend the meeting.

Thus, if they vote at all, the vast majority of shareholders of publicly held corporations vote by proxies solicited by management. And management usually must solicit proxies to obtain a quorum so that business can be transacted at the meeting. The quorum requirement is typically a majority of the shares entitled to vote. Cf. § MBCA 7.25(a).

How and by whom is the proxy solicitation process regulated in publicly held corporations?

The process is regulated by federal (not state) law. Specifically, it is regulated under § 14(a) of the Securities Exchange Act of 1934 ("34 Act") and the rules thereunder, which are called the "**Proxy Rules**." If you think about it, it should seem a bit strange that the process is regulated under federal rather than state law. As you probably know the federal securities laws are mostly about buying and selling securities. The proxy rules are not about raising money or buying and selling stock. They are about corporate governance, an area traditionally regulated by the states.

Technically, there is no such thing as federal corporate law. But in some areas the securities laws spill over and regulate certain aspects of general corporate law. That raises the question:

Why was an additional layer of regulation imposed at the Federal level on the solicitation of proxies?

The answer is found in the legislative history of the 34 Act. The Congressional hearings which preceded passage of the 34 Act showed that there were significant abuses in the process and that state law was virtually void of any regulation of the shareholder voting process. Federal law, or more specifically the proxy rules, were passed to fill the gap. As a result, in publicly held companies—the GMs, Exxons and IBMs of the world—voting at shareholder's meetings are governed by federal law, rather than by Delaware or other state law. It is obviously more efficient to regulate proxy solicitations by large companies at the Federal level, since the activity obviously crosses many state borders.[4]

In Section 14(a) of the 34 Act, Congress gave the SEC the authority to regulate the process of voting by proxy. Section 14(a) of the 34 Act is strictly an **enabling provision**. The statute itself does not prohibit or require anything. It simply gives the SEC the authority to regulate the process and mandates that the SEC adopt rules governing the process.

The point is, you must look to the **rules** to find the substantive regulation—what is required and what is prohibited. Specifically, Regulation 14A, a series of 14 rules and two schedules that govern the solicitation of proxies. These rules have the force of law.

Do the proxy rules apply to all companies?

No. The proxy rules only apply to a sub-set of companies known as "companies registered under the 34 Act,"

4. The proxy rules illustrate that while the federal securities laws are primarily aimed at regulating the securities markets, in some areas these statutes spill over and regulate other corporate activities such as the voting process and corporate governance. In some areas it is difficult to determine precisely where general corporate law ends and securities regulation begins.

"reporting companies" or "publicly held companies"—all synonymous terms.

Do not confuse my use of the term "publicly held companies," which I use in this section to refer to companies subject to the proxy rules, with my use elsewhere in the book of the similar term "public company," a term used in this book to distinguish "public companies"—companies which have a market for their shares from "close corporations"—companies which have no market for their shares. The term "publicly held company," is a word of art—a defined term under § 12 of the 34 Act. It means a company that either:

(1) Has a class of securities listed on a national securities exchange—§ 12(b); or

(2) At the end of a fiscal year has 500 or more shareholders and assets of $10 million or more—§ 12(g).

If a company meets either of the above tests the company must register under the 34 Act and, as a result of that registration, it becomes a "publicly held company" for 34 Act purposes. That status subjects the company to a number of obligations and requirements, one of which is the proxy rules.

————

The proxy rules come into play in two different fact situations: (1) contested elections and (2) non-contested elections. Contested elections involve a proxy fight for control of the corporation. In a contested election, not only the directors proposed by management but also an insurgent group, trying to kick out the incumbents and elect its own slate of directors, are soliciting proxies.

Non-contested elections involve the usual annual meeting of shareholders (or sometimes a special meeting), where the shareholders are required by state corporate law to meet and elect directors (and sometimes approve other matters). The only party soliciting proxies in this situation is management. Contested elections (sometimes known as proxy fights) are rare and beyond the scope of the basic business course. This book only discusses the proxy rules in the context of non-contested proxy solicitations.

How do the proxy rules regulate a routine non-contested solicitation of proxies?

The proxy rules do three things: (1) require that the party soliciting proxies file the proxy material with the SEC in advance of soliciting proxies, (2) regulate the type of information that the proxy material can contain as well as the format in which the information is presented and (3) impose liability if the proxy soliciting material is materially false or misleading.

In basic concept and approach, the proxy solicitation process is regulated in much the same way as the process of going public. The proxy rules were modeled after the 33 Act registration requirements which govern public offerings (a process discussed later in § VIII.G, *infra.*) Both the proxy rules and § 5 of the 33 Act require the preparation and delivery of a comprehensive disclosure document. In public offerings the disclosure document is called a prospectus. In the solicitation of proxies the disclosure document is called a proxy statement. Both require full and accurate disclosure of detailed material information.

A **proxy statement** is a comprehensive disclosure document which must accurately and truthfully provide all of the information relevant to the matters to be voted on at the meeting. The linchpin of proxy regulation is Rule 14a–3, which provides that no one may solicit a proxy unless the solicitation is accompanied or preceded by a proxy statement. Solicitation is broadly defined as the first step in a campaign to solicit votes. Rule 14a–3 also requires the proxy statement to be accompanied or preceded by an annual report to shareholders, containing specified financial data. Rule 14a–4 regulates the form of the proxy card on which shareholders indicate their approval or disapproval of each matter voted on at the meeting.

Pursuant to Rule 14a–6, definitive copies of the proxy statement and form of proxy must be filed with the SEC at or before the time they are first mailed to shareholders. If the proxy solicitation relates to any matters other than the election of directors, approval of accountants or shareholder proposals, preliminary copies of the proxy statement and form of proxy must be filed with the SEC at least ten days prior to mailing. The SEC staff often comments on, and sometimes insists on changes, in the proxy material before it is mailed.

c. Shareholder Proposals

In addition to regulating the proxy solicitation process and the information contained in the proxy statement, the proxy rules regulate so called "shareholder proposals" under Rule 14a–8. The details regarding shareholder proposals are outside the scope of this book. However, shareholder proposals involve free speech and corporate democracy and they have been increasing in recent years. Thus, some professors like to discuss them and you should know what they are.

What are shareholder proposals?

Rule 14a–8 gives any security holder of a publicly held company who owns at least $1,000 worth of or 1% of the securities eligible to vote at the meeting the opportunity to get a referendum on issues the shareholder proposes at the meeting. Generally, the proposals are sponsored by economic, political or social activists seeking a shareholder vote on a wide variety of causes—*e.g.* management compensation, environmental matters, discrimination (there have been shareholder proposals both for and against affirmative action), gay rights (health insurance for gay partners) and a host of other issues.

When must a shareholder proposal be included in the proxy statement?

Rule 14a–8 contains a detailed set of rules that **permit management to exclude from the proxy statement the following types of shareholder proposals:**

(1) Proposals that are contrary to state law may be excluded. This rule rests on the same fundamental concept of governance discussed earlier. Namely, the corporation is managed by the board of directors and shareholders have no legal right to manage the company.

Thus, a proposal that General Motors stop making Oldsmobiles or shut down its plant in Yipsilante, Michigan because those operations are unprofitable can clearly be excluded. On the other hand proposals to shut down operations because of ethical or safety concerns—*i.e.*

human rights violations, asbestos concerns, etc.—raise close questions.

(2) Proposals that violate the law or rules of the SEC;

(3) Proposals that relate to personal claims or grievances. For example, a party to a sex discrimination suit against the company submits a proposal regarding the company's hiring practices of women;

(4) Proposals that relate to operations that account for less than 5% of the companies business or that have been rendered moot; and

(5) Proposals similar to proposals previously submitted during the past five years, which received less than a specified percentage of votes.

Procedure. Procedurally any shareholder meeting the standing requirement noted above initiates the process by submitting her proposal to the company and sending a copy to the SEC. If the company decides to exclude the proposal it so informs the submitting shareholder and the SEC, setting forth its reasons for exclusion.

The SEC staff acts as the umpire and decides whether or not the proposals must be included in the proxy statement. In at least 99 out of 100 cases the staff's decision ends the matter. But when a proposal is excluded the shareholder does, after exhausting her administrative remedies, have a right to appeal to the courts.

If the proposal is included (and many get on the ballot without company opposition) the proponent can write a 500 word statement in support of the proposal and management can write a similar statement in opposition. Both statements are included in the proxy statement.

d.　Liability for False or Misleading Statements in a Proxy Statement—Rule 14a–9

What happens if the proxy statement is false or misleading?

Rule 14a–9 makes it unlawful to solicit proxies by means of any proxy statement or other communication "containing any statement which is . . . false or misleading with respect to any material fact or which omits to state any material fact."

The SEC can enforce this rule through civil, criminal or injunctive actions. And since the 1964 Supreme Court decision in the case of *J.I. Case v. Borak* (1964), violations of Rule 14a–9 can be the basis of private civil suits by shareholders, individually or as a class.

The *Borak* case held that a shareholder, whose vote to approve a merger was obtained by means of a misleading proxy statement had an implied right of action for damages or other relief. Recognition of this so called "implied right of action" has been an important development in corporate jurisprudence of the 20th century, not only with respect to litigation under Rule 14a–9, but more importantly with respect to litigation under Rule 10b–5, the SEC's general anti-fraud rule, which is discussed in Chapter VII.[5]

5.　There is significant overlap in the elements necessary to state a cause of action under Rule 14a–9 and the broader and more widely used general antifraud rule, Rule 10b–5, which is discussed in depth in Chapter VII, *infra*. Much of what is said there relative to "securities fraud" cases is applicable here relative to "proxy fraud" cases.

What are the elements of a cause of action under Rule 14a–9?

To state a cause of action under Rule 14a–9, a plaintiff must show the following elements:

1. **Jurisdiction**.—The company soliciting the proxies was a company which is subject to proxy rules (*i.e.* meets the tests of § 12(b) or § 12(g) of the 34 Act, discussed above).

2. **Misstatement or omission of fact**.—Obviously the statement or omission must be shown to be false or misleading. This includes lies, half truths and deception—in general the same kinds of misconduct prohibited by Rule 10b–5. See § VII. B.2, *infra.*

In the case of *Virginia Bankshares, Inc. v. Sandberg* (1991) a key issue was not whether the statement was false or misleading but rather whether the statement was a "fact" as opposed to an opinion. The proxy statement soliciting shareholders approval of the proposed merger of a majority owned subsidiary into the parent company, included the following statement: "The Plan of Merger has been approved by the board of directors [of the subsidiary bank] because it provides an opportunity for the bank's shareholders to achieve a high value for their shares." The trial jury found that the directors of the subsidiary did not really believe that statement was true, but made the statement under coercion from the parent company. The Supreme Court held that this statement as to motive was a statement of fact. In other words, if the directors did not believe the statement but nevertheless made the statement, the false statement could be the basis for a cause of action under Rule 14a–9.

3. **Materiality**.—A Rule 14a–9 plaintiff must prove not only that a statement or omission is false or mislead-

ing, but also must prove the materiality of the misstatement or omission.

Materiality is a controlling concept, under both the 33 and 34 Acts. The linchpin of the entire disclosure-based system is that anything material must be disclosed, and conversely anything not material need not be disclosed. This is critical whether we are talking about liability for false and misleading statements in a 33 Act prospectus, violation of the proxy rules, or violation of Rule 10b–5, the general antifraud rule.

While materiality is a threshold issue under all three of the areas of the federal securities laws that we touch on in this book, the most frequently cited test of materiality comes from a case involving the proxy rules, *TSC Industries, Inc. v. Northway, Inc.* (1976). In that case the United States Supreme Court held that:

> An omitted fact is material if there is a substantial likelihood that a reasonable shareholder would consider [the omitted fact] important in deciding how to vote.... Put another way, there must be a substantial likelihood that the disclosure of the omitted fact would have been viewed by the reasonable investor as having altered the total mix of the information made available.

This is a common sense, jury oriented test. The question is: ***Would the reasonable prudent investor, in light of the total mix of information provided, consider the questioned information significant in making her decision*** as to how to vote (or, in the context of Rule 10b–5, whether to buy or sell the securities—see § VII.B.3, *infra*).

4. **Level of fault**.—Recall Rule 14a–9 merely prohib-its and does not expressly provide a remedy if the rule is violated. This raises the questions as to the level of fault required to maintain an action for violation of the Rule.

Does plaintiff have to show that the materially false or misleading statement or omission was made recklessly or intentionally (i.e., some level of scienter); is negligence enough; or is it enough just to show falsity?

The Supreme Court has not yet spoken to this issue, and so far, the lower federal courts are split on the issue. The current majority rule seems to be that the **level of culpability required depends on the remedy sought**.

If the remedy sought is merely an **injunction**—some sort of prospective relief—*i.e.,* postpone the meeting until we can work the matter out—**no level of fault is required**, not even negligence. If the remedy sought is rescission or damages—*i.e.,* undo a done deal, give plain-tiff $100 million in damages, etc.—all courts seem to agree that some **level of fault is required**. But the courts are split as to what the level of fault required is—negligence or scienter.

5. **Reliance/causation**.—Difficult questions can also arise as to the level of causation a complaining share-holder must establish between a misstatement or omis-sion in the proxy statement and approval of the transac-tion complained of. This is particularly relevant in cases where it is likely or certain that the transaction would have been approved, irrespective of how the complaining shareholder would have voted.

For example, in *Virginia Bankshares, Inc. v. Sandberg* Supreme Court spoke to this issue. The transaction challenged was a "freeze-out" merger, pursuant to which, the parent corporation, which owned 85% of subsidiary's stock, was seeking to acquire the interest of the minority shareholders. Since only an 80% vote was required to approve the merger, approval was assured. Nevertheless, the parent submitted the proposal to a vote of the minority shareholders, and the proxy statement was found to contain a material misrepresentation.

The Supreme Court reversed a lower court judgment for the plaintiff, holding that the fact that the parent corporation had the votes necessary to approve the merger, regardless of how the minority shareholders voted, broke the chain of causation.

6. **Remedies**.—The remedies available for violation of the proxy rules include injunctions, rescission and damages, or a combination of these remedies.

C. GOVERNANCE OF LIMITED LIABILITY COMPANIES

The rules governing the management of LLCs are flexible and vary from state to state. Today, most state LLC statutes afford the owners (called "members") the option of:

(1) Managing the business themselves—called a "**member-managed LLC**"; or

(2) Electing managers to manage the business—called a "**manager-managed LLC**."

The governance structure in an LLC is almost always set forth in a contract among the members called an operating agreement in most states. The decision-making authority of the members of a member-managed LLC is similar to that of partners in a general partnership. The decision-making authority of the managers of a manager-managed LLC is similar to that of the board of directors of a corporation. And most of the governance issues in an LLC are determined by contract law. See § V.B.3.a.(3), supra.

CHAPTER VI

WHAT ARE THE LEGAL DUTIES OF THE DECISION MAKERS AND HOW ARE THOSE DUTIES ENFORCED? (herein Fiduciary Duties)

In the last chapter we identified the real people, or groups of real people, who make decisions for business associations. With legal power goes legal responsibility. The decision makers for a business, whether the business is structured as a corporation, a partnership or an LLC are said to have "**fiduciary duties.**" And they may be exposed to liability if they violate those duties.

The word "fiduciary" comes from the law of trusts and, broadly speaking, involves acting for the benefit of someone else. However, fiduciary is a context oriented word which defies explicit definition and applies to a variety of relationships. Just as trustees owe fiduciary duties to beneficiaries and agents owe fiduciary duties to their principals, directors and officers of a corporation owe fiduciary duties to their corporations. The individuals who govern the other types of business associations also owe fiduciary duties to those businesses.

While the label "fiduciary" applies to a wide variety of relationships, the scope of the duty imposed may vary depending on the nature of the relationship. Justice Frankfurter effectively made that point in an often quot-

160

ed statement from his opinion in *SEC v. Chenery Corp.* (1943). He wrote:

> "Directors are fiduciaries ... but to say that a man is a fiduciary only begins the analysis; it gives direction to further inquiry.... What obligations does he owe as a fiduciary?"

This chapter is about the nature and scope of the fiduciary duties of the decision makers in the various types of business associations. The chapter also explores the manner in which fiduciary duties are enforced. They are enforced through a peculiar procedural vehicle developed years ago by courts of equity called the "shareholders derivative suit."

A. FIDUCIARY DUTIES OF CORPORATE DIRECTORS AND OFFICERS

1.   IN GENERAL

The state courts, rather than the legislatures, have primarily defined the scope of the fiduciary duties owed by directors and officers to their corporations.[1] In defining the scope of those duties, the courts have tried to strike a balance between giving managers the flexibility to run the business and holding the managers accountable to the owners of the business. This is not an easy

1. Recently, in response to the corporate scandals discussed earlier, Congress passed the Sarbanes–Oxley law, which in addition to imposing stricter regulation on accountants (See § I.A.5.d, *supra*), supplements state law by regulating certain practices of officers and directors of publicly held corporations. Sarbanes–Oxley mainly addresses specific abuses that came to light in the corporate scandals and it has not yet been fully implemented. Thus, fiduciary duties remain an area mainly regulated under state law.

balance to strike. As a result, the rules are often imprecise and often vary from state to state. Some scholars
have advocated stricter, more uniform and more clearly
defined standards and Sarbanes–Oxley may be a step in
this direction.

In general, the scope of the duties owed by directors
and high-level managing officers, such as the CEO, to
their corporations are substantially the same. Lower
level employees owe a lesser degree of duty, but all
officers and employees are agents of the corporation and
owe the corporation, which is the principal, certain
duties within the scope of their agency.

The law groups the fiduciary duties owed by directors
and officers to their corporations into two basic categories: (1) **the duty of care** and (2) **the duty of loyalty**.

2. THE DUTY OF CARE

The standard which generally governs the scope of the
duty of care required of corporate fiduciaries rests on the
reasonable prudent person standard familiar to students
of tort law. There are two major subsets of the duty of
care: (1) cases involving **action** by the directors or
officers that turns out to be wrong and (2) cases involving **inaction** resulting from inattention or lack of vigi-
lance.

a. Breach of the Duty of Care by Action

In these cases the directors or officers typically make
some type of decision or take some action which, with the
benefit of hindsight turns out to have been wrong and
results in a loss to the corporation. In this type of case,
courts give great deference to the judgment of directors

or officers in matters pertaining to business. The so-called "**business judgment rule**" reflects a judicial "hands off" attitude toward acts or omissions of directors and officers. A good judicial statement of the fundamental notion underlying the business judgment rule is found in *Joy v. North* (2d Cir. 1982):

> While it is often said that corporate directors and officers will be liable for negligence ... all seem agreed that such a statement is misleading. Whereas an automobile driver who makes a mistake in judgement as to speed or distance injuring a pedestrian will likely be called upon to respond in damages, a corporate officer who makes a mistake in judgement as to economic conditions, consumer tastes or production line efficiency will rarely, if ever, be found liable for damages suffered by the corporation.... [T]he fact is that liability is rarely imposed upon corporate directors or officers simply for bad judgement and this reluctance to impose liability for unsuccessful business decisions has been labeled the business judgement rule.

Shlensky v. Wrigley (Ill. App. 1968), which appears in most of the casebooks, is a classic example of a case that involves a dispute over **how the business should be run**. Phillip K. Wrigley owned over 80% of the stock of the corporation which owned the Chicago Cubs baseball team, a team which last won the World Series in 1908 and last appeared in the World Series in 1945. Mr. Wrigley and the directors believed that baseball should be played in the daytime and refused to install lights at Wrigley Field, even though at the time of this case, every other major league team had installed lights and had been playing the majority of their weekday games at night for years.

Shlensky, a minority stockholder, brought a shareholders' derivative suit against Mr. Wrigley and the other directors, to force the Cubs to install lights. Shlensky presented evidence that night baseball would make the Cubs more profitable. Mr. Wrigley and the other directors believed that night baseball might have a detrimental effect on the neighborhood around Wrigley Field. They argued that in the long run, neighborhood deterioration might hurt attendance at Cubs games.

The court dismissed Mr. Shlensky's complaint and held that the court would not second guess decisions of the directors **if there was a rational basis for their decision and there was no fraud, illegality or conflict of interest, even when, with the benefit of hindsight, it is shown the decision was wrong**.

The approach in the *Wrigley* case reflects the approach of almost all courts prior to the 1980s. Many courts still adhere to this approach, which is based on a policy of leaving business decisions to business people. As the *Wrigley* opinion said, courts do not have the training or expertise to second-guess business decisions made by disinterested business people who are acting without fraud or other taint.

In 1985 in *Smith v. Van Gorkom* (Del. 1985), the Delaware Supreme Court rendered a "famous" but controversial decision which narrowed the protection afforded directors' decisions under the business judgment rule. The *Van Gorkom* court took a different approach than the *Wrigley* court. The *Van Gorkom* court was far less deferential to the board's business judgment and was willing to second guess the board.

The facts involved a friendly cash-out merger and a fast-moving series of events which culminated in board approval of the merger. On September 13, 1980, Mr. Van Gorkom, the CEO of Trans Union Corp., a publicly held company, arranged a meeting with Jay Pritzker, a famous and highly successful businessman, to explore whether one of Mr. Pritzker's companies might have an interest in acquiring Trans Union at $55 per share. At the time Trans Union was trading on the New York Stock Exchange at around $38 per share. The $55 per share price was based on an earlier informal study which had concluded that the intrinsic value of the Trans Union stock for leveraged buy out purposes was between $55 and $60 per share.

Following further conversations, on September 18, Pritzker offered to buy Trans Union for $55 per share, the price suggested by Van Gorkom at their initial meeting. He gave Van Gorkom three days to accept or reject the offer. Since this was a transaction which required board (as well as shareholder) approval, Von Gorkom called a special meeting of the Trans Union board on Saturday, September 20, 1980.

The board meeting, described in great detail in the opinion, lasted two hours. Only two of the ten directors knew prior to the meeting that the purpose of the meeting was to consider selling the company. Van Gorkom made a 20–minute oral presentation in which he outlined the terms of the deal. There was no written summary and the merger documents were not available for review.

A Trans Union attorney, who attended the meeting, advised the board that "they might be sued if they did not accept the Pritzkar offer" ($55 per share represented a premium of about 45% over the market price of the stock on the New York Stock Exchange). The deal was ultimately structured in a way that allowed Trans Union to solicit other bidders, who might top the Pritzker offer for a period of 90 days. No one else made an offer during this period. The board unanimously approved the merger. Later, Trans Union's shareholders approved the merger by a margin of 10 to 1.

Plaintiff brought a class action law suit against the members of the Trans Union board, which consisted of five inside and five outside directors. The Delaware Court of Chancellory (trial court) entered summary judgment for the defendants. In a 3–2 decision, the Delaware Supreme Court reversed and remanded. The majority opinion said that prior to approving the merger, the directors had a duty to inform themselves adequately of the terms of the merger and that failure to do so amounts to gross negligence, which is not protected by the business judgement rule.

As the dissenting opinion suggests, the majority in *Van Gorkom* went to great length to emphasize a litany of things the Trans Union board did or failed to do:

(1) inquire into Mr. Van Gorkom's role in suggesting the terms of the merger;

(2) accepted, without question, the chief financial officer's opinion that $55 per share was within the fair

range of intrinsic value established by the company's internal leveraged buy out study;

(3) did not get a "fairness" opinion from an outside investment banking firm;

(4) acted too quickly, without proper notice or deliberation; and

(5) did not review the merger documents.

And the majority ignored a number of facts, which under prior decisions, such as *Wrigley,* would have supported the lower court's verdict under the business judgement rule:

(1) the $55 per share price represented a 45% premium over the $38 per share market price;

(2) the $55 was within the range of intrinsic value established by an internal leveraged buy out study;

(3) the advice by the Trans Union attorney that the directors might be sued if they did not accept the Pritzker offer;

(4) the pressure on the board created by Pritzker's deadline for acceptance;

(5) the knowledge and experience of a well qualified board;

(6) the fact that no competing bidders topped the Pritzker offer during the period in which competing bids were invited; and

(7) the overwhelming approval of the deal by shareholders.

Almost all law schools cover *Smith v. Van Gorkom* in depth in the basic business associations course and most law professors are critical of the decision. One highly respected scholar described *Smith v. Van Gorkom* as "one of the worst decisions in the history of corporate law."

Despite the abundance of scholarly analysis, the impact this case has had on the scope of the business judgment rule is still not fully understood. The following two points about *Smith v. Van Gorkom* might get you points on your exam. First, the Delaware Supreme Court got much more involved in reviewing the directors' decision making process than had been the judicial practice prior to this decision. Recall, in *Wrigley* the court stated judges do not have the training or expertise to second-guess business decisions made by the board. The *Wrigley* court implicitly said it did not want to get involved. In *Smith v. Van Gorkom* the court got totally involved. It seemed to be second-guessing every aspect of the board's decision. Second, the *Van Gorkom* case seems to require the board to scrutinize mergers, acquisitions and other end-game transactions more closely than ordinary operating decisions such as day or night baseball.

Impact of *Van Gorkom* on board behavior. *Van Gorkom* has had a major impact on board behavior and procedures, particularly in the area of mergers and acquisitions. Today, before a board authorizes a major acquisition, it gets a third party to render a "fairness opinion," which values the company being acquired. The board goes through elaborate decision making procedures scripted by their lawyers—*i.e.*, numerous meetings, a voluminous paper trail, etc.

Impact of *Van Gorkom* on state legislatures. *Van Gorkom* has also had an impact on state legislatures. Following this decision, premiums for directors' and officers' liability insurance (D & O insurance) increased dramatically. Today, few qualified people would serve as directors unless they are provided adequate D & O insurance.

The Delaware legislature quickly responded to the so-called "D & O insurance crisis" by adopting a statutory provision which enabled corporations to shield directors from personal liability for breach of their duty of care. See Del. § 102(b)(7). Notice that Del. § 102(b)(7) only applies to duty of care (not duty of loyalty) violations and only applies to directors (not officers). Statutory provisions like Del. § 102(b)(7), which have been enacted by a number of states, negate much of the impact of the *Van Gorkom* decision and make it harder to recover against directors for bad decisions. MBCA § 2.02(b)(4) provides protection similar to that of the Delaware statute against liability for duty of care violations.

b. Breach of the Duty of Care by Inaction

Directors are expected to monitor the performance of the CEO and other senior managers to whom the directors have delegated the day-to-day management of the company. They face potential liability if they go "to sleep at the switch" while officers and other managers harm the corporation. This aspect of the duty of care has been described as follows:

> Every director has an affirmative duty to inform himself/herself about the performance of the company, to attend meetings regularly, to be vigilant, to

make an appropriate degree of inquiry and to act for
the general welfare of the corporation.

However, the scope of a director's duty to monitor is not
clear and courts have been reluctant to impose liability
for director inaction. The following two cases illustrate
issues often encountered in suits involving inaction (lack
of diligence) on the part of the board of directors.

In *Barnes v. Andrews* (S.D.N.Y. 1924), the corporation,
Liberty Starters Corp., was formed to make starters for
Ford automobiles and aircraft. Liberty had raised a substantial amount of money through a stock offering. Mr.
Andrews, a wealthy investor and personal friend of Maynard, the promoter and president of Liberty Starters was
one of the investors in Liberty. About a year after
Liberty was formed Mr. Andrews became a director of
Liberty. Andrews resigned ten months later, which was
about a year prior to Liberty's going into receivership.
Andrews and Maynard frequently drove into the city
together. The opinion states that (1) Andrews attended
all but one of the board meetings during the time he
served on the board, (2) his "integrity was unques-
tioned" and (3) he did from time-to-time inquire in a
general way of Maynard how things were going at Liberty, but he was content to accept general answers (such as
"everything is going fine" or "it looks promising"). He
never pressed Maynard for details, even though the company was producing nothing and "slowly bleeding to
death."

Due to technology problems and disagreements among
the managers, Liberty never produced a single starter. It
went into receivership and many investors, including the

defendant Mr. Andrews, lost money. Barnes, the receiver, sued Andrews for breach of his duty of care.

In this famous opinion, Judge Learned Hand addressed issues dealing with both the scope of a director's duty and causation. First, the opinion held that the scope of a director's duty of care encompasses a duty to inform himself of what was going on with some particularity and that Mr. Andrews breached that duty. Second, Hand's opinion held that Mr. Andrews was not liable because the plaintiff failed to show Andrews' breach of duty was the proximate cause of the injury to the corporation. In other words, the opinion states plaintiff failed to show that even if Andrews had made the inquiry required of a diligent director, he could not have prevented Liberty Starter from going into receivership.

In *Francis v. United Jersey Bank* (N.J. 1981), Mrs. Pritchard inherited 48 percent of the stock in a closely held business from her husband, the founder of the business. The couple's two sons (who owned the rest of the stock) took over management of the business after Mr. Pritchard's death. The sons and other employees allegedly misappropriated large sums of the company's clients' money and the corporation filed for bankruptcy.

Mrs. Pritchard and her two sons were the only directors. The evidence showed that Mrs. Pritchard knew nothing about the business and did nothing to learn about it. In fact, following her husband's death, she became depressed, drank heavily and rarely attended board meetings. The trustee in bankruptcy sued Mrs. Pritchard's estate, alleging that she violated her duty of care.

The court held that Mrs. Pritchard breached her duty of care and that failure to discharge her duty, as a director, caused harm to the corporation. In other words, in this case the plaintiff prevailed on the causation issue as well as on the duty issue.

What is the distinction between the Andrews and United Jersey Bank cases?

Andrews involved operating problems. If, as in *Andrews*, the problem the director fails to discover is a general operating problem, it will usually be difficult for plaintiff to show that if the director had discovered the problem he would have been able to correct it.

In contrast, if, as in *United Jersey Bank*, the improper conduct the director fails to discover is conduct, such as embezzlement, improper loans, self-dealing, etc., it is obvious that had the director discovered the improper conduct, she could have prevented further wrong-doing by threatening to expose the wrongdoers or calling the authorities.

What is the scope of the directors' duty to inquire or to monitor the activities of the officers and other employees of the corporation?

MBCA § 8.30(b) and the case law suggest that, except in special situations, which require a "due diligence" investigation, such as a public offering or a major merger, the directors can rely on information provided them by officers and other employees. As long as the director' reliance is reasonable and in good faith, the directors do not have to independently verify the information given to them by the officers and employees. For example, the directors can rely on information furnished by the CEO as to the status of overall operations and they can rely on figures supplied by the CFO as to financial condition and profitability.

The main limitation to the general rule of reasonable reliance, stated in the preceding paragraph, is triggered if the directors become aware of something (some kind of red flag is raised) that puts the board on inquiry notice. If that happens the board is required to carry out a detailed, systematic investigation.

Despite MBCA § 8.30(b) and the case law, the relatively recent Delaware case of *In re Caremark Intern., Inc.* (Del. Ch., 1996) suggests that the board may have a duty to install some sort of monitoring system to enable it to better discharge its oversight obligation. It should be noted that the broad statements made the *Caremark* opinion are dicta because, in the case before it, the court was merely approving an agreed settlement in which the directors promised to do a better job of monitoring in the future.

3.   THE DUTY OF LOYALTY

In the *Hornbook on Corporation Law*, Professor Gevurtz describes the cases we have just covered (*i.e.* cases in which the complaint is that the directors or officers breached their **duty of care**) as cases where the directors were **"lazy or dumb."** He then describes the cases, which we will cover in this section dealing with the **duty of loyalty** as cases where the officers and directors are **"greedy and put their own financial interests ahead of the interests of the corporation or its shareholders."** This is an effective way to point out the basic conceptual distinction between duty of care and duty of loyalty cases.

Duty of loyalty cases involve conflicts of interest. There are many ways in which a director or officer can breach the duty of loyalty. Stealing company assets or competing with the company, while employed by the company are two examples of breaches of the duty of loyalty. But they are probably too obvious to be on your test. I will focus on the two duty of loyalty applications which are more likely to be tested in your course on business associations and more likely to arise when you get out into practice: (1) **interested director transactions** and (2) **usurping corporate opportunities**.

It is very important to understand at the outset that **business judgment rule protection is not an issue in duty of loyalty cases.** The reason is duty of loyalty cases all involve some level of conflicts of interest and conflicts of interest preclude application of the business judgment rule.

a.   Interested Director Transactions

Conflicts of interest occur in a variety of ways. For example, officers or directors of a company may directly or indirectly own property that they sell or lease to their company, they may enter into contracts with their company to provide goods or services, etc. Most situations where one or more directors or officers, either directly or indirectly, are on both sides of the transaction, are now resolved under so called "conflict of interest" statutes. The application of the conflict of interest statutes is easier to understand in the context of history.

History—The early common law rule of automatic voidability. The 19th century rule governing interested director transactions was that all transactions between directors or officers and their corporations or between corporations with common directors were voidable at the election of the corporation. In other words, under the common law rule a mere showing that a director or officer had a financial interest on both sides of a transaction was enough to void the transaction. It did not matter whether the corporation benefitted from the transaction or that other directors, who had no financial interest in the transaction, approved the transaction. This was called the "voidability per se" rule.

Modern conflict of interest statutes. Beginning in the early part of the 20th century, the states began enacting so called conflict of interest statutes, which changed the common law rule of voidability per se. Today, almost all cases involving interested director transactions are resolved under these statutes. The general approach of these statutes is that even if there is a conflict of interest, the transaction is **not voidable** if certain statutory tests are met.

Analyzing an interested director transaction under a modern conflict of interest statute. While the particulars of the conflict of interest statutes vary, the overall approach followed by most is similar. See, *e.g.,* Del. § 144. Most modern conflict of interest statutes incorporate a three step process of analysis:

(1) Is the transaction within the statute?

(2) What is required by the statute to avoid voidability?

(3) What is the effect of satisfying the statute?

The three step process of analysis under the conflict of interest statutes plays out as follows:

(1) *Is the transaction within the statute*?

A transaction falls within the statute if the transaction is between the corporation and an officer or director of the corporation, who has a **direct or an indirect interest in the transaction.**

If a transaction falls within the statutory definition, you have a conflict of interest. It does not matter that the transaction might have benefitted the corporation or been eminently fair. Under the statutes "conflict of interest" does not mean the transaction is voidable. In fact, the transaction is not voidable if the person with the conflict of interest complies with the statute.

(2) *What is required by the statute to avoid voidability?*

First, full disclosure of all material facts concerning the conflict of interest and the transaction.

Second, ratification of the transaction by a majority of the disinterested directors (or if it is not practical to get board ratification, ratification by a majority of the disinterested shareholders).

Third, if she can not get director or shareholder ratification, the interested party, under some, but not all state conflict of interest statutes can still defeat voidability if she can meet the burden of proving that the transaction was fair. The statutes are state-specific as to whether fairness will suffice in situations where neither board or shareholder approval is obtained.

(3) *What is the effect of complying with the statute?*

If the requirements of the statute are satisfied, the transaction is not voidable, even though there was a conflict of interest.

b. Usurpation of Corporate Opportunities

Another major subset of the duty of loyalty may arise when directors or officers take for themselves business opportunities that might be of interest to the corporations they serve. **Usurping a corporate opportunity violates the basic rule that directors and officers cannot utilize their positions with a corporation to whom they owe fiduciary duties to profit personally at the expense of the corporation**. While easy enough to state, this rule has been difficult to apply, because in deciding specific cases before them, courts try to strike a balance between two conflicting policies:

(1) Discouraging disloyal behavior by officers and directors toward the corporations they serve; and

(2) Permitting directors and officers of corporations to engage in entrepreneurial activities in their individual capacity.

The courts have not developed a clear test to determine which opportunities belong to the corporation and which opportunities the directors and officers may take for themselves. Rather, over the years, the courts have applied several different tests, which are state specific as well as fact specific.

(1) Tests

The tests, applied by the courts over the years include the following:

The interest or expectancy test. The interest or expectancy test restricts a director or officer from taking property or a business opportunity for himself where the corporation has an existing interest in the property or opportunity or has an expectancy growing out of an existing interest. Generally this is the least restrictive of the various tests in terms of the opportunities it allows officers and directors to pursue. However, the scope of the restriction imposed under this test has varied depending on how various courts interpret "interest" or "expectancy."

The line of business test. Under this test, an officer or director must turn over to the corporation any opportunity which is in, or relates to, the corporation's business. The scope of the prohibition under this test may vary substantially depending on how a particular court in a given case interprets the scope of a particular corporation's "business."

The Delaware courts use the line of business test. *Guth v. Loft, Inc.* (Del. 1939) is a famous case in which the Delaware courts applied this test. The defendant, Guth was the president of Loft, Inc., a manufacturer of candy, syrup and beverages. Megargel, who at the time controlled the National Pepsi–Cola Company ("Old Pepsi"), informed Guth of the opportunity to buy the assets of Old Pepsi, which was then in bankruptcy. The assets of Old Pepsi at the time consisted mainly of its secret formula for making Pepsi–Cola and the Pepsi trademarks.

Guth and Megargel formed a new company ("New Pepsi") which bought the assets of Old Pepsi and produced and marketed the soft drink now known as Pepsi–Cola. Guth also used Loft's facilities and resources to improve the Pepsi–Cola formula. Loft sued claiming that Guth had usurped a corporate opportunity.

The Delaware Supreme Court held that Guth had breached his fiduciary duty to Loft and ordered him to transfer his stock in New Pepsi to Loft. The opinion stated that since the opportunity acquired by Guth was so close to the business of Loft, Guth's acquisition of the opportunity was prohibited, even though the opportunity originally came to Guth in his individual, rather than his corporate, capacity. The court also indicated that it would have so ruled even if Guth had not used Loft's facilities and resources in developing the opportunity.

The fairness test. Some courts have stated the test as to whether an officer or director usurped a corporate opportunity is simply a test of basic fairness under the circumstances. Courts applying the fairness test to corporate opportunities look to a variety of factors, such as: (1) did the information come to the defendant by reason of his position with the corporation, (2) how important the opportunity was to the corporation, (3) was the corporation seeking the opportunity, (4) whether the defendant used corporate funds or facilities in acquiring or developing the opportunity, and (5) whether the corporation had the resources to develop the opportunity.

The two-step test. The two-step test combines the line of business test with the fairness test. Under the two-step test the court first considers whether the opportunity was in the corporation's line of business. If so, the court then considers whether it was nevertheless fair for the defendant to pursue the opportunity. The burden of proof as to the first question is on the plaintiff. If the plaintiff meets this burden, the burden shifts to the defendant to show that despite being in the same line of business, defendant's taking of the opportunity was fair based on equitable considerations.

The ALI test. The American Law Institute's Corporate Governance Project ("ALI") has formulated a new approach for analyzing corporate opportunity cases, which was discussed in *Northeast Harbor Golf Club, Inc. v. Harris* (Me. 1995), a case which appears in many casebooks.

In *Northeast Harbor*, Nancy Harris was president of a corporation which owned and operated a golf club in Bar Harbor, Maine. She personally purchased two parcels of land near the club and informed the Club's board of directors of both purchases. She learned of the availability of the first parcel (the Gilpin property) in her capacity as president of the club. She learned of the availability of the second parcel (the Smallidge property) in her individual capacity.

The board voiced no objection when originally told of the purchases. However, years later, when Ms. Harris announced that she planned to develop the properties, the club sued Ms. Harris for usurping a corporate opportunity by buying the two parcels of land.

The trial court held that Harris had not usurped a corporate opportunity because buying land was not in the corporation's line of business and the corporation lacked the financial resources to buy the properties. The Supreme Court of Maine reversed and remanded. The court rejected the Delaware "line of business" test and instructed the lower court to apply the test, set out below, that had recently been formulated by the ALI.

ALI Principles of Corporate Governance § 5.05(b) defines a corporate opportunity as a business opportunity that:

(1) the director or officer becomes aware of in his corporate capacity or through the use of corporate information or property, which the director or officer should reasonably know is being offered to the corporation or reasonably believes would be of interest to the corporation; or

(2) the director or officer knows is closely related to a business in which the corporation is engaged or expects to engage.

If there is a corporate opportunity, then the question becomes whether the taking of the opportunity was approved in the manner fixed by § 505(a), which generally requires the officer or director to make full disclosure and give the corporation the chance to take or reject the opportunity.

(2) Defenses

Is financial inability of the corporation to take advantage of the opportunity a defense?

Some courts have held that a defense based on the corporation's financial inability to undertake the corporate opportunity presented can only be raised in cases where the corporation is legally bankrupt or at least de facto insolvent.

However, other courts have applied a less restrictive test and allow any form of financial inability of the corporation to be used as a defense. Recall in the *Northeast Harbor* case, the trial court cited the lack of the club's financial wherewithal to buy the real estate as one of the reasons it held in favor of Ms. Harris.

Is offering the corporation a chance to acquire the opportunity a defense?

If the corporate opportunity is offered to the corporation—with full disclosure—and an impartial board declines to take the opportunity, that is a **complete defense**. The factual issues, relative to the application of this defense you might see on an exam are whether: (1) the board was, in fact, **impartial**; and (2) **full disclosure** was, in fact, made.

This defense significantly lessens the impact of the corporate opportunity doctrine because it **merely requires the director or officer to offer the opportunity to the corporation** before personally taking advantage of the opportunity.

(3) Remedy

The usual remedy if a corporate opportunity is usurped is to place the property or opportunity wrongfully acquired and any profits derived therefrom in a **constructive trust** for the benefit of the corporation. Usually the corporation must reimburse the officer or director for his acquisition costs. Some courts have allowed punitive damages in cases involving bad faith.

B. FIDUCIARY DUTIES OF CONTROL SHAREHOLDERS

Control shareholders also owe certain fiduciary duties to their corporations. The fiduciary duties of control shareholders differ from the fiduciary duties of directors and officers in both nature and scope.

1. DEFINING CONTROL

Who is a control shareholder?

The definition of a control shareholder, sometimes called an affiliate, is a shareholder or affiliated group of shareholders **with demonstrated ability to influence a majority of the board**.

The clearest evidence of control is someone who owns a majority of the outstanding stock—*i.e.,* 51% or more. And in certain close corporations majority stock ownership may be required. On the other hand, in publicly held corporations with widely dispersed shareholders, far less than 51% would likely constitute control. A control person may be a parent corporation, an individual or a so called control group—*e.g.,* closely aligned family members, the CEO and his top lieutenants, etc.

The test is **de facto control**. If, as a practical matter, a person can walk into the board room and say, "I want this done" and what he wants done consistently gets done, without argument, that person is a control person.

2. CONTROL SHAREHOLDERS' FIDUCIARY DUTIES

If a person is identified as a control shareholder or a member of a control group, does that person owe fiduciary duties to the corporation and its minority shareholders?

Control shareholders owe fiduciary duties to the corporation and its minority shareholders. The fiduciary duties of control shareholders do not parallel those of directors and officers. Rather, the nature and scope of a control shareholder's fiduciary duties vary depending on the nature of the transaction and whether the corporation is a public or closely held corporation.

I will discuss the nature and scope of the fiduciary duties of control shareholders in three situations. The situations discussed are not the only ones in which issues dealing with control shareholder's fiduciary duties might arise, but they are three common situations which are often discussed and tested.

(1) Dealings between a parent and a majority-owned subsidiary,

(2) Freezeout merger transactions, and

(3) Sale of control.

a. Dealings Between a Parent and a Majority–Owned Subsidiary

A parent corporation, by definition a control person, dictates how the subsidiary will operate and usually executives of the parent control the board of the subsidiary. This creates multiple conflicts of interest and often raises the following threshold question:

Should the questioned transaction be given a presumption of propriety under the business judgment rule or should the transaction be subject to fairness review as a conflict of interest situation?

Sinclair Oil Corp. v. Levien (Del. 1971), a case found in most casebooks, speaks to this question. The Delaware Supreme Court held that transactions between parent and subsidiary companies are subject to fairness review only if the minority shareholder shows "self-dealing" in which the controlling parent prefers itself at the expense of minority shareholders. Another way of stating the test is **whether through the exercise of influence by the parent (*i.e., "self-dealing"*), the parent received a benefit and the subsidiary's minority shareholders suffered a detriment**.

The *Sinclair* case illustrates the application of the **benefit and detriment** test by distinguishing between two sets of transactions challenged by minority shareholders of Sinven, Sinclair's 97% owned Venezuelan subsidiary:

(1) Sinclair caused Sinven not to enforce certain contracts for the sale of oil at specified prices made with wholly owned subsidiaries of Sinclair. The court treated the nonenforcement of these contracts as self-dealing transactions (*i.e.*, Sinclair received a benefit and Sinven suffered a detriment). The burden then shifted to Sinclair to show its decision not to enforce the contracts was intrinsically fair, and Sinclair did not meet that burden. The practice was, therefore, subject to fairness review by the court.

(2) Sinven had a policy of paying high dividends. Over a seven year period the subsidiary had paid $38 million more in dividends than it had earned. The burden was on the minority shareholders to show self-dealing—a burden the minority shareholders

failed to meet. Since all of Sinven's shareholders (minority and majority) received the same proportionate share of dividends plaintiffs did not meet its burden of showing self-dealing. Therefore the dividend policy was afforded the presumption of propriety under the business judgment rule.

While the Delaware benefit **and** detriment test is now the majority rule, there is a minority rule which imposes on the parent the burden of showing intrinsic fairness, if the transaction (1) causes harm to the minority shareholders **or** (2) enables the majority shareholder to obtain an exclusive benefit.

In other words, under majority rule, minority shareholders must show **both** a benefit and detriment to impose the burden of proving intrinsic fairness on the controlling majority shareholder. On the other hand under the minority rule, minority shareholders can impose the burden of showing intrinsic fairness on the controlling majority shareholder by showing **either a benefit** to the majority **or a detriment** to the minority.

b. Freeze Out Mergers Transactions

The corporate statutes of every state contain merger statutes which allow two or more corporations to merge into a single corporate entity. We will learn more about mergers in Chapter X. For now, we simply need to realize that the merger statutes can be used to eliminate the interests of minority shareholders. Mergers effected for that purpose are called "freeze out," or "cash out" mergers.

The end result of a "freeze out" merger is the minority shareholders receive cash for their interests and the majority shareholder ends up owning 100% of the equity of the subsidiary. Obviously, the minority stockholders are entitled to receive a fair price for their shares. The majority has enough votes to approve the freeze out mergers even if the minority objects.

In freeze out mergers the parent corporation has a clear conflict of interest and there is obvious potential for abuse. This is because the majority shareholder (usually a parent corporation) wants to pay the minority shareholders as little as possible for their interests. Thus, freeze out mergers often generate litigation and minority shareholders have a choice of remedies which have been asserted in litigation involving freeze out mergers.[2] In this chapter our focus is on minority shareholders' most common remedy, actions in state court against the parent (*i.e.* the control shareholder) for breach of fiduciary duties.

Weinberger v. UOP, Inc. (Del. 1983), a major decision handed down by the Delaware Supreme Court in 1983, is found in most casebooks. This decision not only clarified the law in Delaware but also influenced the law in other states. In addition, the principles of this case have been applied not just to freezeout mergers but in other areas as well.

2. Remedies include suits for violation of the SEC's proxy rules as discussed in *Virginia Bankshares, Inc. v. Sandberg* (1991) and suits for violation of rule 10b–5 as discussed in *Santa Fe Industries, Inc. v. Green* (1977). Both these cases are discussed in detail elsewhere in this book.

Signal, which owned 50.5% of UOP's outstanding stock, decided to acquire the remaining 49.5% of the stock held by minority shareholders in exchange for cash. Arledge and Chitea, two Signal employees who sat on the UOP board, did a feasibility study in which they concluded that acquiring the remainder of the UOP stock at up to $24 a share would be a good investment for Signal. Signal offered $21 a share for the minority interest based on a fairness opinion prepared by Lehmann Brothers. At the time the UOP stock was trading in the range of $14 to $15 per share. The 6 non-Signal directors met and approved the plan of merger (the 7 Signal directors abstained). Later the merger was also approved by a majority of the minority shareholders of UOP.

Weinberger, a minority shareholder of UOP, sued Signal, UOP and various directors for breach of fiduciary duty. In his class action law suit, he alleged the minority shareholders were not paid enough for their shares of UOP.

The lower court held for the defendant, but the Delaware Supreme Court reversed and remanded. In its opinion the Delaware Supreme Court established what has come to be known as the "**entire fairness test**." The two prongs of the entire fairness test are: **fair dealing** and **fair price**. The court held that this acquisition failed both prongs of the test. In holding that the UOP acquisition failed the fair dealing prong of the entire fairness test the Delaware Supreme Court considered:

- The unreasonable time constraints placed on the UOP board (the deal initiated by Signal was presented to and approved by the UOP board in four business days);

- Lehman's fairness opinion, which was prepared on a hurry up basis, at the request of Signal;

- Less than full disclosure, because Arledge and Chitea's feasibility study, in which they concluded a price of $24 per share would be a fair price, was not disclosed to UOP's board of directors or shareholders.

In addition, the court held that this deal also failed the fair price prong of the entire fairness test. This part of the decision was based on issues outside the scope of the basic business association course (and this book). Today the entire fairness test is not limited to freeze out merger cases, but is also used in other areas where fairness review is required.

c.   Sale of Control

Another situation in which issues relating to a control shareholder's fiduciary duties sometimes come into play involves the sale of control. For example, assume that the stock of ABC Corporation is trading at $12 a share. Harry owns 51% of ABC's stock. The remaining 49% is owned by numerous public shareholders. Joe wants to buy control of ABC. Joe agrees to pay Harry $20 a share for his controlling interest in ABC. The $8 per share over and above the market price is called a **control premium**.

A control premium is the excess over and above the market value of a block of stock that comes with controlling the corporation's business. Control is a valuable commodity. It is the key to the corporation's treasury, assets and earning power. Common sense should tell you that control may be worth a premium over market price. My example raises the following question:

Does Harry have to share the $8 a share he received as a control premium with the minority shareholders?

As a general rule, the answer is **no**. The mere fact a control shareholder gets a premium for his control stock does not in and of itself create a cause of action in favor of the corporation or the minority shareholders. A shareholder can sell his stock for whatever price he can get for the stock, including a control premium, subject to certain exceptions.

The exceptions are situations recognized by the case law, where the sale of control violates fiduciary duties owed by the controlling shareholder to the corporation or the minority shareholders. Two exceptions to the general rule are:

- A control person cannot sell to a person he has reason to believe will loot the corporation; and

- A control person cannot divert a corporate opportunity to himself.

(1) Sale to Looters

A control person cannot sell control of the corporation to persons she has reason to believe will loot the corporation. Since there are not many buyers who announce that they want to buy control of the company so they can loot it, the issue in these cases usually boils down to the question—What is the scope of the sellers duty of inquiry regarding the buyer?

DeBaun v. First Western Bank & Trust Co. (Cal. App. 1975) is a classic example of a looting case. Johnson, the founder of a successful close corporation, owned 70 of the 100 outstanding shares. When Johnson died, the Bank, as Johnson's executor, sold his shares to a company controlled by Mattison, who looted the corporation. In about a year he turned a corporation with a positive net worth of $220,000 into one with a negative net worth of $218,000—a negative turn-around of about $450,000.

The bank failed to adequately investigate the buyer, Mattison. Public records in Los Angeles County revealed a mass of information on Mattison, including 38 unsatisfied judgments (some for fraud). An investigation would have revealed that Mattison did not have the wherewithal to buy the corporation, without dipping into the corporation's assets and retained earnings.

The minority shareholders DeBaun and Stephans, who owned 20 and 10 shares, respectively, sued and recovered the from the Bank on a derivative theory. They recovered the net asset value of the Corporation when Mattison bought in, plus an amount equal to anticipated after-tax earnings and the sum required to pay existing claims incurred while Mattison was running (looting) the company. In a looting case, if the plaintiff can prove specific damages she can recover either from the looter or the former controlling shareholder, who sold to the looter. Here the Bank, which sold to a looter without making a reasonable investigation, was liable for all damages proximately caused by its breach of duty.

(2) Diverting a Corporate Opportunity

A control shareholder who diverts a corporate opportunity, in which all shareholders might have shared, to himself violates his fiduciary duties and may have to share the control premium with minority shareholders.

The case included in most casebooks to illustrate the application of this rule is *Perlman v. Feldmann* (2d Cir. 1955). The opinion is less than a model of clarity, and scholars have been debating the exact basis for the holding for years.

The relevant facts are Feldmann and members of his family owned approximately 37% of the outstanding stock of Newport Steel Corporation, a publicly held company. Feldmann was also the president and chairman of the board of Newport Steel. His status as a control person was not disputed in the case.

Newport manufactured steel, which during the Korean war was in short supply. The buyer, Wilport Company, a syndicate of end users of steel products, wanted to acquire a dependable new source of supply. There was evidence that Wilport or another potential buyer had proposed to acquire Newport through a plan of acquisition in which all of Newport's shareholders (majority as well as minority) would have participated. For purposes of this discussion we assume that the original proposal was tantamount to an offer to acquire all of Newport's outstanding stock.

Feldmann rejected that proposal but made a counter offer. He agreed to sell Wilport his 37% controlling interest in Newport for $20 per share. That price included an $8 per share control premium over and above the then current market price of about $12 per share. Minority shareholders, who did not participate in the deal brought a shareholders' derivative suit. Reversing the

Federal district court, the Second Circuit held that Feldmann had violated his fiduciary duty to the minority shareholders and required him to share his control premium with the minority shareholders.

The opinion contains several broad statements, some of which, as pointed out by the dissent, do not accurately express the law of fiduciary duties. While there has been lively scholarly debate for years over the rationale of this decision, if you accept the factual premise that Feldmann, a control person, diverted a corporate opportunity to his own benefit, the decision appears sound.

C. FIDUCIARY DUTIES OF PARTNERS

The scope of the fiduciary duties owed by partners to the partnership and to each other is broader than the scope of the fiduciary duties owed by directors and officers to their corporations. The common law foundation on which partners' fiduciary duties rest was established in 1928 in the landmark decision of *Meinhard v. Salmon*.

In that case, in one of the most frequently cited and influential passages in partnership or corporate law, Justice Cardozo described the scope of a partner's fiduciary duties as follows:

[C]opartners, owe to one another, while the enterprise continues, the duty of finest loyalty. Many forms of conduct permissible in a workaday world for those acting at arm's length, are forbidden to those bound by fiduciary ties. . . . Not honesty alone, but the punctilio of an honor the most sensitive, is then the standard of behavior.

Today, Cardozo's famous "punctilio of an honor" statement is viewed by many scholars as too extreme and indefinite to represent a workable standard for defining the duties of partners. Such duties are now generally characterized as duties of "utmost good faith," "loyalty" and "care." The scope of these duties is further refined in § 404 of RUPA. Under § 404, the duty of loyalty prohibits misappropriation of partnership property, usurpation of partnership opportunities, having an interest adverse to the partnership or competing with the partnership. The standard imposed by the duty of care is gross negligence. And partners have an obligation of good faith and fair dealing in the discharge of all of their partnership duties. Finally, these duties may not be waived or eliminated in the partnership agreement, but the partnership agreement may set standards which can be used in defining the scope of these duties.

D. FIDUCIARY DUTIES IN CLOSE CORPORATIONS

Directors, officers and control shareholders of close corporations are obviously subject to at least the traditional fiduciary duties of corporate directors, officers and control shareholders discussed in § VI.A and B, *supra.* The overarching question considered in this section is:

Are directors, officers and control shareholders in "close corporations" subject to stricter fiduciary duties than those imposed on directors, officers and control shareholders generally?

An analysis of the differences in the way "close" and "public" corporations are governed (See generally

§ V.B.2, *supra*) and the differences in the nature of the problems typically faced by shareholders of close and public corporations, leads to the conclusion that the answer to this question should be yes. As discussed in the preceding chapter, the primary dangers faced by minority shareholders in close corporations are (1) the **liquidity problem** and (2) the threat of **oppression** and **freeze out.**

For example, assume *A*, *B* and *C* start a business which they incorporate as ABC Inc. *A*, *B* and *C* each own 33.3% of the corporation's voting stock and each is employed by the corporation. As is typical of close corporations, ABC Inc. pays no dividends, but most of the company's current earnings are distributed to the owners through payment of salaries and perks, such as retirement benefits. There is a disagreement and *A* and *B* remove *C* from the board. They then fire *C* as an employee of ABC Inc. Following *C*'s termination of employment, *A* and *B* continue their policy of paying no dividends and distributing most of the company's earning to themselves through salaries and perks. In this situation, *C* would have a hard time making a case that *A* and *B* violated the traditional duties of care or loyalty, which do not prohibit *A* and *B* from doing what they have done.

If the parties had organized their business as a partnership, *C*'s removal would have triggered an action for accounting of partnership profits and payment for his partnership interest. Neither the MBCA or state corporate statutes contain provisions which obligate a corporation to repurchase stock from a shareholder similar to the provisions applicable to partnership dissociation contained in § 601 of RUPA, which we will learn about in

Chapter X. In recent years some courts have recognized partnership-like fiduciary duties among participants in close corporations.

A well known case, found in many casebooks, because of its discussion of the similarities between close corporations and partnerships is *Donahue v. Rodd Electrotype Co.* (Mass. 1975). In *Donahue*, the plaintiff was the widow of a long-time employee of the company, who over the years had acquired 50 shares of the company's stock. The remaining 198 shares were owned by Harry Rodd and his three sons. The sons had taken over management of the company, Harry, age 77, still owned 81 shares. He was ready to retire, but wanted some money. The corporation agreed to buy 45 of Harry's shares for $800 per share (the book value of the shares). The widow Donahue tendered her 50 shares to the corporation, demanding that it buy her shares at the same price it agreed to pay Harry for his shares. When the corporation refused, the widow sued, alleging breach of fiduciary duty to a minority shareholder.

The lower courts, noting that the purchase of Harry's stock was in good faith and at a fair price, held for defendant. The Supreme Court of Massachusetts reversed, and in so doing, established what is known as the **"equal access rule."** The court specifically limits application of the equal access rule to close corporations, as defined in its opinion.

Under the equal access rule controlling shareholders owe a fiduciary duty to minority shareholders to give them an equal opportunity to sell their shares to the corporation on the same terms as the controlling shareholder. As a remedy, the court allowed the corporation to choose between buying Donahue's shares at $800 per share or rescinding the agreement to buy Harry's stock at that price.

Shortly after *Donahue,* the Supreme Court of Massachusetts rendered another important decision dealing with the scope of fiduciary duties in close corporations. In *Wilkes v. Springside Nursing Home, Inc.* (Mass. 1976) the court both affirmed the general concept which underlies the *Donahue* decision and, at the same time, limited the application of *Donahue.*

Wilkes involved a classic close corporation squeeze-out. Four individuals were equal owners of a corporation that owned and operated a nursing home. All four were directors and employees of the corporation. The corporation paid no dividends, but paid equal salaries to each of the four owners for work performed at the nursing home. Wilkes had a falling out with the other three shareholders. They removed Wilkes from the board and fired him as an employee. Wilkes sued for breach of fiduciary duties.

The Massachusetts Supreme Court tempered the scope of its ruling in *Donahue* by fashioning a balancing test. The court stated that in certain "legitimate spheres" such as employment matters, dividends, etc., the majority has discretion to manage the business in the way it sees fit, even if minority shareholders are harmed in the process. The *Wilkes* holding requires the majority to show a legitimate business purpose for its action (*i.e.*, in this case firing Wilkes). If, the majority meets its burden, the burden then shifts to the minority to show that the

objective sought to be achieved by the majority could
have been accomplished in a manner that was less harm-
ful to the minority's interests. In the *Wilkes* case, the
controlling shareholders were unable to show a legitimate business purpose for firing Mr. Wilkes. Therefore,
the court did not have to deal with the balancing issue.

Not all jurisdictions agree with the view that shareholders in closely held corporations owe one another
expanded fiduciary duties in the nature of those owed by
partners to each other. The Delaware Supreme Court
rejected this notion in *Nixon v. Blackwell* (Del. 1993), a
case with facts similar to those in *Donahue*. In *Nixon,* a
closely held corporation through its employee stock ownership plan and key man life insurance provided employee-shareholders the opportunity to cash out their ownership interests in the corporation on death or retirement.
Non-employee shareholders, who lacked any market for
their shares sued. The trial court held that providing
liquidity for employee-shareholders, while not providing
similar liquidity to non-employee shareholders, constituted a breach of fiduciary duty. The Delaware Supreme
Court reversed stating that it would be inappropriate for
courts to create ad hoc rules to protect minority shareholders, which were not contracted for or provided for in
the statute.

Some states have embraced the notion of expanded
fiduciary duties in close corporations, as reflected in
Donahue and other cases, while others have not. Most
states have not yet ruled one way or the other. This is an
emerging issue and the depth to which you will be
required to understand this issue in your basic business

course will depend on the emphasis placed on this issue by your professor.

Professors who emphasize this area may be trying to make a point about basic process. Historically, the law of fiduciary duties was developed (and as a work in progress is being developed) by the courts under two separate models: (1) The **corporate model** where the main concern was the scope of the duties of care and loyalty owed by directors and officers to the corporate entity and (2) the **partnership model** where the main concern was with the way the partners treat one another. The close corporation is a hybrid and the courts are trying to develop workable rules that govern this relationships by borrowing from both the corporate and the partnership models.

E. FIDUCIARY DUTIES IN AN LLC

The last section suggested the scope of fiduciary duties in close corporations is not yet fully developed. The scope of fiduciary duties owed by members and managers of LLCs is even less developed. It is beyond the scope of this book to speculate on how this area of the law will develop in the years to come. However, we can identify the main issues likely to play out as the courts (and perhaps the legislatures) go through the difficult process of defining the scope of fiduciary duties in the LLC. Some of the key issues, they will likely face, include the following:

(1) The diversity of the LLC statutes;

(2) The impact of provisions in the operating agreement on the scope of fiduciary duties; and

(3) Whether the courts choose to follow a corporate or partnership model in defining the scope of fiduciary duties in LLCs.

Diversity of LLC statutes. LLC statutes vary widely in the way they describe the fiduciary duties owed by members and managers of LLCs. And because LLCs are so new there are few definitive judicial decisions that establish clear cut criteria for defining the scope of such duties.

The Uniform Limited Liability Company Act ("ULLCA") in § 409 expressly provides for fiduciary duties in a manner similar to § 404 of RUPA. ULLCA § 409(b) limits the duty of loyalty to (1) accounting to the LLC for any property or profit derived in conducting or winding up the business, (2) refraining from dealing with the LLC while having an interest adverse to the LLC and (3) refraining from competing with the LLC. In § 409(c) the duty of care is limited to gross negligence, reckless conduct, intentional misconduct, or knowing violation of the law. Members in member-managed LLCs and managers in manager-managed LLCs are both subject to these duties. Finally, ULLCA § 103 limits the manner in which the scope of fiduciary duties may be limited or modified in the operating agreement.

In sharp contrast to the ULLCA, the Delaware Limited Liability Company Act ("DLLCA") does not specify any fiduciary duties for members or managers and expressly states that maximum effect will be given to freedom of contract. See § 18–1101(b). Section 18–1101(c)(2) specifically states that "[t]he member's or manager's or other person's duties may be expanded or restricted by provisions in a limited liability agreement." While I know of no Delaware case law interpreting this provision, the Delaware Supreme Court decision, *Elf Atochem North America v. Jaffari* (Del. 1999), suggests that under DLLCA the parties may eliminate fiduciary duties.

Delaware and the ULLCA represent opposite ends of a wide spectrum of ways in which the LLC statutes of the various states define the scope of fiduciary duties. The ULLCA has not been widely accepted and there is much variation regarding fiduciary in the various states. Obviously, a higher degree of uniformity is desirable.

The impact of the operating agreement. Over half the state LLC statutes provide that the scope of fiduciary duties may be modified or eliminated by provisions in the operating agreement. This is in sharp contrast to partnership law, under which as you will recall, while partners can contract around most of the default rules in the statutes, they cannot eliminate their fiduciary duties.

A number of state LLC statutes contain provisions, similar to Delaware § 18–1101(c), which allow the operating agreement to modify or define the fiduciary duties of members or managers without restriction. If read literally and fully enforced by the courts, provisions such as Delaware § 18–1101(c) would permit LLCs to operate free of any fiduciary duties. Your author, being part of a generation of lawyers steeped in the tradition of *Meinhard v. Salmon*, has difficulty with a concept that allows the parties unfettered ability to restrict or eliminate fiduciary duties. More importantly, your professor is likely to have her own views on this issue.

The model applicable to LLCs. Finally, the question, raised in § VI.D., *supra*, regarding the scope of fiduciary duties in close corporations, is also relevant to the scope of fiduciary duties in LLCs.

Will fiduciary duties, if any, imposed by the courts on members or managers of LLCs, be modeled after the fiduciary duties imposed on corporate officers and directors or those imposed on partners in a general partnership?

Some writers have suggested that corporate-type fiduciary duties should be imposed on managers of manager-managed LLCs while partnership-type fiduciaries should be imposed on members of member-managed LLCs. This suggestion seems overly simplistic, particularly in view of the fact that virtually all LLCs are closely-held businesses. And, more importantly, there is presently no case law that supports this proposition.

Since your professor will not likely know exactly what the scope of fiduciary duties in LLCs is, it is not likely that she will expect you to know. This is currently a developing area of the law. However, she will likely expect you to understand the issues and see the analogies between LLCs and the older forms of business associations, because the courts and legislatures are likely to draw from either or both corporation law and partnership law in developing rules that govern the scope of fiduciary duties in LLCs.

F. HOW VIOLATIONS OF FIDUCIARY DUTIES ARE ENFORCED
(herein Shareholders' Derivative Suits)

1. THE GOVERNANCE DILEMMA

We have seen that directors and officers owe fiduciary duties to the corporation, the breach of which gives rise to a cause of action in favor of the corporation. We have also seen that the power of management, vested in the directors and officers, includes the power to bring law suits to redress injuries suffered by the corporation.

Most derivative litigation involves claims that directors or officers breached fiduciary duties owed to the corporation. When these duties are breached the corporation (an entity separate and apart from the officers and directors who manage it and the shareholders who own it) is hurt and has a right to sue. But when the claim is against the directors or officers themselves, the law cannot trust the officers and directors to authorize the corporation to sue because they have an obvious conflict of interest. If the officers and directors elected to sue, they would, in effect, be suing themselves. This dilemma is caused by the way corporations are governed and is referred to as the "governance dilemma."

2. THE NATURE OF A SHAREHOLDERS' DERIVATIVE SUIT

To deal with this "governance dilemma," courts of equity many years ago developed a procedural device called the *"shareholders' derivative suit."* This is an action in which an individual shareholder (who under normal circumstances would not have the power to cause the corporation to sue) sues on behalf of the corporation. The cause of action belongs to the corporation and, with rare exceptions, any recovery belongs to the corporation. The shareholder merely serves as the self-appointed enforcer of a corporate right.

Conceptually, a shareholders' derivative suit is two suits in one: (*Suit One*) the shareholder sues the corporation, in equity, seeking to force the corporation to (*Suit Two*) bring suit against the directors and officers for violating their fiduciary duties. Today, both suits are consolidated into one action, but thinking in terms of the historical notion of two suits in one, makes the conceptual framework and peculiar procedures of a shareholders' derivative suits easier to understand.

Who are the necessary parties?

Obviously, the plaintiff is the shareholder attempting to vindicate a wrong done to the corporation. The directors and officers, who allegedly breached their fiduciary duties, are, of course, defendants. But the corporation must also be a party to the case. In derivative litigation, not only is the corporation an indispensable party, it is on both sides of the case—both a plaintiff and a defendant, as follows:

Plaintiffs: Shareholder & Corporation v. **_Defendants_**: Corporation & *A, B, C, D* & *E* (directors).

Often the corporation is called a **nominal** defendant and the individual directors, who allegedly breached their fiduciary duties, are called the **real** defendants.

There are two legal reasons that the corporation has to be both a plaintiff and a defendant: (1) As an entity affected by the judgment the corporation must be before the court and (2) joining the corporation ensures that the judgment will be res judicata against the corporation.

3.   THE DIFFERENCE BETWEEN DIRECT AND DERIVATIVE SUITS

There are two types of suits shareholders can bring against their corporation—**direct suits** and **derivative suits**. As previously pointed out **derivative suits** are suits in which the shareholder asserts a corporate cause of action and seeks recovery on behalf of the corporation. Suits for breach of fiduciary duties owed to the corporation by directors and officers are an example.

Direct suits, on the other hand, are suits in which the shareholder sues the corporation to enforce her rights as a shareholder. Recovery in a direct suit belongs to the shareholder, either individually or as representative of shareholders similarly situated. Examples include suits to protect voting rights, to compel payment of dividends, to redress fraud on shareholders by the purchase or sale of securities, to compel dissolution of the corporation, etc.

The distinction is clear in most cases, even in cases where both the corporation and the shareholders are harmed. For example, assume the business of a corporation is severely harmed as a result of the gross negligence of an officer. In that situation the shareholders will also suffer harm since the value of their shares will likely decline as a result of the officer's negligence. However, courts have uniformly held that shareholders can not bring direct actions for decline in the value of their shares resulting from harm to the corporation.

Sometimes the distinction can get blurred. If the essence of the claim is indirect damage suffered by the shareholder resulting from director conduct that harms the corporation, the action is derivative. On the other hand, if the essence of the shareholder's claim is that the directors actions directly impacted her rights as a shareholder, the action will be classified as direct, even though conduct complained of also had an adverse impact on the corporation. This distinction can be subtle and, in part, may depend on how the shareholder pleads her case.

For example, in *Smith v. Van Gorkom*, discussed earlier, the plaintiff complained that the directors breached their duty of care by voting to accept a merger proposal. The suit was not about the impact of the directors' decision on the corporation's future operations or profitability. Instead, the suit focused on whether the shareholders could have received a price higher than $55 per share for their shares. Thus, the linchpin of the suit went to the value of the shareholders' shares and the shareholders were allowed to bring a direct suit.

Eisenberg v. Flying Tiger Line, Inc. (2d Cir. 1971) was an even closer case. A shareholder challenged a corporate reorganization in which shareholders in an operating company became shareholders in a holding company. The court allowed this suit to be brought as a direct action because the reorganization deprived the shareholder of any voice in the affairs of the operating company. This case contains a good judicial discussion of the basic differences between direct and derivative litigation.

The *Eisenberg* case also illustrates why the direct/ derivative distinction is important. Since the suit was classified as a direct action, the plaintiff did not have to post a security for costs bond. There are a number of procedural hoops (which I will discuss later) that plaintiffs must jump through in derivative suits. Many of these procedural hoops can be avoided if the case can be brought as a direct suit.

What is a class action and how does it compare with a derivative suit?

A **class action is a direct suit**, not a derivative suit. Derivative suits and class actions are different procedural devices used to assert different types of substantive claims. In a class action, a representative of the class is suing on his own behalf and on behalf of others with the same claim (*i.e.,* similarly situated). All members of the class are asserting personal claims; no one is asserting a claim on behalf of the corporation. Class action law suits are governed by a different set of procedural rules, which are outside the scope of the basic business course and this book.

However, class actions share one common characteristic with shareholders' derivative suits. In both, a litigant is representing someone else. This common characteristic makes both controversial. Just as all members of the class have an interest in a class action because they all share in the recovery, all shareholders of a corporation have an interest in the outcome of a shareholders' derivative suit because whatever the corporation recovers, at least in theory, goes to the shareholders. The following examples illustrate why both class actions and shareholders' derivative suits are controversial.

Class action: Suppose an item is subject to price controls. You buy that item and later find out the company overcharged you by $10. While this might make you angry, no rational person would bring a lawsuit for $10.

But if a lawyer sees that you are one of 2 million customers, each overcharged by $10, the economics change dramatically—your $10 claim becomes a potential claim for $20 million. Another common example would be asbestos litigation on behalf of a class harmed by this toxic tort.

Shareholders' derivative suit: Exactly the same economics drive shareholders' derivative suits. For example, *X*, who owns 200 shares of IBM sues IBM derivatively for violation of fiduciary duties and gets a judgement for $100 million. IBM has millions of shareholders and hundreds of millions of shares outstanding. Thus, the pro rata share of the $100M judgement which would inure to *X*'s benefit as one of several million IBM shareholders would be quite small—possibly as little $100.

Why would a plaintiff spend the time and effort to bring either a class action or a shareholders derivative suit when the plaintiff's personal stake in the recovery is so small?

The obvious answer is **attorney's fees**. Attorney's fees are the economic engine that drives both class actions and shareholders' derivative suits. The answer becomes obvious when you understand the process of **entrepreneurial litigation**. In most of these cases a lawyer learns of the potential derivative claim or class action and then "finds" a client to serve as plaintiff.

The plaintiff's attorney acts as a combination bounty hunter and independent entrepreneur who performs the function of deterring undesirable conduct in corporate America. The lawyer, not the client, controls the case, finances the case and the lawyer gets a large share of what is recovered.

The entrepreneurial aspect of this type of litigation is very real. The lawyer must finance the case. These cases require a substantial investment of both time and money by the lawyer. To be successful, an entrepreneurial lawyer has to know how to pick good cases and has to be good at what he does. If the lawyer doesn't win or get a favorable settlement he does not get paid for his time on the case or reimbursed for the expenses he has advanced. Thus, poor lawyers tend not to last very long in this area, but lawyers who are successful are the highest paid lawyers in the world.

4. PROCEDURAL REQUIREMENTS IN SHAREHOLDERS' DERIVATIVE SUITS

a. The Demand Requirement

The demand requirement is the key requirement in derivative litigation. While modern procedural rules governing the demand requirement vary in detail from state to state, the bottom line is that the plaintiff must allege that he has made a demand on the board of directors to bring suit or state with particularity why the demand was excused. The conceptual foundation on which the demand requirement rests is the governance dilemma discussed earlier. It gives the board of directors, which is charged with managing the corporation, an opportunity to decide whether or not a suit is in the corporation's best interest.

How does the demand requirement play out?

The demand requirement requires that Plaintiff write a letter to the board of directors demanding that they bring suit. Generally, the letter alleges a wrong and the relevant facts supporting the allegation in much the same way as is done in a complaint. When the board receives plaintiff's demand letter, they have two obvious choices:

(1) Accept the demand—bring suit, or

(2) Reject the demand—not sue.

If the board **accepts** the demand and decides to sue there is, of course, no need for the derivative suit. The board will hire its own lawyer and take over the suit.

If the board **rejects** the demand and can show that the rejection was "**in good faith**" and "**by an independent board**" then the derivative suit cannot go forward. The decision to reject the demand is given the presumption of propriety under the business judgement rule.

The bottom line is, if he makes a demand, plaintiff's attorney is likely to find himself in a catch 22. If the board accepts the demand, he loses control of the case (and the opportunity to earn the attorneys fee which drives these cases). If the board rejects the demand plaintiff's attorney is faced with the tough burden of overcoming the business judgement rule. He must show that the board was not independent (for example, a majority of the directors were involved in the wrongdoing) or that there was no rational basis for the decision not to sue. Thus, plaintiff tries to get around the demand requirement by **showing excuse**.

When can the demand be excused?

The main ground for excusing demand is **futility**. The case of *Marx v. Akers,* discussed below, surveys the three major approaches to excusing demands. Before I discuss the New York approach (adopted in *Marx)* I will discuss the other two approaches discussed in the *Marx* opinion.

The Delaware approach was set out in *Aronson v. Lewis* (Del. 1984), a shareholders' derivative suit in which the plaintiff sued all of the directors of Meyers Parking Systems, Inc. The suit alleged that a 5 year employment contract with Fink, a 75-year-old retiring director, who owned 47% of the stock of Myers, provided excessive compensation. Plaintiff did not make a demand on the board before filing suit. The complaint alleged that demand would be futile because all the directors approved the transaction, and all were chosen and dominated by Fink.

In holding that plaintiff's complaint failed to allege adequate facts to excuse the demand, the Delaware Supreme Court articulated a test which has come to be known as the "Delaware two-part test" for determining futility:

Demand is excused if the plaintiff can state with particularity, facts that create a reasonable doubt (1) that a majority of the directors on whom demand would have been made are disinterested or (2) that the challenged transaction was protected by the business judgment rule.

In other words, to show futility under the Delaware two part test, plaintiff must point to specific facts (before discovery) that tend to show either that (1) the board is not disinterested or independent or (2) the underlying transaction was improper as tested under the business judgment rule.

The Model Act adopts a universal demand approach. MBCA § 7.42 requires that a plaintiff wanting to file a shareholders' derivative suit must always first make a written demand on the board of directors (called a universal demand). The plaintiff must then wait 90 days after making the demand to bring suit, unless the board rejects the demand sooner or the wait would cause irreparable harm to the corporation.

After the 90–day waiting period expires, the shareholder can bring a derivative suit. If the board rejected the demand, plaintiff must plead particular facts that show either the board was not disinterested or that the rejection was not in good faith (similar to the *Aronson*). See MBCA § 7.44.

The New York approach was articulated in *Marx v. Akers* (N.Y. 1996), a derivative suit with facts similar to *Aronson*, against IBM's board of directors. The IBM board consisted of 18 directors, 15 were outside directors and the remaining 3 were inside directors (employees of IBM). The suit was for corporate waste (payment of excessive compensation to the IBM executives). The court held that the 3 inside directors were tainted by self-interest and implicitly held that a demand on these 3 would be futile and thus excused. But the court went on to hold that the remaining 15 directors were not tainted and since they comprised a majority of the board, demand was not excused.

After surveying the Delaware and Universal Demand approaches discussed above, the *Marx* court rejected both and adopted the following approach for New York. In New York, demand is excused if any of the following is alleged with particularity in the complaint:

(1) A majority of the board is interested in the challenged deal;

(2) The board did not fully inform itself about the challenged deal; or

(3) The challenged deal was so unfair on its face that it could not have been the product of sound business judgment.

b. The Special Litigation Committee

What is the special litigation committee and how does it work?

The **special litigation committee** rests on the same conceptual foundation as the demand requirement: namely, preservation, to the extent possible, of the governance role of the board in deciding whether the corporation should bring a lawsuit.

Basic principles of corporate governance, incorporated in the corporate statutes of all states, authorize the board to select from their members smaller groups—called committees—to deal with a specific area—*e.g.*, compensation committee, acquisition committee, etc.

Based on this notion, corporate defense attorneys in the 1970s came up with a way for the "innocent minority" of directors to make the decision whether the corporation should sue the other board members. The board creates a committee consisting of some or all of the directors not implicated in the alleged wrong and delegates to that committee the power to decide if the corporation should pursue a lawsuit against the majority.

The composition of committee is critical. Often, the committee is composed of people who were not directors at the time of the alleged wrongdoing. It is always composed of individuals who were in no way involved in the alleged wrongdoing. The special litigation committee typically hires counsel to investigate the facts that lead to the derivative suit. The committee, with the aid of the attorney and often other experts, than investigates the facts and evaluates the merits of the case—projected costs, potential benefits to the corporation, etc. The committee then incorporates its findings into a report which it submits to the court along with the committee's recommendation as to whether the suit should be continued or terminated—couched in terms of the best interests of the corporation.

Assume that the special litigation committee's recommendation is to dismiss the law suit. Studies have shown that dismissal is almost always the committee's recommendation. The attorney for the corporation then makes a motion to dismiss based on the committee's recommendation. This raises the following question:

How does the court respond to a motion to dismiss the shareholders' derivative suit, backed by a recommendation of the special litigation committee?

Obviously, you have to be a little skeptical as to whether the special litigation committee is truly unbiased and whether its recommendation is based solely on what is in the corporation's best interest. Directors are, after all, judging their fellow directors. This concern over the special litigation committee's true independence coupled with other policy concerns inherent in the special litigation committee technique has resulted in a diversity of judicial approaches. The three main approaches are as follows:

The New York approach. In New York, under *Auerbach v. Bennett* (N.Y. 1979), unless the plaintiff can prove that the special litigation committee lacked independence or failed to operate on an informed basis, the committee's recommendation is entitled to the presumption of propriety afforded by the business judgement rule. In other words, if the committee systematically follows proper procedures—*i.e.,* meets regularly, systematically reviews the facts, relies on opinions of independent counsel, makes a detailed record, etc.—and has a rational basis for their decision—*e.g.,* the potential claim lacks merit, litigation expenses might exceed potential gains to the corporation, the suit would create bad publicity for the corporation or damage employee moral, etc.—the court will follow the committee's recommendation and dismiss the suit. This approach, called the *Auerbach* Rule, is the approach most favorable to the defendant.

The minority approach. The supreme court of Iowa in *Miller v. Register and Tribune Syndicate, Inc.* (Iowa 1983) adopted a simple approach favorable to the plaintiff. This approach basically states that if the board is disqualified from recommending dismissal, than any committee appointed by that board would be likewise disqualified. This is clearly a minority rule.

The Delaware approach. In 1981 in *Zapata v. Maldonado* (Del. 1981), the Delaware Supreme Court adopted an approach between the two extremes discussed above. This has emerged as the **majority rule**.

The *Zapata* case was a shareholders' derivative suit against the entire board of directors of Zapata Corporation for self-dealing. Plaintiff alleged the board moved up the expiration date of some options so the directors could exercise the options and thus enrich themselves at the expense of the corporation.

Four years into the suit, the board appointed directors, who were not on the board when the wrongdoing occurred, as a special litigation committee. The committee conducted an investigation and recommended that the suit be dismissed.

Zapata established a two part test to determine whether or not a special litigation committee's recommendation to dismiss would be followed:

(1) First, the defendants have the burden of proving the committee members' independence and the procedural completeness of their investigation; and

(2) Second, if the special litigation committee's recommendation passes the first part of the test, the court exercises its own independent discretion in determining whether or not it is in the corporation's best interest to dismiss the suit.

Under the second prong of the *Zapata* test, the court applies its own business judgment as to whether the suit should go forward, rather than giving the special litigation committee's recommendation the presumption of propriety under the business judgment rule.

Some scholars have criticized the *Zapata* decision on the ground that the case vitiates the business judgment rule as to litigation decisions. This is true, but it is also true that this a more limited intrusion on the business judgment rule than would be a decision vitiating the business judgment rule as to how the business should be operated (*i.e.*, day and night baseball).

Also, the *Zapata* test only applies in cases where demand has been excused. Three years after the *Zapata* decision, in *Aronson v. Lewis*, discussed above, the Delaware Supreme Court significantly limited the number of situations in which demand would be excused. Thus, *Aronson* has limited the importance of the *Zapata* rule.

c. Other Procedural Requirements

Shareholders' derivative suits trigger a number of other procedural requirements. The specific requirements vary significantly from state to state. Some are found in the states' corporate statutes, while others are found in the states' rules of civil procedure. All directly or indirectly relate to the three main concerns courts have with respect to shareholders' derivative suits—the governance dilemma, strike suits and conflicts of interest. The "other procedural requirements" are rarely covered in any depth in the basic business course, except by professors who have a particular interest in procedure. They are beyond the scope of this book. I will, however, mention two significant "other procedural requirements" in a cursory way.

The contemporaneous ownership rule. Most state statutes require that the plaintiff be a shareholder when the wrong occurred. This is sometimes referred to as a standing requirement. The details on what is required varies from state to state. MBCA § 7.41(1) is fairly typical. Some state statutes go further than MBCA § 7.41 and require that the plaintiff continue to be a shareholder through trial and/or final judgment.

Security for expenses. Some states require that plaintiff, as a condition to bringing a derivative suit, post security to cover the defendant corporation's litigation costs. The obvious purpose behind this requirement is to weed out strike suits. Security-for-expense statutes have been a powerful disincentive to derivative litigation because both the costs of posting a bond and the risks of having to pay defendant's expenses are high. Today, only a minority of states have security for expense statutes. Delaware has no such statute. Most of the security-for-expense statutes exempt shareholders who own more than a specified minimum of the corporation's stock (*i.e.*, 3% or 5%) from this requirement.

———

As the above discussion reflects, the procedural rules surrounding derivative litigation (*i.e.*, the demand requirement, the deference given recommendations of the special litigation committee, the security-for-expense statutes, etc.), are diverse and state specific. Consequently, the manner in which you handle these requirements will depend upon your professor's emphasis. However, whatever the emphasis in your particular class, if you understand the process underlying derivative litigation and understand the so called "governance dilemma"— the tension between the directors' authority to make corporate decisions and the shareholder's right to bring shareholders' derivative suits—you should be able to effectively work your way through any of the specific issues involving shareholders' derivative suits that might be tested.

CHAPTER VII

WHAT PROTECTION DOES THE LAW GIVE TO PERSONS WHO BUY OR SELL SECURITIES?
(herein Rule 10b–5)

In the last chapter we learned that shareholders, as owners, have certain rights derived from ownership. Among those rights are protection from incompetent or disloyal directors and officers who violate certain duties, which the law has labeled fiduciary duties.

In this chapter we change focus and look at another set of rights and remedies available to shareholders. Rather than looking at shareholders as owners entitled to certain ongoing rights as an attribute of ownership we look at them as **investors** who make decisions to buy or sell stock. In this capacity shareholder-investors might be induced to buy or sell stock in a particular company by false or misleading statements or material omissions. We will refer to this kind of conduct as "fraud." But fraud is a broad context oriented term, we will need to define with more particularity.

What protection does the law afford investors against fraud in connection with the purchase or sale of securities?

The law provides investors many remedies against fraud. First, it affords remedies under the common law of fraud and deceit—tort law. Also most states have so called deceptive trade practices statutes and state securities (or "Blue Sky") laws which provide remedies for fraudulent conduct. These remedies are outside the scope of this book.

Today, the main remedy—a remedy which dwarfs all the others in importance—is a body of case law which has developed around a rule adopted by the SEC under the Securities Exchange Act of 1934 ("34 Act"). This body of jurisprudence which goes by the unassuming name of **Rule 10b–5**, is the primary focus of this chapter.

A. RULE 10b–5—OVERVIEW

Rule 10b–5 must be understood. It transcends the specialized body of jurisprudence called "securities law" and is part of a more general body of jurisprudence called "general corporate law." As you know, business associations are mainly governed by state law. However, questions arising under Rule 10b–5 are governed by federal law. The body of jurisprudence developed around Rule 10b–5 by the federal courts has probably had more impact on corporate conduct during the last 50 years than any other single rule of law.

1. HISTORY

The 33 and 34 Acts contain a number of anti-fraud provisions aimed at "fraud" in certain specific situations (*i.e.*, the sale of securities by issuers going public, the solicitation of proxies, fraud by broker/dealers, etc.). But in 1942, an SEC investigation revealed that the president of a publicly held company in Boston was making false statements about the company's earnings, while buying the company's stock. The SEC staff realized there was a loophole in the statutes—they did not contain a broad anti-fraud provision which prohibited fraud in the **purchase or sale** of securities by anyone.

The SEC closed that loophole. Using the catchall authority of § 10(b) of the 34 Act, which gives the SEC authority to promulgate rules that prohibit:

"manipulative or deceptive devices or contrivances . . . in connection with the purchase or sale of any security"

the SEC staff proposed a new rule which prohibited "fraud" by "anyone" in connection with the purchase or sale of a security. The Commission adopted the new rule without debate. The new rule was named Rule 10b–5, because it was the fifth rule adopted under the enabling authority of § 10(b).

About 4 years after its adoption, a federal district court held that violation of Rule 10b–5 gives rise to a private remedy in favor of injured investors. And as they say, the rest is history. Rule 10b–5 covers an extraordinarily wide range of transactions and activities and a significant body of case law has developed around the Rule.

2. APPLICATION—IN GENERAL

Rule 10b–5 is by far the broadest provision in the federal securities laws. It applies to both issuer transactions and trading transactions.

The fraud may be perpetrated by anyone. It might be perpetrated by the corporation itself in connection with a public offering or in connection with the solicitation of proxies. The same disloyal or incompetent directors we saw in the last chapter violating their fiduciary duties might also be committing various acts of fraud. The fraud might be committed by investors, as when investor A sells outstanding securities to investor B by means of misstatement or deceit.

No business or transaction is too small to escape the reach of Rule 10b–5. Rule 10b–5 applies whether the securities are publicly traded or closely held and whether the transaction is subject to SEC registration or exempt. All you need to bring Rule 10b–5 into play is a purchase or sale of securities through the use of the mails or the instrumentalities of interstate commerce.

For example, assume A and B each own 50 shares of the 100 shares of stock a company whose sole asset is a lemonade stand. B, who operates the lemonade stand, talks A into selling B his 50 shares by lying about how much lemonade the company sold last year. A probably has a cause of action under Rule 10b–5.

Operative language of the rule; securities fraud defined. In considering the application of the rule you need to begin by looking at the specific language of the rule. The three operative clauses of the Rule prohibit:

(a) any device, scheme or artifice to defraud;

(b) any omission or misstatement of a material fact;

(c) any act or practice that would operate as a fraud or deceit.

In this chapter, I use the word "fraud" as a shorthand reference for the acts, practices or omissions prohibited under the three operative clauses of the Rule.

Nobody, not even the Justices of the Supreme Court, know exactly what the three operative clauses of the Rule mean. Through interpretation, the Justices make up the meaning as they go along.

The language of the rules three operative clauses is potentially broad enough to "cover the world" and the factual patterns that might give rise to an action under Rule 10b–5 are infinite. It covers all forms of fraud, manipulation and deception. The SEC is content to let the courts apply the rule on a case-by-case basis. This approach results in uncertainty and a high degree of subjectivity but it also provides the flexibility that the SEC and federal prosecutors obviously want in administering the rule.

Many areas of securities law and general corporate law require analysis of detailed statutory regulations. This is not the case with Rule 10b–5. When analyzing a Rule 10b–5 problem think in terms of **common law** analysis. The courts, not the SEC or Congress, have defined the scope, consequences and limitations of this rule. You will not find any detailed or arcane rules in this area. All you find is the broad and vague language of the Rule itself and a lot of case law interpreting that language in an infinite variety of fact situations. Do not think of Rule 10b–5 as merely as a legal rule but as a body of jurisprudence. As to securities transactions, Rule 10b–5 has largely superceded most of common law fraud in the second half of the 20th Century. Both at exam time and when you get out in practice, when you see a fact pattern where someone is buying or selling securities, **always consider the possible application of Rule 10b–5**.

While Rule 10b–5 has been applied in a wide variety of factual contexts, the two most common applications of Rule 10b–5 cases (the only applications covered in this book or likely to be covered in the basic business course) are so called (1) securities fraud cases and (2) insider trading cases.

Securities fraud case is the broad label used to describe the most common application of Rule 10b–5. These are cases where somebody lies, tells half truths, puts out false financial statements, phony press releases, files false documents with the SEC, uses a prospectus or proxy statement containing false or misleading information, etc.

Insider trading case. While not as common in terms of number of cases brought, insider trading is the category of cases for which 10b–5 is best known, because many of the insider trading cases have been brought against rich and famous people and have, therefore received much media attention. A good example is the recent insider trading investigation of Martha Stewart, which is discussed later. "Insider trading" is the label used to describe cases where someone buys or sells securities on the basis of undisclosed information available only to the "insider." The gist of insider trading cases is not a misrepresentation, but rather non-disclosure when there is a duty to disclose.

B. SECURITIES FRAUD CASES
(herein Elements of a Rule 10b–5 Case)

The gist of this application is some kind of misrepresentation—somebody lies, tells half truths, puts out false financial statements, phony press releases, etc. Recently we have seen a lot of that—*e.g.*, Enron, Tyco, WorldCom, etc. Most of the companies and individuals involved in these situations have been prosecuted criminally and/or sued civilly under Rule 10b–5.

For purposes of organization and analysis, it is helpful to break the 10b–5 cause of action down into its elements. Different writers classify the elements of a 10b–5 cause of action in slightly different ways or they use slightly different labels for the elements. Any classification is nothing more than an analytical tool. The most common classification used in explaining the Rule's application consists of eight elements, as follows:

(1) **Jurisdictional Means**

(2) **Fraud**

(3) **Materiality**

(4) **Culpability—Scienter**

(5) **In Connection with the Purchase or Sale of Securities**

(6) **Standing—Plaintiff Must have Bought or Sold Securities**

(7) **Causation/Reliance**

    (a) **Transaction Causation**

    (b) **Loss Causation**

(8) **Damages**

1.   JURISDICTIONAL MEANS

By its express terms Rule 10b–5 requires that the purchase or sale of securities be made through the use of "interstate commerce or the mails." These are called the **jurisdictional means**. While a requirement, this element is seldom an issue, because due to the way it has been interpreted the requirement is almost always satisfied. The misstatement or omission need not be made in the phone call or letter. Any use of the mails or the telephone at any time in connection with a securities transaction will satisfy this requirement.

The telephone call or letter does not have to cross state lines; nor does the actual offer to buy or sell securities have to be by mail or telephone. For example, the buyer and seller can work in the same building and the offer and sale can be in a face to face conversation in that building. But if one party calls the other to arrange the meeting or to clarify some detail or if a check or stock certificate is transmitted by mail, the requirement has been satisfied. See, *e.g.*, *Dupuy v. Dupuy* (5th Cir. 1975), a case in which phone calls between two brothers in the same apartment complex in New Orleans, negotiating the sale of an interest in a closely held family business, were enough to satisfy the jurisdictional requirement.

2. FRAUD

In shorthand terms we refer to the type of misconduct prohibited by Rule 10b–5 as "fraud." But "fraud" is a term whose meaning depends on the context in which it is used. In the context of Rule 10b–5 "fraud" means committing any of the acts, omissions or practices specified in the three operating clauses of the rule, quoted verbatim above.

What specific conduct do these clauses prohibit?

Lies. Lies are obviously prohibited. But there are lies and there are lies.

Does there have to be an evil motive behind the lie?

No. In *Basic, Inc. v. Levinson* (1988), an important Supreme Court decision on several points, Basic Industries, a publicly held company was negotiating a merger. The deal was a friendly acquisition by which a larger company would acquire Basic. Negotiations were obviously being conducted in secret. If the deal got done, the shareholders of Basic would get a premium for their shares.

While these negotiations were in process, trading in Basic Industries picked up and the stock rose in price. A representative of the New York Stock Exchange asked the president of Basic, who was involved in the negotiations, if he knew why trading volume had increased and why the price was moving up. The president's answer was that he did not know. And he denied that the company was in negotiations to be acquired.

That was a lie. But there was no evil motive behind the lie. The president was lying to protect the confidentially of sensitive merger negotiations, which if consummated (which they eventually were) would result in the shareholders getting a premium for their stock. Although the president was lying to protect the best interests of the company and its shareholders, in *Basic, Inc. v. Levinson* the Supreme Court held that this lie was enough to invoke liability under Rule 10b–5.

Manipulating, misleading, or deceiving acts or statements all invoke liability under Rule 10b–5. Obviously, these terms are like "obscenity"—sometimes hard to define but lawyers need to learn to recognize them when they appear in a given fact situation. Likewise students need to learn to recognize them at exam time to spot potential Rule 10b–5 issues.

Half truths. The hornbook definition of a half truth is: A statement that is technically correct but it omits a fact that is necessary to make the statement not misleading.

Example: Assume in *Basic, Inc. v. Levinson* the guy from the stock exchange asked the president: "Are you negotiating a merger?" The president answers, "no," because the company was not negotiating a "merger" in the technical legal sense. It was negotiating a "sale of assets."

Technically this is not a lie, because legally a sale of assets is not a merger. But in the context of the question (which related to a transaction having a potential impact on the price of the stock), the answer was a half truth. In terms of potential impact on the price of the stock, a sale of assets, at a premium, is the functional equivalent of a merger.

Opinions, predictions and other soft information. Sometimes courts must decide whether a particular statement is a statement of fact as opposed to a mere opinion or prediction. Numerous cases have characterized broad qualitative statements such as "this should be our most profitable year ever" or "this product should be our best product ever" as mere unactionable opinions or puffing. But the Supreme Court in *Virginia Bankshares, Inc. v. Sandberg* (1991) held that a statement that a price offered to shareholders in a freeze out merger was "high" could constitute an actionable false statement if the speaker knew that the statement was untrue.

In recent years, not only the courts, but also the Congress and the SEC have become more permissive with respect to so called soft information. The SEC, which for years opposed providing earnings projections, valuation reports and other soft information in documents filed with the commission, came to realize that such information is exactly the type of information that sophisticated investors find most useful. Today the SEC not only allows, but in some cases, requires such information. The SEC has provided protection against liability by creating "safe harbor." The Private Securities Litigation Reform Act of 1995 incorporated many of these safe harbors into the statutes. In general, the safe harbor rules now provide protection for forward looking information if the provider of the information had a reasonable basis for the opinion or prediction and the provider believed the opinion or prediction.

Silence or nondisclosure. Silence can be actionable when there is an affirmative duty to speak. We will explore the question of when there is an affirmative duty to disclose later when we discuss the application of 10b–5 to insider trading cases.

The deception requirement established by the United States Supreme Court in the case of *Santa Fe Industries, Inc. v. Green* (1977) limited the scope and better defined the application of Rule 10b–5.

Recall in the last chapter we learned about fiduciary duties and about the **stringent procedural requirements that surround the main remedy for breach**

of fiduciary duties—the shareholders derivative suit. Prior to the *Santa Fe* case, several lower federal courts (and the Supreme Court), rendered a number of decisions which held that Rule 10b–5 afforded a federal remedy against corporate officers, directors and control shareholders for breaches of fiduciary duties, if in some remote way the breach of fiduciary duties could be connected to a purchase or sale of securities. The effect of applying Rule 10b–5 in this way would be: (1) to federalize a large portion of the law of fiduciary duties, which traditionally had been part of state corporate law and (2) to enable plaintiffs to do an end run around the stringent procedural requirements that surround shareholder derivative suits.

The best example of this old expansive application of Rule 10b–5 can be found in *Superintendent of Insurance v. Bankers Life & Casualty Co.* (1971), a case decided by the Supreme Court in 1971. In that case an insurance company owned some government bonds. A person named Begole acquired the insurance company from Bankers Life. After acquiring control of the insurance company, Begole had the insurance company sell the bonds. Begole then looted a significant amount of cash, including the cash received for the bonds, from the company and fled the country.

The Supreme Court held this constituted a violation of Rule 10b–5. The "fraud" was Begole's failure to tell the board, which authorized the sale of the bonds, that he intended to steal the proceeds. The court found a nexus between the sale of the bonds and the looting, even though the fraud had nothing to do with the sale of the bonds, but rather had to do with Begole's looting the proceeds derived from the sale. While *Santa Fe v. Green* did not specifically overrule the *Bankers Life* decision, all experts agree that *Bankers Life* is **not** the law today. The case illustrates how the law has changed.

In *Santa Fe v. Green,* Santa Fe Industries owned 95% of the stock of Kirby Lumber Co. It sought to acquire the remaining 5% of Kirby's stock held by the minority stockholders pursuant to a "short form" merger governed by the Delaware short form merger statute. Under this procedure the minority shareholders, including Mr. Green, were cashed out at a price arrived at on the basis of an appraisal prepared by Morgan Stanley. Santa Fe complied with the Delaware short form merger statute, which does not require a vote of shareholders. After completing the merger, Santa Fe informed Kirby's minority shareholders of the merger, told them that they would be getting $150 per share for their stock and advised them of their statutory right of appraisal, the remedy provided under Delaware law, if they felt they were entitled to more.

Morgan Stanley, an investment banking firm, had appraised Kirby's assets—its land, timber, oil and gas properties, etc. The appraisal valued these assets at $125 per share and the price paid for the Kirby shares was $150 per share. Santa Fe sent the minority shareholders copies of the Morgan Stanley appraisal along with other relevant information. This information convinced one of the minority shareholders, Mr. Green, that the value of Kirby's assets was not $150 per share but rather $770 per share.

Rather than pursuing his appraisal rights in state court, Mr. Green brought an action in federal court which sought to set aside the merger because it violated Rule 10b–5. Green's complaint stated, and the theory of his case was, that the Kirby shares were worth $770 a share. He claimed that the price Santa Fe paid the minority shareholders was too low and was based on a fraudulent valuation. And he alleged this amounted to fraud prohibited by Rule 10b–5.

This case was decided on the pleadings. It is important to understand that the complaint did not allege any material misrepresentations or omissions. The premise on which this case was decided is that there was full disclosure—no lies, no material omissions, no half truths, etc. The gist of the minority shareholder's complaint was simply, **we are being forced to sell our shares to the parent corporation at an unfair price**.

The Supreme Court held for the defendant. In holding that the plaintiff had failed to state a cause of action under Rule 10b–5, the *Santa Fe* Court says 10b–5 is a **disclosure rule not a fairness rule**. If there has been full disclosure there is **no violation of Rule 10b–5**, even though the underlying transaction is unfair. The Supreme Court did not tell Mr. Green that he did not have a remedy if the price is unfair. They simply said you are in the wrong court Mr. Green. Go to state court to redress this kind of a grievance.

The basic teaching of *Santa Fe* is that **Rule 10b–5 is not a fiduciary duty rule, it is not a fairness rule— it is a disclosure rule**. *Santa Fe* draws a clear line in the sand. Cases on one side of the line are classified as "fiduciary duty or fairness cases" and go to state court. Cases on the other side of the line, which are about "deception," can go to federal court under Rule 10b–5.

While *Santa Fe v. Green* defines the problem, the case does not solve the problem, because **fairness and deception do not exist in water tight compartments**. There is significant overlap in the two categories of cases. Some form of deception is probably present in almost every case where someone breaches his fiduciary duties. People who loot companies, self-deal or overreach do not typically disclose to others that this is what they are doing. That failure to disclose may be deception and if there is sufficient causal connection between the deception and the misconduct one might have a action under Rule 10b–5.

Santa Fe told us we **have to have deception but it did not tell us what constitutes deception nor did it speak to the degree of causal connection required**. Thus, the scope of the decision is subject to both interpretation and debate. The Supreme Court's opinion left the task of drawing the line created by *Santa Fe* to the lower courts.

Bottom line. *Santa Fe* took many cases which in the 1960s and early 1970s would have been brought in the federal court out of that arena and put them back in the state court. Today while no court would likely make the stretch the *Bankers Life* court made to bootstrap a fiduciary violation case into a 10b–5 case, the lower federal courts are still trying to draw the line between "deception cases" and "fairness cases." And the courts are not in agreement as to where to draw this elusive line. This is an active area of litigation and thus, likely to be discussed and perhaps tested in the basic business course.

Finally, in connection with this line of inquiry, consider the *Weinberger* case, discussed in § VI.B.2.b, *supra.* *Weinberger*, decided by the Delaware supreme court six years after *Santa Fe* (and similar to *Santa Fe* on its facts) established the "entire fairness test" in Delaware. Thus, today it may be less important to get under Federal law, now that state law seems to provide an adequate remedy. On the other hand, given a choice most plaintiffs would still likely prefer to bring their cases under Rule 10b–5 rather than suing in state court because suing under Rule 10b–5 may enable plaintiffs to do an end run around many of the stringent procedural requirements that surround shareholder derivative suits such as (1) the contemporaneous ownership rule, (2) the demand requirement, (3) posting security for costs, etc.

If you understand how *Weinberger* and *Santa Fe* fit together you have made progress in "learning the process." While the rules may change, particularly in developing areas of the law, the process remains the same. Most professors try to teach the "**process**" and at exam time they try to test the students' understanding of the process.

3. MATERIALITY

To form the basis of liability under Rule 10b–5, a misstatement or omission must rise to the level of materiality. Materiality is a controlling concept under both the 33 and 34 Acts, whether we are talking about liability for false and misleading statements in a 33 Act pro-

spectus, violation of the proxy rules or violation of Rule
10b–5. The basic test of materiality is the same in all
these areas.

While determining the materiality of a given fact can
be difficult since the factual variations are infinite, the
legal test of materiality is well settled. It was formulated
by the U. S. Supreme Court in *TSC Industries, Inc. v.
Northway, Inc.* (1976), a case brought under Rule 14a–9,
the proxy fraud rule. The test, which is equally applicable in Rule 10b–5 cases, was quoted verbatim in
§ V.B.4.d, *supra.*

Under the *TSC Industries* test, a fact is material if
there is a **substantial likelihood that a reasonable
investor would find the fact important in deciding
whether to buy or sell a security**.

When viewed in an academic setting, the *TSC Industries* test appears to be a reasonable, jury oriented, objective test. However, in a real world trial of a securities
fraud case, the test favors the plaintiff.

Why does this test favor the plaintiff?

Because plaintiff's lawyer, in the presence of the jury,
will typically ask the following question with respect to
the piece of information whose materiality is challenged:

"Would you have liked to have had this information
when you bought the stock?"

When the question is put that way, after the fact, the
answer will almost invariably be "yes." Though the jury
will be instructed to view the materiality of information
omitted as of the time of the purchase or sale, few jurors
are capable of ignoring events which occurred subse-

quent to the time of purchase or sale that make the information clearly material. We will focus on two legal issues pertaining to materiality that frequently arise in cases and on exams.

The probability/magnitude test. How do we determine the materiality of facts relating to the possibility of a future event occurring, when the materiality of the event would be clear, but at the time of the purchase or sale, it was not clear whether the event would occur.

A good example occurred in *Basic, Inc. v. Levinson*. Here a corporation denied that it was in merger negotiations when the corporation was in fact negotiating a merger which ultimately resulted in shareholders receiving a premium of about 50% on their stock over the pre-merger market price. At the time of the misstatement, however, it was not clear that the merger would be consummated. A statement disclosing the merger negotiations, had the merger failed to materialize, would just as likely have resulted in liability.

In *Basic,* the Supreme Court applied the so called **probability/magnitude test**. Under the probability/magnitude test as of the moment of the event the jury is supposed to balance the probability that the event will occur against the magnitude of the event if it occurs. The conceptual framework is easy to understand—the lower the probability, the higher the magnitude necessary to find materiality and vice versa.

On its face, particularly in an academic setting, weighing probability and magnitude seems to make sense. But in a real life litigation situation, irrespective of the instruction that says the jury should apply the test at the time of the transaction, can the jury ignore the accomplished fact that the merger did go through and that shareholders who held their shares until the merger occurred got a 50% premium? Most practicing lawyers, as well as many scholars, doubt they can. That having been said, probability/magnitude is the test to use on your exam if you encounter a developing situation in which you must determine the materiality of information pertaining to an event that may or may not happen.

The bespeaks caution doctrine. Another issue that often comes up in the context of materiality involves projections or opinions followed by warnings the projections or opinions might not pan out. It is called the "**bespeaks caution doctrine**." The 34 Act has been amended to incorporate provisions of the Private Securities Litigation Reform Act of 1995 which added a safe harbor that codifies the bespeaks caution doctrine for forward looking statements.

The main issues under the bespeaks caution doctrine relate to the scope of its application. The cautionary statement must be detailed and specific, there must be a reasonable basis for the statement, and the statement must be made in good faith.

4. SCIENTER

The operative language of Rule 10b–5 does not specify the level of fault required. Prior to *Ernst & Ernst v. Hochfelder* (1976), a U.S. Supreme Court decision, the circuit courts around the country were divided. Some said plaintiff had to show an intentional violation to recover under Rule 10b–5, while others said that negligence was enough.

Ernst & Ernst v. Hochfelder held that in order to maintain an action under Rule 10b–5, the plaintiff must show that the defendant acted with **scienter**. *Hochfelder* was an action by defrauded customers of a stock brokerage firm, whose president and controlling shareholder, Nay, stole money from clients' escrow accounts. At the time of the lawsuit, Nay had committed suicide and the brokerage firm was bankrupt. The suit was against the brokerage firm's auditor, Ernst & Ernst. Plaintiff argued that Ernst & Ernst was negligent in conducting its audit of the brokerage firm, and that such negligence was actionable under Rule 10b–5.

The Supreme Court reversed the Seventh Circuit and held that **without scienter there can be no violation of Rule 10b–5.** The court derived the "scienter" requirement from the language of Section 10(b), the enabling section, and the legislative history of the 34 Act. From these sources the Court concluded that Congress did not intend to create 10b–5 liability for mere negligence.[1]

While the opinion in *Hochfelder* clearly rejected negligence as the proper state-of-mind and required scienter as the standard, the court gave us only a vague hint of what is meant by scienter. In a footnote, the Court described scienter as "a mental state embracing **an intent to deceive, manipulate or defraud**." Unfortunately, that definition raises almost as many questions as it answers.

1. *Hochfelder* is one of several cases in which the Supreme Court has limited the scope of Rule 10b–5's application on the basis of the language in the enabling section 10(b)—"manipulative or deceptive device or contrivance"—which, as interpreted by the court, is narrower than the language in the Rule itself.

The following two questions relative to scienter are particularly important:

First, does scienter require a showing of bad faith, evil motive or intent to cause harm?

Basic, Inc. v. Levinson answers that question. Recall *Basic* was the case where the president of the company lied to protect the confidentiality of sensitive merger negotiations. There was no evil motive or desire to further some self serving scheme behind that lie. The president was acting in a sensible businesslike way, trying to protect the best interests of the company and its shareholders. He was not lying to line his own pockets or maliciously cause harm.

In *Basic,* the Supreme Court implicitly said none of that matters. Good faith, business judgement, etc. are not defenses in the context of Rule 10b–5. **Rule 10b–5 merely requires that the statement was false. It does not require bad faith, evil motive, or malice.**

Second, will reckless disregard of the truth support liability under Rule 10b–5?

In *Hochfelder,* the Supreme Court left open the question of whether making a statement in reckless disregard of the truth is sufficient to support a Rule 10b–5 action. The circuit courts, that have considered this question subsequent to *Hochfelder,* have held that recklessness is enough to support a violation of Rule 10b–5. The courts are not, however, in agreement as to what constitutes "reckless" in the context of Rule 10b–5.

There has been considerable litigation and much scholarly writing on the reckless issue. While there is variation in the rhetoric used to describe the standard of recklessness required, a majority of the courts and writers, that have spoken on the issue, seem to be saying reckless means: **If you speak, knowing that you do not know whether what you are saying is true or false, but you speak anyway, without qualification, that is reckless, and reckless is enough to invoke potential liability under Rule 10b–5**.

5.   IN CONNECTION WITH THE PURCHASE OR SALE OF A SECURITY

Obviously, Rule 10b–5 does not apply to all frauds. The fraud must occur "**in connection with the purchase or sale of securities**." For example, if the CFO of a company embezzles $5 million, he has committed a crime, a tort, and violated his fiduciary duties, but he has not violated Rule 10b–5, because no purchase or sale of securities took place in this example. Two other basic and rather obvious points flow from the "in connection with" requirement.

(1) For Rule 10b–5 to apply, there must be a purchase or sale of a "security." The rule does not prohibit fraud in connection with the purchase or sale of used cars, real estate or other types of property. When the thing bought or sold is corporate stock, which is the case in most 10b–5 cases, a security is obviously involved. But, as discussed elsewhere, there are other types of interests which fit within the broad definition of a security. The point to remember is that the definition of a "security" is the same for purposes of invoking Rule 10b–5

under the 34 Act as it is for invoking the registration requirement under the 33 Act.

(2) Rule 10b–5 applies to purchases or sales exempt from the registration requirement of the 33 Act as well as purchases or sales which require registration. Therefore the distinction between sales by the issuer of new securities and resales by investors of outstanding securities, while extremely important for 33 Act purposes, is not important under Rule 10b–5. Rule 10b–5 applies to both types of transactions. For example, if a sale is made by an issuer by means of a false or misleading registration statement, plaintiff would have a cause of action under Rule 10b–5 as well as under § 11 of the 33 Act. There is an overlap of remedies, but the difference is Section 11 imposes strict liability, while Rule 10b–5 requires scienter.

In addition, the "in connection with" requirement relates to the connection between the purchase or sale and the fraud or misconduct. This aspect of the "in connection with" clause is similar to **proximate cause,** a necessary element in tort cases. Remember from torts there has to be a causal connection between the wrong and the injury. Rule 10b–5 works the same way. There has to be causal connection (a "nexus") between the purchase or sale of securities and the misconduct.

6.   STANDING—PLAINTIFF MUST HAVE BOUGHT OR SOLD SECURITIES

In *Blue Chip Stamps v. Manor Drug Stores* (1975), the Supreme Court held that, in order to have standing to sue under Rule 10b–5, the plaintiff must have been a buyer or seller of securities. In a case where plaintiff's decision ***not*** to sell or **not** to buy is induced by fraud, plaintiff cannot maintain an action under Rule 10b–5.

For example, assume that in the fall of 2001 Enron Corporation put out a false and misleading press release, which grossly overstated earnings, understated debt and lied about the company's business and prospects. In reliance on that press release one group of Enron employees bought stock in the company. This group would have standing to sue under Rule 10b–5. But assume another group of employees, who owned stock in Enron prior to the press release, decided, in reliance on the press release, not to sell their stock. The stock subsequently became worthless after the fraud was exposed and Enron went into bankruptcy. This group would not have standing to sue under the rule of *Blue Chip Stamps,* even though the group which did not sell might have been damaged by the false press release as much as the group which bought.

You also need to understand the converse of the *Blue Chip Stamps* holding: **The defendant does not have to be a purchaser or seller of securities**. Only the plaintiff has to meet the buyer or seller requirement. Consider our earlier example of the Enron false release, which caused plaintiffs to buy stock in the open market. Even though Enron did not buy or sell any stock itself, Enron would be potentially liable, under Rule 10b–5, for false statements it made in the press release, provided that plaintiff can show a causal connection between Enron's misconduct (the false statements in the press release) and plaintiff's purchase or sale of securities.

7. CAUSATION/RELIANCE

Causation, an element of common law fraud, is also an element of a Rule 10b–5 cause if action. In securities fraud cases causation encompasses two separate, but related concepts—"**loss causation**" and "**transaction causation**."

Loss causation embodies the concept that the defendant's fraud caused, or at least materially contributed to, the plaintiff's pecuniary loss—*i.e.,* the false statement caused the decline in the price of the stock. Assume for example, that X Airline puts out an annual report which materially overstates its earnings for the fiscal year ending June 30, 2001. During the fall of 2001, after the earnings misstatement is discovered the price of X Airline's stock declines materially. However, in the interim, the terrorist attack of September 11, 2001 occurred, which resulted in declines in airline travel and massive operating losses for X Airline. This is an obvious example of what in torts is known as an intervening cause. In securities litigation, it is called a lack of loss causation.

In re Apple Computer Securities Litigation (9th Cir. 1989) involved a more sophisticated application of loss causation. The application in that case requires introduction to another concept called the "Efficient Market Hypothesis," which is a catchy name given to a theory that says that stock prices in active trading markets respond rapidly to all available information about a stock—both true information and false information. That concept underlies the "fraud on the market" presumption discussed below.

In the *Apple* case, Apple Computer put out what the trial court found to be a materially misleading press release which overstated the potential capabilities of two new products—the Lisa Computer and a compatible disk drive called Twiggy. There is a good reason that most of you have never heard of these two products introduced in the 1980s. They both turned out to be flops, which had a material adverse impact on Apple's earnings and the price of its stock.

The Ninth Circuit reversed a trial court's multimillion dollar verdict against Apple for material misstatements in the press release. The reversal was based on reasoning flowing from the Efficient Market Hypothesis. The court stated that during the same time frame as Apple put out its overly optimistic release about Lisa and Twiggy, independent analysts were putting out releases of their own which were skeptical of these products. The releases put out by the independents were not as widely disseminated as the Apple release. They were published mainly in technical journals, rather than the Wall Street Journal, but the conflicting information and opinions were publicly available and the court believed that the market professionals had absorbed all of the conflicting information. Thus, under the Efficient Market Hypothesis all of the conflicting information was reflected in the price of the stock. In other words, Apple was able to get a reversal on the theory—we lied, but the market did not believe us—and thus there was no loss causation.

Transaction causation is often termed "reliance" because the plaintiff's reliance on the false statement is the usual way in which the false statement caused plaintiff harm—*i.e.*, reliance on the false statement caused plaintiff to enter into the transaction. Thus, transaction causation, which in essence is just another way of saying plaintiff relied on the fraud, relates to the nexus between the fraud and the investment decision.

The fraud on the market theory is a means of proving transaction causation (or reliance, which we said earlier are one and the same) when there is an active trading market for a security. Rule 10b–5 applies to face-to-face transactions as well as transactions in the organized trading markets. In face to face transactions, reliance means exactly what it means at common law. Plaintiff has to show she was aware of the misstatement and was deceived by it. However, most Rule 10b–5 cases do not involve direct dealings between plaintiff and defendant. Rather they involve persons buying or selling in active trading markets such as stock exchanges.

What if the plaintiff (or some members of the class in a class action) was not aware of the specific misrepresentation?

Basic, Inc. v. Levinson provides the answer to this question. Recall that in *Basic,* management issued statements which falsely denied that Basic was in merger negotiations. After the merger, in which Basic shareholders received a 50% premium over the market price of the stock before the merger, was announced, a class action law suit was filed on behalf of all persons who had sold their stock between the time of the false statements and announcement of the merger. Although the false denial of the merger negotiations was published in the Cleveland Plain Dealer and other newspapers, it was virtually certain that many of the plaintiffs in the class never read or heard of Basic's denial before selling their shares. *How can those plaintiffs satisfy the element of reliance or transaction causation?*

In *Basic,* the U.S. Supreme Court told us the reliance requirement can be satisfied by a presumption known as **fraud on the market theory**, in the following words:

"The fraud on the market theory is based on the hypothesis that, in an open and developed securities market, the price of a company's stock is determined by the available information regarding the company and its business.... Misleading statements will therefore defraud purchasers of stock even if the purchasers do not directly rely on the misstatements.... The causal connection between the defendants' fraud and the plaintiffs' purchase of stock in such a case is no less significant than in a case of direct reliance.... "

The fraud on the market theory does not obviate the need to prove materiality, scienter, or loss causation. All it provides is a means of proving transaction causation or reliance by a rebuttable presumption in situations where the stock in question is widely traded in an active market. The presumption applies to stocks traded over a stock exchange or in the NASDAQ, automatic quotation system. Whether it applies to other markets is still unclear. When it applies, the fraud on the market theory creates a powerful presumption that is hard to overcome.

8.   DAMAGES

Private Rule 10b–5 plaintiffs have a full range of equitable and legal remedies. Section 28(a) of the 34 Act has been read to say that (1) the goal is **compensatory damages** and (2) **punitive damages** are not available under Rule 10b–5.

The most common measure is **out of pocket damages—the difference in the amount paid for the security and its actual value as of the time of the transaction**. However, courts are not limited to that measure of damages.

Also, in the 1980s, Congress amended the 34 Act to allow the SEC to enforce insider trading violations, through statutory civil actions for treble damages. Today, while most 10b–5 insider trading cases (the next application of Rule 10b–5 discussed) are brought by the SEC, most civil securities fraud cases are brought by private plaintiffs.[2]

C. INSIDER TRADING

Among the general public, the best known application of Rule 10b–5 is probably **insider trading**. This is due in large part to the fact that a number of insider trading cases have been brought against high profile celebrities and have received extensive media coverage. Insider trading is a relatively new area of the law, which developed in stages over the last 45 years. The practice of insider trading, except in certain face to face transactions, was not even illegal until the 1960s and the rules that currently govern were laid down by the courts in the 1980s and 1990s. Today, the rules that govern insider trading are fairly well established. To better understand the

2. All criminal cases based on Rule 10b–5, including securities fraud and insider trading cases, are brought by the Justice Department.

current rules and how they apply, we need to understand what insider trading means and how the current rules developed.

1. WHAT IS INSIDER TRADING?

"Insider trading" is simply a short-hand description of a fact pattern where an officer or director of the company, a rank and file employee (such as a secretary or a guy in the mail room), or an associate in a law firm or accounting firm that represents the company acquires material information about the company. The information could be good or bad news, but it is **news that will likely cause the price of the stock to move** up or down—*e.g.*, the company is about to be acquired at a premium, it is about to get a very large new contract, it is about to file for bankruptcy, etc.

Before that information is made public, that person (the "insider") buys or sells the stock and later makes a profit when the news is made public. Or the recipient of the information tips someone else (a "tippee") who buys or sells the stock on the basis of the inside information and makes a profit.

In the insider trading cases, we are not dealing with lies, misrepresentations, half truths or the like. Rather we are dealing with **complete silence**—lack of disclosure.

The insider trading prohibition applies in face-to-face transactions. But most of the trades in insider trading cases occur over a stock exchange or NASDAQ. The so called "insider" has no idea who the person on the other side of the trade is. The insider's motive is to make money, but it is not to cheat or mislead the person on the other side of the trade, whose identity is almost never known to the inside trader.

2. WHAT LAWS OTHER THAN RULE 10b–5 MAY APPLY TO INSIDER TRADING?

a. Insider Trading Under State Law

While Rule 10b–5 is now the main rule used to police insider trading, through criminal and civil actions brought in Federal courts, we can get a better perspective of what is involved by first looking briefly at how state law treats insider trading. Most casebooks take this approach and include *Goodwin v. Agassiz* (Mass. 1933), which reflects how insider trading is dealt with under state law. Because of the similarity in the facts of this case and the seminal federal case on insider trading, *Texas Gulf Sulphur*, which we will discuss later, *Goodwin* not only provides a good history lesson but also illustrates the current contrast between the state and federal law of insider trading.

In *Goodwin v. Agassiz*, plaintiff Goodwin sold 700 shares of Cliff Mining Co. on the Boston Stock Exchange. Defendant Agassiz, the president and a director of Cliff Mining, bought those shares on the same exchange. Agassiz had inside information—a geologist's report that indicated the property in which Cliff Mining had the mineral rights might be rich in iron ore. Goodwin and Agassiz did not know one another and had never spoken. Their respective buy and sell orders simply reached the floor of the Boston Stock Exchange at about the same time through normal brokerage channels and were matched. The Massachusetts Supreme Court held for the defendant and refused to impose liability. The opinion emphasized the anonymous and impersonal character of transactions that occur over a stock exchange.

Goodwin v. Agassiz represents the current rule of insider trading under state law. **There is no liability for insider trading under state law with one exception**. The exception, discussed in *Goodwin*, is called the "**special facts doctrine**," which comes from *Strong v. Repide* (1909), a famous early case. The special facts doctrine is a common law doctrine which says: **An officer or director is under an affirmative duty to disclose special facts when buying shares from existing shareholders**. The elements necessary to state a cause of action under the special facts doctrine are all captured in the above sentence:

(1) Only officers and directors are subject to the doctrine.

(2) While originally the special facts doctrine only applied to **purchases**, today it applies to **purchases** or **sales**.

(3) While the special facts doctrine was originally only triggered by facts that were truly extraordinary, today **any material information** will trigger the doctrine.

(4) Finally, and most importantly, there has to be **privity**—face to face dealings between the officer or director and the party on the other side of the transaction.

Since the **special facts doctrine** only applies to **face to face** transactions, not dealings over a stock exchange, the special facts doctrine did not apply in the *Goodwin* case.

b.   Section 16(b) of the 34 Act

Goodwin v. Agassiz still reflects the current state law of insider trading. But federal law, today, is different because of Rule 10b–5 and the body of jurisprudence which has developed under that rule with respect to insider trading. However, until 1961 the federal rule was the same as the rule under state law—no liability except under the special facts doctrine—subject only to § 16(b) of the 34 Act.

Long before 1961, Congress was aware that insider trading was a problem. The hearings which preceded passage of the 34 Act revealed flagrant insider trading abuses. The legislative history of the 34 Act clearly shows that while Congress knew that insider trading was a problem which undermined the integrity of the securities markets, it did not know how to deal with the problem.

Congress's only attempt to deal with the problem was § 16(b) of the 34 Act, which the legislative history describes as a "crude rule of thumb." Section 16(b) is still used as a crude but potent remedy for capturing profits made as the result of short term trading by certain high level people. You could not find two provisions more different in concept or application than § 16(b) and Rule 10b–5.

Section 16(b) imposes strict liability on any director, officer or 10% shareholder of a company, subject to § 16(b), who makes a profit (as defined for purposes of § 16(b)) within a six month period from the purchase or sale or the sale and purchase of equity securities of her company. No fraudulent intent is required. If a person subject to § 16(b) waits six months and one day between trades she can engage in the world's worst fraud without liability under § 16(b). On the other hand, if the purchase and sale occur within six months of one another and there is a profit, then there is liability regardless of how well intended or reasonable the transactions might have been.

The legislative history clearly reveals the philosophy behind § 16(b) was to impose **strict liability** so as to remove all temptation on the part of high-level insiders to trade short term in the stock of their corporations. The remedy requires the § 16(b) insider who profits from trades within six months of one another to turn all profits over to the corporation. The mechanism for enforcing § 16(b) is a statutory shareholders' derivative suit, and the economic engine which drives § 16(b) lawsuits is the liberal attorney's fees authorized by the statute.

Section 16(b) liability is computed by matching the price received in any purchase or sale, regardless of order, during any six-month period in which the sales price is higher than the purchase price and there is no offset for losses. This is called the lowest-in, highest-out formula. It is designed to squeeze out all possible damages resulting from violations.

The rules which govern the application of § 16(b) are arcane and, for the most part, counterintuitive. They are devoid of logic and recognize no equitable exceptions. The bad news is that this makes § 16(b), which on its face seems simple, one of the most complex provisions of the Federal Securities Laws. But the good news is that details pertaining to § 16(b)'s application are beyond anything usually covered in the basic business course. Unless you have a professor that emphasizes § 16(b), all you really need to remember about 16(b) is (1) that **persons subject to § 16(b) should always wait at least six months between trades** and (2) how § 16(b) differs from Rule 10b-5 in concept and application.

How does § 16(b) differ from Rule 10b-5?

(1) Section 16(b) only applies to companies registered under the 34 Act (*i.e.*, the same subset of companies subject to the proxy rules are subject to § 16(b)).

(2) Only directors, officers and 10% shareholders of "publicly held" companies are subject to § 16(b). As you will see, this is much narrower than the class of persons subject to Rule 10b-5 liability.

(3) While § 16(b) imposes automatic strict liability regardless of any wrong doing or intent, Rule 10b-5 requires trading based on material, non public information, a fiduciary duty of confidentiality and scienter.

Today, the number of suits brought under § 16(b) is only a small fraction of the number of suits brought under Rule 10b-5.

3.   HOW DOES RULE 10b-5 DEAL WITH INSIDER TRADING?
(Evolution of the Current Insider Trading Rules)

a.   The Disclose or Abstain Rule and *Texas Gulf Sulphur*

In 1961, President Kennedy appointed William L. Cary, a famous professor of corporate and securities law at the Columbia law school, Chairman of the SEC. Long before being appointed Chairman of the SEC, Professor Cary had developed the notion that insider trading ought to be illegal even if the trades took place on a stock exchange. He had written law review articles explaining his view, but no one outside of academia paid much attention.

However, once professor Cary became Chairman of the SEC, he was in a position to make his view the SEC's view, which he did. Needless to say, that got the people's attention. Professor Cary's view (the SEC's view) of what the prohibition of insider trading should be was first articulated in an administrative proceeding by the SEC against a broker/dealer, called *In re Cady Roberts*.

In re Cady Roberts involved what today would be considered a crude and clear cut insider trading violation, but in 1961, when the case arose, this was not known to be illegal. Cowden, a partner in Cady Roberts, was on the board of Curtiss Wright Corp. He attended a board meeting at which the Curtiss Wright board voted to cut the dividend. At a morning recess of the board meeting Cowden called and told one of his partners at Cady Roberts, Gintel, that Curtiss Wright was going to announce a dividend cut later in the day. Gintel sold Curtiss Wright stock in his own account and the accounts of several Cady Roberts customers, before the dividend cut was announced.

The SEC held that Cady Roberts had violated Rule 10b–5. The opinion, written by Chairman Cary, stated that Gintel had an affirmative duty to either disclose the material facts he knew or refrain from trading until those facts became public. This has come to be known as the **disclose or abstain rule**.

The **rationale** for the SEC's decision in *Cady Roberts* was simply that it is **unfair** for "anyone" who acquires inside information to exploit that information when the typical shareholder does not have access to the same information. This came to be known as the **equal access rule**. As we shall see, **the rationale for the disclose or abstain rule is no longer fairness and equal access. And the prohibition no longer applies to "anyone."** But that is getting ahead of the story.

Cady Roberts illustrates a practice sometimes employed by the SEC, when they want to change or clarify the law. The SEC brings an administrative proceeding, decides the case and writes an opinion announcing its position. In a broker/dealer proceeding such as *Cady Roberts*, the SEC staff is the prosecutor and the commission is the judge. You cannot find a friendlier forum than that. The SEC knew that, to carry any weight, its position would have to stand up in court.

The case in which the SEC tested its new position on insider trading was the seminal case of *SEC v. Texas Gulf Sulphur* (2d Cir. 1968). In November, 1963, Texas Gulf Sulphur Co. ("TGS") was exploring for minerals near Timmons, Ontario in Northeastern Canada. They drilled a hole and took a core sampling, the now famous K–55–1 core sample, which on visual inspection suggested the land might contain exceptionally high deposits of silver, copper, zinc and other hard minerals. Shortly after the K–55–1 core sample was drilled it was time to shut down operations for the winter. TGS moved the rig, sent the core sample to Utah to be assayed, and began quietly buying up mineral rights from landowners in the area. Only a few select people at TGS were told of the core sample and they were instructed to maintain absolute silence. However, the news did get up the corporate ladder to a few people at TGS.

During the period between November 12, 1963, when the core sample was first examined in the field and April 16, 1964, after operations resumed and rumors of a large mineral discovery began to surface, several TGS employees, from the field geologist to the president, who had knowledge of K–55–1, bought TGS stock or options. Some of those people also told friends—golfing buddies, relatives, girlfriends, etc.—about the core sample and those people (designated "tippees" by the court) also bought TGS stock or options.

The SEC brought an action under Rule 10b–5 against the TGS employees (and their tippees) who bought TGS stock or options with knowledge of the K–55–1 core sample, before the news was made public. The Second Circuit held that the defendants had violated Rule 10b–5, stating:

"Anyone in possession of material non public information has a duty to disclose that information before trading in the stock" and "Rule 10b–5 is based in policy on the justifiable expectation of the securities marketplace that all investors trading on impersonal exchanges have relatively equal access to material information . . . . "

Note that the rationale in *Texas Gulf Sulphur* was the same as in *Cady Roberts*—**fairness** and **equal access to information**.

While *Texas Gulf Sulphur* was generally well received in the legal community, following the case, lawyers and their clients faced a serious line-drawing problem. Obviously, a corporate officer who buys or sells stock in his company, knows more about the business and prospects of the company than an ordinary shareholder in middle America, who happened to be on the other side of the transaction. No knowledgeable investor, who bought or sold stock, could know for sure that liability might not attach on the basis that he knew more about the security than the person on the other side of the transaction.

There was also an outpouring of scholarly articles on insider trading in law reviews. And a backlash began to develop as many scholars questioned the assumptions underlying the prohibition against insider trading. Most scholars agreed with the concept, but many argued that a law based simply on the broad and undefinable concept of fairness was too open-ended, too unpredictable and not in touch with the reality of the market place, which always was and always will be information driven. Fairness is often the goal of the law, but rarely is it the defining legal standard. It is simply too amorphous a concept—like beauty, fairness can only be defined through the eyes of the beholder.

While these and other issues were being debated in academia and the board rooms of corporate America, a new character, who would be the catalyst for the next change in the rules governing insider trading came on the scene. His name was Vincent Chiarella.

b. Finding the "Fiduciary Nexus"—*Chiarella v. United States*

Chiarella v. United States (1980) is the foundation on which most of the current rules on insider trading rest.

The facts of the case are simple. Mr. Chiarella was an employee of Pandick Press, a printer of prospectuses, proxy statements, tender offer documents, etc. The takeover boom of the 1980s had begun and Pandick was one of the financial printers "bidder companies" hired to print the offering material which the securities laws[3] required them to use in connection with tender offers to acquire so-called "target companies."

As a security measure, the names of both the "bidder" and "target" companies were not revealed until the final printing—the night before the tender offer was announced. In preliminary drafts the names of the "bidder" and "target" companies were coded. Mr. Chiarella was able to figure out the code and identify the target companies in five cases over a 14–month period. He bought stock of the target companies before the tender offer was announced and sold the stock at a profit following the announcement. He made insider trading profits of about $30,000 before an SEC investigation uncovered his insider trading scheme.

Mr. Chiarella was indicted and criminally convicted of violating Rule 10b–5. But the United States Supreme Court reversed the conviction and in so doing, changed the rules that govern insider trading. This decision by a divided court, while approving the basic disclose or abstain rule of *Texas Gulf Sulphur*, **completely changed the analytical framework for resolving insider trading cases**. One of the dissenting opinions in this case also provided the foundation for additional changes

3.   The so called Williams Act, enacted in 1968, amended the 34 Act by requiring persons making tender offers for publicly held companies to file certain documents with the SEC. See § X. B.3.b, *infra*.

in the rules governing insider trading, which were yet to come. I will therefor discuss both the majority opinion and Justice Burger's dissent.

The majority opinion. In overturning Chiarella's conviction, the majority opinion significantly limited the class of persons subject to the disclose or abstain rule. Recall in *Texas Gulf Sulphur*, the rationale behind the disclose or abstain rule was equal access to information. Under the holding of that case the mere possession by anyone of material information not available to other traders was sufficient to trigger the duty to disclose or abstain. In *Chiarella*, the majority said that rule is too broad. In the words of the majority, when "fraud" is based on non-disclosure (as it always is in insider trading cases): "there can be no fraud absent a duty to speak." In other words, **the Court held the disclose or abstain rule is limited to persons in a fiduciary relationship with one-another.**

After *Chiarella*, we must find a **fiduciary nexus** (*i.e.,* a duty of confidentiality) between the person with the inside information (*i.e.,* the "insider") and the other party to the transaction. This fiduciary nexus is the foundation on which the duty to disclose or abstain rests, according to *Chiarella*. Today this is called the "**fiduciary nexus**" or the "**classical**" theory of insider trading.[4]

Applying the fiduciary nexus theory, the Supreme Court reversed Chiarella's conviction because the jury instruction (based on the equal access rule), which prohibited anyone with inside information from trading, was

4. To distinguish this theory from an alternative theory for imposing liability, called the "misappropriation theory," which I will discuss in the next subsection.

too broad. *Chiarella* completely changed the framework of analysis in insider trading cases. After this decision, the name of the game became—find the fiduciary nexus.

How do you find a fiduciary nexus between the buyer and seller of the securities?

When an employee is trading in the stock of her own company, finding the fiduciary nexus is not a problem. *Chiarella* would not have changed the result of *Texas Gulf Sulphur*, where all the buyers were employees of TGS or tippees of such employees. The sellers by definition were shareholders of TGS. There is "a relationship of trust and confidence" (*i.e.*, a fiduciary relationship) between shareholders and the insiders who obtained confidential information by reason of their position with that corporation.

employee → corporation ← shareholder

All employees of the company whose stock is being bought or sold are covered—the **CEO** to the **clerk in the mail room**. If you are an employee of a company and have material undisclosed information about your company, you are subject to the disclose or abstain rule and may be liable civilly or criminally if you violate that rule. The notion that triggers application of Rule 10b–5 is that all employees have a duty of confidentiality to the company for which they work.

The duty of confidentiality and resulting duty to disclose or abstain also extends to attorneys, accountants, public relations firms and investment bankers (and all employees of such firms) engaged to do work for the company in whose stock they trade. These people are sometimes called "constructive fiduciaries" or "temporary insiders." The notion that triggers their duty is the same as that which triggers the duty of employees. By virtue of their engagement, these temporary insiders have a duty of confidentiality that runs to the company.

Under this test Mr. Chiarella would not be covered. Mr. Chiarella was buying stock of the target company. While Rule 10b–5 would have applied to any purchases by Mr. Chiarella of the bidder company's stock, neither Chiarella, his employer Pandick or Pandick's client (the bidder company) owed a fiduciary duty to the target company, the company whose stock Mr. Chiarello was buying. Thus, the fiduciary nexus was broken and Mr. Chiarella was not prohibited from trading in the target company's stock as shown by the following diagram.

Fiduciary Nexus Test Met

Attorney ↘

Employee → Bidder Company → Shareholder

Test not met in Chiarella case

Chiarella(buyer) → Pandick → Bidder Company

      (break in fiduciary nexus)

Target Company ← Shareholder (seller)

Chiarella is the law today and most insider trading cases are brought under the classical or fiduciary nexus theory established in that case. *Chiarella* was a major step in the development of the law of insider trading. But the *Chiarella* case is not the end of the story. If the Chiarella case had come up today, Mr. Chiarella would have gone to jail. He would be convicted today, not under the fiduciary nexus theory, but under an alternative theory of liability called the "**misappropriation theory**," which was established by the U.S. Supreme Court in *United States v. O'Hagan* (1997), the next case discussed. While the *O'Hagan* case was not decided until 17 years after *Chiarella,* the misappropriation theory had its genesis in Justice Burger's dissent in *Chiarella.*

The Burger dissent. In their briefs to the Supreme Court, the government attorneys, probably suspecting that a majority of the justices might not buy the equal access rule, presented the court with an alternative theory for upholding Chiarella's conviction. It has come to be called the **misappropriation theory**. It probably got its name from language in Justice Burger's dissenting opinion in which the Chief Justice said he would have upheld Chiarella's conviction based on the alternative theory, which Burger characterized as follows: [Chiarella] "misappropriated—stole to put it bluntly—valuable nonpublic information entrusted to him in utmost confidence." The majority, however, refused to consider this theory because it had not been presented at trial.

In the 17 years between *Chiarella* and *O'Hagan,* although it had opportunities to do so, an apparently divided Supreme Court refused to consider the misappropriation theory. During that time, 5 of the circuit courts upheld the misappropriation theory, but 2 of the circuits rejected the theory. This split of authority in the circuit courts set the stage for the Supreme Court to rule on the

validity of the misappropriation theory in the case of
United States v. O'Hagan.

c. The Misappropriation Theory—*United States v. O'Hagan*

The *O'Hagan* case involves the sad story of a crooked
lawyer. The facts closely resemble those in *Chiarella.*
O'Hagan was a partner in a large Minneapolis law firm,
Dorsey & Whitney ("D & W"). D & W represented Grand
Met, an English company planning a tender offer for
control of Pillsbury Corporation. O'Hagan apparently
learned of the transaction from his partners at D & W.
O'Hagan had lost a lot of money in the stock market and
had embezzled money from clients of D & W. Hoping to
make enough money to cover the shortfall in his clients'
accounts, O'Hagan bought Pillsbury stock and options,
which he later sold after news of the Grand Met tender
offer was announced. He made a profit of $4.3 million.

However, his windfall was short lived because the
federal prosecutors came after him with a 57–count criminal indictment, which included violation of Rule 10b–5
grounded on the misappropriation theory (the only aspect of the case here discussed). He was convicted in the
trial court but the Eighth Circuit reversed the conviction.
The Supreme Court reinstated the conviction and held
that Rule 10b–5 liability may be predicated on the "misappropriation theory." The opinion explains the difference between the **"fiduciary nexus theory,"** which the
court refers to as the **"classical theory"** of insider
trading and the **"misappropriation theory,"** which
some people refer to as **"outsider trading."**

The classical theory is based on fraud on the other party to the transaction, while the misappropriation theory is based upon fraud on the source of the information. The facts of *O'Hagan* illustrate the application of the misappropriation theory. The bidder company (source) **entrusts** the D & W law firm (recipient) with material confidential information. An agent of the recipient (Mr. O'Hagan) misuses the information by buying stock in the target company in violation of a duty of confidentiality owed by the recipient to the source of the information.

Violation of this duty of confidence (the act of misappropriation) triggers the duty to disclose or abstain. So when O'Hagan traded the stock of the target company, he violated the disclose or abstain rule. His trades violated Rule 10b–5, even though no fiduciary nexus could be established between Mr. O'Hagan and the parties on the other side of the trades.

Saying the same thing a little differently, under the misappropriation theory, you are not looking for a fiduciary nexus, as you are in the classical theory. Instead, you are looking for an act of misappropriation that violates the duty of confidentiality owed by the recipient of the information to the source of the information.

When and how does a duty of trust and confidence arise between the source and the recipient of information?

To trigger the duty to disclose or abstain under the misappropriation theory, there has to be a relationship of trust and confidence between the recipient and the source of the information. Clearly there was such a relationship in the *O'Hagan* and *Chiarella* cases. But in some cases, questions arise as to whether such a relationship exists.

The courts have not yet given us a test for determining whether or not such a relationship exists, particularly in nonbusiness settings. But in October 2000, the SEC gave us guidance in the form of a new rule, Rule 10b5–2, which sets forth three nonexclusive bases for determining that a relationship of trust and confidence exists:

    (1) When the person receiving the information agreed to keep the information confidential;

    (2) When the persons involved in the communication had a history or pattern of sharing confidences; and

    (3) When the person who provided the information was a spouse, parent, child, or sibling of the person who received the information, unless it is shown that there was no reasonable expectation of confidentiality.

d. Tippers and Tippees—*Dirks v. SEC*

Chiarella and *O'Hagan* established the rules that today govern the scope of the duty to **disclose or abstain** imposed on the **original recipients** of "inside information." But recall, *Texas Gulf Sulphur*, the fountainhead case on insider trading, prohibited such trading not only by the original recipients of the inside information, but also by others to whom the information was passed. The *Texas Gulf Sulphur* court labeled these persons "**tippees**."

This subsection explores the scope of liability of tippees—*i.e.*, the brother-in-law, the golfing buddy or the girlfriend. It also explores the scope of liability of the persons who passed on the information on to the tippee, labeled "**tippers**" by the *Texas Gulf Sulphur* court.

The case which established the rules that today govern in the area of tipper/tippee liability is *Dirks v. SEC* (1983). The company in this case, Equity Funding Co., was more or less the Enron of the 1970s. It was in the business of selling insurance, variable annuities and related financial products. Its stock, listed on the New York Stock Exchange, had risen dramatically.

Raymond Dirks, the defendant in the case, was a well known investment analyst and a principal in a New York brokerage firm. Dirks' specialty was analyzing stocks of insurance companies. He had, in the years preceding the case, put many of his clients into Equity Funding and they, as well as Mr. Dirks, personally, had made a lot of money from appreciation in the stock. However, at the time this case arose, Dirks himself no longer owned any Equity Funding stock.

Secrist, a former officer of Equity Funding, met with Dirks and told him that Equity Funding's stock was grossly over valued and that the company was engaged in a massive fraud on the investing public. Secrist also told Dirks that he had tried to get the SEC to investigate, but that it did not do so. Though skeptical in the beginning, Dirks decided to go to the Equity Funding's Los Angeles headquarters and investigate. From his investigation he concluded Equity Funding was indeed overvalued and had engaged in fraudulent practices.

On reaching that conclusion, Dirks did two things: (1) he went to the Wall Street Journal, gave it the information, and eventually convinced it to write a series of articles exposing Equity Funding, and (2) while he was investigating and convincing the Wall Street Journal to write the story, but before the story was published, Dirks advised several of his clients to sell to sell Equity Funding. Several of Dirks' clients sold their Equity Funding holdings before the Wall Street Journal story was published. After publication, the price of Equity Funding's stock dropped dramatically.

The SEC then brought an administrative proceeding against Mr. Dirks for violating Rule 10b–5 by tipping his clients. In the administrative proceeding, the SEC alleged that Dirks violated Rule 10b–5, as a tippee. But the SEC went on to say in its complaint, that while he should not have tipped his clients, because of the good work Mr. Dirks had done in exposing the fraud at Equity Funding, his penalty should be a mere censure (a slap on the wrist) rather than a fine or suspension.

Mr. Dirks, obviously a proud man, was not grateful for the SEC's leniency or appreciative of its compliments. He apparently felt his good reputation had been impugned and appealed the SEC's ruling all the way to the United States Supreme Court.

The Supreme Court held in favor of Dirks, and in so doing gave us the rules on tipper/tippee liability that apply today. The opinion states that to impose liability on a tippee, you have to show two things: (1) that the tipper (Secrist—in this case) breached a fiduciary duty and (2) that the tipper tipped for the purpose of obtaining some sort of personal benefit. This has come to be known as the **personal benefit test**.

The SEC's case failed to satisfy either prong of the test. Secrist was an ex-employee of Equity Funding and thus no longer in a fiduciary relationship with Equity Funding. Obviously he did not misappropriate anything from the source of the information. And he was not tipping for personal benefit. He asked nothing in return and was merely "blowing the whistle" to expose a fraud. Therefore, Dirks received the information legally and could do with it what he wanted. He was not liable as a tippee. Also, while the issue was not before the court, clients to whom Dirks passed on the information were not liable as sub-tippees. Nor was Secrist liable as a tipper. As we will learn later, if you can establish tippee liability—both the tipper and the tippee, as well as any sub-tippees, will be liable. We will get back to that point later. First, consider the following question:

Can we change the facts of the Dirks case and establish tipper/tippee liability?

Yes. If we change the facts by (1) making Secrist a current employee of Equity Funding, when he told his story to Dirks and (2) having Secrist ask for something in return such as immunity from prosecution in exchange for the information.

In the revised facts since Secrist is a employee we can establish a **fiduciary nexus** between him and the party on the other side of the trade. And by cutting a deal in exchange for the information he would meet the **personal benefit test**.

The rules as to the liability of tippers and tippees play out the same whether the tipper's duty to disclose or abstain arises under the fiduciary nexus (or classical) theory or under the misappropriation theory. If the tipper (1) violates a duty of trust and confidence imposed under either theory by tipping and (2) the personal benefit test is met and (3) the tippee trades, both tipper and tippee may be held liable, either criminally or civilly.

How is the "personal benefit" test met?

There are several ways of meeting the "personal benefit" test. The three main ways the test has been met are: (1) selling the information, (2) giving the information to enhance one's reputation or standing or with the expectation of receiving a reciprocal benefit and (3) giving the information to someone with whom the tipper has a personal relationship. Under the case law, the personal benefits test has generally been relatively easy to satisfy.

Are eavesdroppers who trade on the basis of inside information they overhear subject to insider trading liability?

No. A person who trades on inside information he overhears in a restaurant, elevator, etc. is not liable for insider trading. The classic example is found in *SEC v. Switzer* (W.D. Okla. 1984), where the famous coach overheard a CEO and his wife talking about a transaction which would likely cause the price of the stock of the CEO's company to rise, while sunbathing in the stands at a track meet in Norman, Oklahoma. The most interesting aspect of that case was the evidence, introduced by the SEC, which the jury chose to ignore (*i.e.*, telephone calls between the coach and the CEO the night before the track meet and upgrading of the CEO's season tickets at OU football games from 10 to 50 yard line seats). But according to Coach Switzer's version of the facts, which the jury believed, the coach just got lucky and escaped liability under the eavesdropper rule.

Remote tippees—How far down the line does liability extend?

All the way down the chain. Often there are chains of tipping—*i.e.,* tippee #1 becomes a tipper by passing the inside information on to tippee #2, etc. A case in point is *SEC v. Musella* (S.D.N.Y. 1989). There the manager of the steno pool at a major New York law firm which was working on a lot of takeovers, like Mr. Chiarella, figured out the identity of the target companies. He followed the usual pattern of buying shares in the target prior to the announcement and selling at a profit following announcement of the takeover bid.

In this case, he also told his friend the cab driver, who told his friend, the policeman, who told his brother, the president of an investment club in a New York suburb. The court found all of the tippers and tippees in the chain, including the members of the investment club, liable. The government overcame a defense by the investment club members that they had no idea where the information came from, by convincing the court that conscious indifference, when there was reason for suspicion, was enough to support insider trading liability.

e.   Pushing the Envelope in Insider Trading—The Martha Stewart Case

The highly public prosecution of media maven Martha Stewart, which arose out of an insider trading investigation, raised certain questions about insider trading, although Ms. Stewart was not actually charged with insider trading.

Ms. Stewart owned 3928 shares of a biotech company called Imclone, which had applied for FDA approval of an anti-cancer drug it had developed. The president of Imclone, Sam Waksal, was a social acquaintance of Ms. Stewart and both Stewart and Waksal used the same stock broker. Waksal learned that the FDA was about to refuse approval of the cancer drug, and he believed that once news of the refusal became public the price of Imclone's stock would drop significantly. So Waksal and members of his family sold or attempted to sell, some of the Imclone stock.

Ms. Stewart, while en route to Mexico for a vacation, got a voice mail message on her telephone from her stockbroker (who was also Waksal's broker) that he thought "Imclone is going to start trading downward." When Ms. Stewart returned the call, she did not speak to the stockbroker but did speak to his assistant. The assistant told her that Waskal and members of his family were selling. Ms. Stewart instructed the broker to sell. He sold all of Ms. Stewart's shares at slightly more than $58 a share. A few days later, when news that the FDA had refused approval of the anti-cancer drug became public, the Imclone stock dropped to about $15. Thus, Ms. Stewart averted a loss of about $170,000—not a great deal of money for Martha Stewart.

A threshold legal question was, did Ms. Stewart trade on the basis of inside information? Recall the definition adopted in the *Texas Gulf Sulphur* case: ***"Information intended to be available only for corporate*** pur-

poses." That is generally thought to be information that comes from within the company, such as forthcoming earnings or acquisitions.

Ms. Stewart did not have that kind of information. She simply had **"market information."** She knew Waksal and members of his family was selling. Is that kind of market information enough to form the basis for a criminal insider trading case? That question was not answered in the Stewart case because Ms. Stewart concocted a story about a pre-existing stop-loss order to sell which the jury found to be untrue. The point is Ms. Stewart was not charged with insider trading. Rather she was charged with obstruction and making false statements to the government.

While Ms. Stewart was convicted of these obstruction-type charges in her high-profile trial, since the issue concerning market information was not answered, the Stewart case adds little to our knowledge of the law of insider trading. However the case illustrates that the SEC and Federal prosecutors are constantly seeking to expand the insider trading prohibition, particularly in cases against high-profile defendants.

4. SUMMARY OF THE CURRENT RULES GOVERNING INSIDER TRADING UNDER RULE 10b–5

As reflected in the above discussion, the law of insider trading developed in stages. In the 1960s, the SEC and the federal courts through *Texas Gulf Sulphur,* constructed a disclose or abstain rule which subjected anyone who traded on the basis of material nonpublic information to insider trading liability. In the 1980s and

1990s, under decisions of the Supreme Court, mainly *Chiarella, O'Hagan* and *Dirks,* the scope of the ban on insider trading was narrowed and more clearly defined.

The linchpin of insider trading liability under Rule 10b–5 is the misuse of material, nonpublic information by persons with a fiduciary duty of confidentiality. Today, there are two theories under which a person can violate a duty which triggers the disclose or abstain rule: (1) when a **fiduciary nexus** is established between the inside trader and the other party to the transaction and (2) when the trader violates a **fiduciary duty owed to the source of the information**. The persons prohibited from trading or tipping are now more clearly defined, as follows:

a. **Employees** of the company in whose shares they trade, from the CEO to the clerk in the mail room are all bared from trading on the basis of inside information because a fiduciary nexus runs between the employees and the other parties to the trade, who by definition, are shareholders of the company.

b. **Temporary** or **Constructive Insiders** are non-employees of the company, who by virtue of the nature of their work for the company, have access to confidential corporate information. Such persons include employees of law firms, accounting firms, public relations firms, investment bankers and the like.

c. **Persons Who Misappropriate Information** entrusted to them by the source of the information. The classic example is the wayward attorney O'Hagan, a partner in the law firm representing the bidder company in a tender offer, who bought stock and options of the target company. While O'Hagan owed no fiduciary duty to the other party to the transaction (shareholders of the target company), the act of misappropriating confidential information from the source of the information triggered the duty to disclose or abstain and resulted in Rule 10b–5 liability.

d. Tippers and Tippees. The disclose or abstain rule not only prohibits trading, but also prohibits tipping persons who trade, on the basis of confidential nonpublic information. Under the *Dirks* test, if the tipper acquired the inside information in violation of a fiduciary duty and passes the information on to someone else to obtain a personal benefit, both the original tipper and tippee as well as any subsequent tippers and tippees in the chain are subject to insider trading liability.

Persons who have no fiduciary relationship with the corporation whose shares are traded or with the source of the confidential information are not subject to the disclose or abstain rule and can legally trade or tip without Rule 10b–5 liability. Such persons include the eavesdropping coach, the securities analysts who dug up information on Equity Funding and a host of others, who through hard work, persistence, skill, or luck have better information about the value of the stock they buy or sell than the party on the other side of the trade.

CHAPTER VIII

HOW DO BUSINESSES RAISE MONEY?

A. INTRODUCTION

All businesses, large and small, need money ("capital") to operate and grow. The capital may be generated internally by the business itself or it may be obtained externally through investors and/or lenders.

The amount and source of the capital needed by a business may determine the form of business association selected for that particular business. Recall in Chapter II an LLC was chosen as the business structure for the Taco Stand, a business with relatively modest capital needs, which were supplied by the people who would actually run the business. By contrast, the High Tech Start–Up was a business that required substantial capital over a relatively long period of time. The bulk of the funds needed to start that business and operate the business until it began generating a positive cash flow were provided by a venture capital firm whose exit strategy was to harvest value through a public offering. The business association chosen for the High Tech Start–Up was a corporation.

This chapter contains a basic overview of a subject generally called "corporate finance." Corporate finance deals with the process of **establishing a financial**

framework and **raising funds** for a business. Many legal issues arise in connection with this process, which in the jargon of business is called "capitalization and financing." This area is often confusing to students without a business background because many of the concepts are unfamiliar and much of the language is new. We will only touch on certain basics in this area, which you may encounter in business associations. Almost all law schools offer advanced courses in corporate finance and securities regulation. Students who think they may have an interest in practicing business law should consider taking these courses.

In this chapter, I will first discuss some of the major underlying concepts and define some of the basic terms related to corporate finance. I will then discuss three specific substantive areas: (1) the authorization and issuance of stock; (2) preemptive rights and dilution; and (3) the process of raising equity capital and how that process is regulated under the Securities Act of 1933.

B. SOURCES OF FINANCING

The three principle ways in which all businesses raise money are: (1) retained earnings, (2) borrowing and (3) selling equity in the business.

1. Retained Earnings. One obvious way for a business to finance its operations is through the use of profits from the business. This is the largest source of financing. How do the big drug companies fund their research and development? How does Microsoft pay all those bright computer technology types who develop their software? How does Exxon pay for all their oil wells, pipelines and refineries? Most of these operations are financed from the billions that these successful companies generate through operating profits and related cash flow. Using retained earnings does not create many legal problems or need much further discussion.

Obviously the ability of a particular business to generate internal funds from operations depends on (1) the earnings of the business, (2) its stage of development, and (3) the amount needed to operate and grow the business. For example, in the hypothetical involving the Taco Stand in Chapter II, the business plan anticipated that the business would generate sufficient cash flow to finance its operations by the time the initial $100,000 raised from the sale of equity was depleted. The plan was to use the profits, over and above what was distributed to the principals by way of dividends and salaries, to operate and grow the business. That is probably a sound business plan for financing a single taco stand. If the goal were to establish a chain of taco stands, a more elaborate plan for raising the necessary funds would be necessary.

2. Borrowing. Businesses can raise money by borrowing, which is called debt financing. The money borrowed must, of course, be repaid with interest. If the money borrowed can not be repaid the borrower will loose the business or be forced into bankruptcy. A problem with borrowing is that banks and institutional lenders like to make loans to borrowers who do not really need the money or who have unencumbered assets which they can pledge to secure repayment of the loan. For example, Southwest Airlines would have little trouble borrowing several million dollars to buy ten new commercial jets, given its strong balance sheet and demonstrated ability to generate profits. Also a mortgage on a commercial jet is good security for the lender. On the other hand the Taco Stand and High Tech Start-up, discussed in Chapter II, would have a hard time securing loans because they are in an early stage of development and have no proven record of earnings or assets that they can mortgage to secure their loans.

3. Equity Financing. A business association may obtain money from persons who buy interests in the business. In consideration for the money these buyers invest in the business, they acquire interests in (*i.e.,* become the owners of) the business. These interest owners may be persons who will be active in managing the business, passive investors, seeking a return on their investment, or a combination of the two.

Equity ownership in any business entitles the owners to a bundle of rights and powers. The three basic rights and powers are:

(1)   The right to a share of the profits of the business,

(2)   Ownership of a share of the assets of the business, and

(3)   The power to participate in the management of the business.

These attributes of equity ownership are allocated differently in different types of business associations. And you should understand the difference in the manner in which the bundle of rights and powers (called the "attributes of equity ownership") are bundled and allocated among the various persons involved in the business. This is a basic concept that underlies many areas of business associations. You will probably find the basic business course easier if you understand this concept.

Unincorporated businesses. In a partnership the allocation of the attributes of equity ownership are usually fixed in a contract by and among the partners called a partnership agreement. The partnership agreement can specify what portion of the profits and distributions each partner is entitled to and what rights of management the various partners have. If the partnership agreement contains gaps, the applicable state partnership statute provides default rules that fill in the gaps.

The attributes of equity ownership are allocated in much the same way in an LLC. The allocation is usually fixed in a contract by and among the members of the LLC, which in most states is called an operating agreement. If the operating agreement contains gaps, the state LLC statute provides default rules that govern.

Corporations. In corporations, the attributes of equity ownership are allocated differently. There is no contract among the owners which defines the attributes of equity ownership of each owner. Rather, ownership interests in the corporation are allocated through the issuance of shares of stock. The number of shares owned by a particular owner determines that owner's pro rata share of the attributes of equity ownership (*i.e.*, dividend rights, distribution rights and voting rights). As more fully explained by Professor Gevurtz in the *Hornbook on Corporation Law*, the basic idea behind shares of stock is to create fungible units, each with the same attributes of ownership.

The concept of specifying the rights of equity owners through their relative ownership of fungible shares of stock is useful, particularly in publicly held businesses which have a constantly changing group of owners. It avoids the need for investors to read the governing agreements before they invest. It also eliminates the need to amend these agreements each time a new investor invests or one owner transfers her interest to another owner. Further, in a corporation these different aspects of equity ownership can be bundled and packaged in different ways by creating different types of securities, such as common stock and preferred stock. This greatly facilitates financing by enabling the managers of the corporation to tailor a capital structure that fits the needs of the business, the desires of the various constituencies within the corporation, and the preferences of the marketplace. This flexibility of capital structure, along with limited liability, explains why virtually all publicly held businesses are organized as corporations, despite the disadvantage of double taxation.

In summary, allocating the attributes of equity ownership in unincorporated businesses involves artfully drafting partnership agreements or operating agreements, an essential lawyering skill of the corporate lawyer, but probably beyond the scope of the basic business course (unless you have a professor who emphasizes drafting skills). On the other hand, allocating the attributes of equity ownership in a corporation is largely a matter governed by corporate law. Most issues pertaining to capitalization and financing arise in the context of corporations. So the rest of this chapter will focus on corporations.

C. BASIC DEFINITIONS—TERMS AND CONCEPTS

The following are some of the key terms used in corporate finance. Many of these terms and concepts may be unfamiliar to students without a prior business background. All need to become part of every student's basic business vocabulary.

Capitalization and financing. The process of raising capital (*i.e.* money) is called **financing**. **Capitalization** is a less precise term, the meaning of which varies depending on the context in which it is used. I use the term capitalization in a broad sense—*i.e.*, in the sense of a corporation's **capital structure**. A corporation's capital structure usually consists of both ownership interests **(equity)** and obligations **(debt)**.

Debt. The most important thing to remember about debt is that it is an obligation which must be repaid. The most common form of debt is simply loans from friends or relatives, banks, private investors, venture capitalists or shareholders. Debt, of course, is a liability on the balance sheet, where it is usually classified as long-term or short-term depending on whether the debt is due within a year of the balance sheet date.

Most loans are evidenced by **notes**. In larger corporations, debt may be evidenced by **bonds** or **debentures**. Bonds or debentures are usually issued in transactions in which a corporation borrows a large sum of money from numerous persons, each of whom make relatively small loans on identical terms, through the purchase of such bonds or debentures. For example, when a person buys a government bond, that person is making a loan to the government. Unless your professor makes a point of the distinctions, the distinction between notes, bonds and debentures is outside the scope of the basic business course. All are instruments that evidence debt.

Equity. As stated above, equity means ownership. In a corporation equity is represented by shares. "Shares" are defined in Model Business Corporations Act ("MBCA") § 1.40(22) as the "units into which the proprietary interests in a corporation are divided." In plain English this means shares of stock are the units of ownership into which a business formed as a corporation are divided.

The same general statutory scheme relative to shares of stock found in MBCA is found in all state corporate statutes. A corporation can issue more than one type of stock, if the articles of incorporation authorize it to do so. The most basic type of shares authorized in the articles of incorporation and issued by the corporation is called **common stock**. Most small corporations do not issue anything but common stock. If a corporation issues more than one class of stock, typically it will issue preferred stock in addition to the common.

What are the differences between common stock and preferred stock?

Common stock. Owners of common stock have the fundamental rights to vote and to receive distributions (*i.e.,* dividends or liquidating distributions) contingent upon earnings and claims of creditors and preferred stockholders. See, *e.g.,* MBCA § 6.01(b). Common stock can best be described as the residual interests in the corporation—what is left after all claims of creditors and preferred stockholders have been satisfied. Dividends are not guaranteed. They are payable only at the discretion of the board of directors. While common stock has the lowest priority and carries the highest degree of risk, it also enjoys the greatest potential for reward if the business is successful. Typically, common stockholders control the corporation through all or most of the voting power. Common stock has by far the greatest potential to appreciate in value.

Preferred stock. While legally classified as equity, preferred stock is, in fact a hybrid between debt and common stock. The best way to understand the essence of preferred stock is to focus on the differences between preferred and common stock. As the name implies, preferred stock has certain preferences over common stock, which are discussed in the next paragraph. On the other hand, preferred stock is usually nonvoting. Thus, preferred stockholders usually have no say in management. Also, since preferred shares are usually redeemable at a fixed price, they have little potential for appreciation compared to common shares.

While preferred stock may include numerous preferences, the two most common are dividend preferences and liquidation preferences. Since preferred stock is considered equity, preferred stockholders, unlike bondholders, do not have a right of payment and failure to pay dividends on preferred stock is not a default by the corporation. The decision whether or not to pay dividends on preferred stock, like dividend decisions as to common stock, is within the discretion of the board of directors. However, the preference requires that preferred stockholders be paid dividends (the rate of dividends on preferred stock is usually fixed) before any dividends can be paid to common stockholders. In addition, if the preferred stock is "cumulative," when a dividend on preferred stock is not paid in any year, the dividend accumulates and all accumulated dividends on the preferred stock must be paid before any dividends can be paid on the common stock. Dividend preferences generally benefit holders of preferred stock when the corporation succeeds.

Liquidation preferences generally benefit holders of preferred stock when the corporation fails. The liquidation preference is usually structured so that a fixed price must be paid to preferred stockholders before any amount is paid to common shareholders in the event of liquidation.

Securities. The broad term used in corporate law to encompass all of the various types of interests, both debt and equity, that a corporation may issue is "securities."

D. THE DEBT–EQUITY MIX
AND LEVERAGE

Establishing the most appropriate mix of debt and equity for a particular company involves consideration of numerous business and legal issues by the business people charged with the task of formulating a capital structure and the lawyers who advise them. Answering exam questions in the basic business course simply requires that you understand the following:

First, the biggest disadvantage to borrowing is that the loans have to be paid back, with interest. If a corporation cannot meet its debt obligations as they mature, that company will likely become insolvent. On the other hand, dividends on stock are not fixed obligations. A company unable to pay dividends may have some unhappy stockholders, but it will not necessarily go into bankruptcy.

Second, there are tax advantages to debt. Interest on debt is deductible, while dividends on stock are not.

Third, leverage can be the greatest advantage of debt financing or it can be the greatest disadvantage—depending upon how things work out. "**Leverage**" is an economic principle which explains how the use of debt in a capital structure may improve the owners' return on their investment. The greater the ratio of debt to equity, the greater the leverage.

For example, assume the capital structure of a business is $100,000, all equity, and that business earns $20,000 before interest and taxes in a given year of operation. That business has earned a return on equity of 20% (*i.e.*, $20,000/$100,000). Now assume the capital structure of the business consists of $50,000 equity and $50,000 debt, bearing interest at 10% per year. The business earns $20,000, before interest and taxes during the year. Earnings must be reduced by the $5,000 in interest expense, however the $15,000 earned after payment of interest constitutes a return on equity of 30% (*i.e.*, $15,000/$50,000).

Leverage accentuates the negatives in unprofitable companies in the same way that it accentuates the positives in profitable companies. For example, again assume the capital structure of a business is $100,000, all equity. But assume the business loses $10,000 before interest and taxes during a given year. This is a 10% loss on equity. If that company's capital structure consisted of $50,000 in debt bearing 10% interest and $50,000 in equity the loss would grow to $15,000 reflecting interest costs. And the loss on equity would be 30% ($15,000/$50,000). In short, leverage accentuates both good and bad results.

Fourth, while debt and equity constitute the generic components of capital structure, the distinction sometimes becomes blurred. For example, some hybrid securities such as preferred stock with a convertible feature have attributes of both debt and equity and are not easy to pigeon hole.

E.   AUTHORIZATION AND ISSUANCE OF STOCK

Debt financing (*i.e.*, borrowing), is primarily governed by contract law and debtor-creditor law, both of which are outside the scope of this book. On the other hand, equity financing, which involves the authorization and issuance of stock, brings into play a number of issues covered in the basic business course.

1.   ISSUANCE OF SHARES

The power to issue the shares lies with the board of directors. "**Issuance**" simply means the sale by the corporation of its shares in a classic exchange transaction—the corporation obtains money, property or services in consideration for the shares and the buyers of the shares become stockholders—the owners of the corporation. Only the corporation can issue shares. A later transfer of shares from one shareholder to another is not an issuance.

The corporation only receives consideration for its shares at the time of original issuance. After original issuance, a trading market, which consists of investors selling shares to other investors, usually develops in the outstanding shares. While, for a number of reasons, the corporation likes the price of its stock to be high, the corporation does not receive any consideration as a result of purchases and sales in the trading market nor, is the corporation directly affected by the trading market transactions in either a legal or accounting sense.

2. AUTHORIZATION OF SHARES

Before the corporation can "issue" shares, the shares must be "authorized." The state corporate statutes do not dictate the number of shares that may be authorized. That number is set forth in the articles of incorporation. See, *e.g.*, MBCA § 6.01: "The articles of incorporation must prescribe the number of shares ... the corporation is authorized to issue." All state corporate statutes contain similar provisions. "Authorized" is a word of art in corporate law which refers to authority granted by the articles of incorporation. When a corporation has issued all the shares authorized by its articles it must amend the articles to authorize the issuance of additional shares.

In the terminology of corporate law, shares are usually authorized and something else. For example, "**authorized and outstanding**" means the shares are owned by the shareholders. "**Authorized but unissued**" means the shares have been authorized but not yet issued. They are available for future issuance. Corporations usually authorize more shares than they initially plan to sell to avoid having to amend the articles. If shares have been authorized and issued, but are subsequently reacquired by the corporation they are called "**treasury shares**."

In addition to fixing the number of authorized shares, the articles define the basic attributes of the shares. If there is only one class of shares—*i.e.*, common stock—the provision defining the attributes of the shares is quite simple. If, on the other hand, the articles provide for different classes of common stock or for preferred stock with different rights, preferences and restrictions, the articles must set out the rights and preferences of the different classes. See MBCA §§ 6.01–6.02.

3. CONSIDERATION FOR SHARES— WATERED STOCK LIABILITY

The basic rule under most modern corporate statutes is that a corporation can issue stock in exchange for whatever consideration the board of directors decides to accept, subject to, in many states, two possible limitations related to the **amount** and **type of the consideration**.

a.   Type of Consideration

Until the mid–1980s most state corporate statutes (and in some cases state constitutions) contained provisions similar to the following, which limited the type of consideration corporations could receive in exchange for stock:

the consideration paid for the issuance of shares **must consist of money paid, labor done or property actually received**.

In plain English such provisions did not allow stock to be issued in consideration for promises to pay money in the future (*i.e.*, promissory notes), promises to render future services, etc. In 1984 the MBCA was amended and today the MBCA permits stock to be issued in consideration for:

> "any tangible or intangible property or benefit to the corporation . . ., including . . . promissory notes . . . [and] contracts for services to be performed. . . ." See MBCA § 6.21(b).

Under the current MBCA rule it is permissible to issue 100,000 shares to *A* in consideration for $100,000 cash, 100,000 shares to *B* in consideration for a promissory note for $100,000 and 100,000 shares to *C* as partial consideration for a three year employment contract. However, many states still follow the old rule which limits the type of consideration. Those states would not allow the issuances to *B* and *C* because the type of consideration given in exchange for the shares would be deemed improper. In other words, the rule on this point varies from state to state.

b. Amount of Consideration

The traditional rules governing the amount of consideration a corporation is required to receive for its stock are more complex. They involve the so called "legal capital rules," which rest on the concepts of "par value" and "watered stock liability." The legal capital rules have been universally criticized by scholars and were abolished in the MBCA in 1984. However, the legal capital rules are still the law in over half the states. Some professors want their students to understand the concepts of par value and watered stock liability, while others dismiss these concepts as relics of the past.

Par value. Par value is simply a dollar amount assigned to the shares, which is specified in the articles. While par value is the lowest price for which the corporation can issue its shares, the drafters of the articles can make that dollar amount whatever they choose—it can be $1,000 per share, $.01 per share or any other number. **Par value bears no relationship whatsoever to market value**. Thus, if the par value is set in the articles as $100 per share, the corporation cannot, without potential liability to the recipients of the shares, issue shares for less than $100 per share.

Par value constitutes a minimum issuance price. The corporation is free to charge more than par for its stock. Par value only has an impact on the price at which the corporation can originally issue its shares. It has no impact on the price at which shareholders may subsequently resell their shares.

If the notion that the minimum price a corporation may charge for issuance of its shares is a dollar amount selected from thin air and placed in the articles seems strange, this is because it is strange. The rule is based on a 19th century primitive accounting system that was probably never valid and is certainly not valid today.

It is easy enough for lawyers to comply with the state's par value rule—simply specify a low par value (such as $.01 per share) in the articles and sell the stock for more ($10 per share, $100 per share or whatever) or issue shares "without par value" in states where the corporate statute permits "no par stock."

Watered stock liability. When stock is issued at less than par value the shareholders to whom the stock was issued incur what is known as potential "watered stock liability." The shareholders who receive the so called "watered stock" may be liable to the corporation or its creditors in an amount measured by the difference between par value and the amount they actually paid for the stock.

Even though: (1) the 19th century rationales on which watered stock liability used to rest have long since been discredited, (2) the problem of potential watered stock liability can be easily avoided by simply establishing a low par value for the shares (and issuing the shares for consideration in excess of par), and (3) many states have amended their corporate statutes to eliminate the concept of par value, watered stock problems still sometimes occur and some professors still like to discuss (and test) concepts related to watered stock liability.

In some states, watered stock liability can be a trap for the unwary as illustrated by the 1988 case of *Hanewald v. Bryan's, Inc.* (N.D. 1988), a case found in many casebooks.

In that case, Keith and Joan Bryan, the founders of Bryan's Inc., issued themselves a total of 100 shares of $1,000 per share par value stock for no consideration. They personally loaned the corporation $10,000 and personally guaranteed a bank loan by the corporation of $55,000. The corporation then purchased the assets of plaintiff's retail store in consideration for cash and a promissory note. The corporation also signed a five year lease on the plaintiff's building. Later, the corporation defaulted on the promissory note and the lease.

In a suit by plaintiff against the Bryans for watered stock liability, the court held the Bryans personally liable because they failed to pay par value for their shares. In other words they lost the shield of limited liability to the extent that the consideration they paid for their shares was less than par value. The court's rationale was simply that the governing North Dakota corporate statute required that the shareholders pay a minimum of par value for their shares.

This case illustrates how par value and watered stock liability can be a trap for the unwary. By simply establishing a low par value for the stock and issuing shares to themselves at a price above par, the Bryans could have escaped liability without changing the underlying economics of the transaction.

The 1984 revision of MBCA eliminated par value and watered stock liability. Over 20 states have revised their corporate statutes to eliminate par value in accordance with the 1984 MBCA model. Statutes based on the 1984 MBCA model essentially create a new regime for issuing stock which eliminates the concept of par value and watered stock liability.

Fully paid and nonassessable opinions. Some believe that issues related to par value and watered stock liability are only raised by "out of date" professors, who like to teach historical concepts of marginal relevance today. While there may be some basis for this belief, you should realize that you may encounter such issues when you get out in practice. Usually when a company brings in new investors through a public offering or private placement, the investors require a legal opinion, that the new shares being issued are "**fully paid and nonassessable.**"

This legal opinion is like an insurance policy—if the stock is not fully paid and nonassessable and the new shareholders incur personal liability as a result, the new shareholders will have an action for malpractice against the law firm which rendered the opinion. Young associates in the corporate departments of the law firms rendering the "fully paid and nonassessable" opinion are often assigned the task of researching a corporation's records to support these opinions.

F. ISSUING MORE SHARES— PREEMPTIVE RIGHTS AND DILUTION

When a corporation issues additional shares, the issuance of the additional shares reduces the existing shareholders' percentage of ownership. For example, assume Alpha Corporation has 3,000 shares of common stock outstanding, which are owned by three shareholders *A*, *B* and *C*. Each owns 1,000 shares or 33.33%. If Alpha subsequently issues an additional 1,000 shares of common stock to *X*, the percentage ownership of *A*, *B* and *C* is reduced to 25% each. This reduction of percentage of ownership is called **dilution**.

Shareholders may be protected against dilution under corporate law through a doctrine known as **preemptive rights**. A preemptive right is the right of a shareholder to subscribe to a pro rata portion of any new shares that the corporation proposes to issue that might operate to decrease the existing shareholders' percentage of ownership in the corporation. The basic idea is to protect the shareholders from dilution by giving them the opportunity to maintain their proportionate ownership in the company throughout the life of the corporation. They are not compelled to buy the additional shares, but they have a right to do so.

While preemptive rights began as a common law doctrine, today, the existence or nonexistence of preemptive rights is governed by the articles of incorporation. Whether a particular corporation has preemptive rights varies from state to state due to differences in the default rules under the corporate statutes of the various states. In some states, preemptive rights do not exist unless they are specifically provided for in the articles (these are called "**opt in**" statutes). In other states, preemptive rights exist unless they are specifically rejected in the articles (these are called "**opt out**" statutes).

For example, § 6.30 of MBCA provides: "The shareholders of a corporation do not have a preemptive right to acquire the corporation's unissued shares except to the extent that the articles of incorporation so provide." This is an example of an **opt in** statute–if the articles of incorporation are silent there are no preemptive rights.

Preemptive rights do not attach to all new shares issued by a corporation. There are several transactions in which the issuance of new shares do not trigger preemptive rights, even in corporations where preemptive rights generally exist. Such transactions include the following: (1) shares issued to employees, when approved by a

majority of the shareholders entitled to vote; (2) shares
sold other than for cash—*e.g.*, for property, to effect
mergers, compromise indebtedness, etc.; and (3) shares
of a different class—*e.g.*, holders of common stock do not
have preemptive rights if the corporation decides to issue
preferred stock.

Several considerations, outside the scope of this book,
enter into the decision whether or not to grant preemptive rights to the shareholders of a corporation. For
example, if it is anticipated that the corporation may in
the foreseeable future raise money through a private
placement or public offering, preemptive rights will be a
nuisance which might inhibit or delay financing. Preemptive rights may be a useful device in a close corporation,
but even in a close corporation, a shareholders' agreement may be a more efficient means of protecting shareholders from dilution than statutory preemptive rights.

G.   RAISING CAPITAL—REGULATION
UNDER THE SECURITIES
ACT OF 1933

Often a company needs more money to operate and
grow than it can generate from retained earnings and
ordinary bank borrowing. When this is the case, the
business must raise money by selling additional equity
securities ("equity financing"). Several legal issues, that
might arise in connection with the process of equity
financing will be discussed in this section.

Two possible sources of equity financing are: (1) individuals or other companies, who have some relationship
with the company or institutional investors, who like the

company's prospects for growth and profitability and are willing to invest and (2) venture capital firms, which are in the business of making equity investments in nonpublic companies. Raising money from these sources will likely involve some type of "private placement."

A third source of financing is selling part of the company to the public. In Wall Street jargon, this is called "going public." The first time a company sells stock to the public, it is called an "initial public offering" or "IPO." The IPO is typically the transaction through which a company, almost always with the aid of an "underwriter," transforms itself from a "closely held" to a "publicly held" company. **Public offering, IPO, private placement** and **underwriter** are terms that should become part of your business vocabulary.

Two significant consequences result from a successful IPO. First, assuming a trading market develops (which usually happens following an IPO), the shares owned by the founders and other owners of the company cease to be illiquid shares of closely held company and become liquid shares of a publicly held company.[1]

Second, by going public the company becomes subject to an additional level of regulation. Most of the additional regulation is imposed under the federal securities laws.[2] In prior sections of this book, we have already seen some of the regulations imposed by the **federal securities laws** on publicly held companies—*i.e.* the continu-

1. In the case of "restricted" securities and securities held by "affiliates" (control persons) some restrictions on the ability to sell the securities remain. See § VIII.G.3.c, *infra.*

2. All states also have securities laws, called "Blue Sky Laws." The state Blue Sky Laws vary widely and are beyond the scope of this book.

ing disclosure obligations, the proxy rules, the Sarbanes–Oxley law. Rule 10b–5 applies to publicly held companies as well as closely held companies.

Today, in some areas, corporate law is so intertwined with securities law that they are virtually inseparable. Students in the basic business course are not expected to become full blown securities experts. However, due to the relationship between the securities laws and general corporate law in certain areas, students must have some familiarity with the federal securities laws and a general understanding of when and how these important statutes come into play. The main focus of this subsection is on the **Securities Act of 1933**. As the following overview reflects, the 33 Act regulates the process of going public or otherwise raising capital.

1. OVERVIEW OF THE 33 AND 34 ACTS

The two most important federal securities laws are the **Securities Act of 1933 ("33 Act")** and the **Securities Exchange Act of 1934 ("34 Act")**. While most of securities regulation is beyond the scope of this book, as already noted, you need to be aware of certain aspects of these two statutes. First and foremost, you need to recognize the federal securities laws recognize two distinct settings in which transactions involving securities occur:

Issuer transactions or primary market transactions involve capital raising by issuers. The company (called the "issuer") is raising money by selling newly issued securities, almost always with the help of an investment banker or underwriter. The net proceeds from such sales go to the company (*i.e.*, the issuer of the securities).

Trading transactions or secondary market transactions. After the company goes public, investors begin trading in the now outstanding securities and a so-called secondary market develops. The secondary market consists of trading transactions in which investor *A* sells outstanding securities of the company to investor *B*, and the seller, not the company, gets the proceeds from the sale Trading transactions do have an indirect impact on the company, because higher stock prices increase the overall market valuation of the company.

Both the primary market and secondary market are regulated by the Federal Securities Laws but they are regulated differently, although there is overlap. Rule 10b–5, extensively discussed in the last chapter, which applies to both issuer transactions and trading transactions, is an example of such overlap.

The 33 Act regulates issuer transactions. The 33 Act, our focus in this section, comes into play only when the company sells its securities to investors. It is a highly integrated, narrowly focused statute that deals with primary market transactions.

The 34 Act primarily regulates trading transactions. The 34 Act regulates buying and selling outstanding securities after their original issuance. It contains a hodgepodge of provisions aimed primarily at regulating trading in outstanding securities and the institutions— such as the stock exchanges, broker/dealers, etc.— through which trading transactions take place. It also imposes certain continuing disclosure obligations on so-called "publicly held companies" whose securities are traded in the secondary market.

Both the 33 and 34 Acts were passed in response to the stock market crash of 1929 and the Great Depression which followed—the 33 Act in the first session of the first New Deal congress and the 34 Act in the second session of the same congress. Both statutes are administered by the Securities and Exchange Commission ("SEC"), which was created by the 34 Act.

The speculative bubble witnessed in the 1990s and the declines in stock market values during the first three years of the 21st century pale by comparison to the stock market bubble of the 1920s and the market crash of 1929. The hearings that preceded passage of these statutes found that $50 billion of new securities were issued in the United States in the 1920s and that fully half, or $25 billion, proved to be worthless. The hearings also revealed numerous instances of fraud and manipulation in the unregulated securities markets of the 1920s, which contributed to the collapse of the stock market in 1929 and the great depression of the 1930s.

2. THE REGISTRATION REQUIREMENT UNDER THE SECURITIES ACT OF 1933

The 33 Act comes into play when companies raise money by selling securities. The 33 Act is a disclosure statute. Its basic purpose is to assure the availability of true, correct, reliable and complete information about the securities being offered to the public. In other words, the philosophy of the 33 Act is that investors should be provided full and accurate information about the securities being offered. It is then up to the investors to make their own investment decisions.

a. The Registration Process

The 33 Act implements the policy of full disclosure through a **registration requirement** and an **antifraud requirement**. Most of the 33 Act is concerned with the registration requirement. Section 5 requires registration of public offerings of newly issued securities. It is helpful to think of § 5 as the heart of the 33 Act and to think of all other sections of the 33 Act, with the exception of § 17 and § 12(a)(2) which relate to the antifraud requirement, as limiting, implementing or qualifying § 5 in some way.

The 33 Act is a complex statute with many subtle definitions and esoteric distinctions. In addition, the 33 Act is written in a way that assumes the reader of the statute has an understanding of the process by which securities are sold to the public through underwriters— the so-called process of "going public."

The 33 Act regulates the process of going public. The details, which are dealt with in the course in securities regulation, are beyond the scope of the basic business course. However, students in the basic business course need to develop a general understanding of the following three issues: (1) What does registration entail, (2) What is the liability for failure to comply with the 33 Act, and (3) When is registration required?

What Registration Entails. Section 5 is the beginning point for virtually all questions under the 33 Act. It prohibits offers unless a registration statement has been filed with the SEC and prohibits sales until the registration statement has become effective. It also requires delivery of a prospectus to all purchasers of the securities. That statement raises as many questions as it answers—*i.e.,* ***What is a registration statement? What is a prospectus? What does filing and going effective mean?***

A **registration statement** is the disclosure document, required by the 33 Act, in which the company is legally required to bare its soul—tell investors all relevant material information about the securities being offered and the company offering the securities.

The major portion of the registration statement is the prospectus. The **prospectus** is the part of the registration statement delivered to investors. While the prospectus is a selling document, it is, first and foremost, a liability document which must tell the whole truth. If the prospectus does not tell the whole truth (but rather is false or misleading in some material way), there is potential for criminal penalty and draconian civil liability.

Filing and **going effective** relate to the process of preparing and filing the registration statement with the SEC, administrative review of the registration statement by the SEC staff and the eventual effectiveness of the registration statement. Section 5 divides the process of going public into three stages—the pre-filing stage; the waiting period (the period between filing and effectiveness); and the post-effective period. Both the ground rules for making offers and sales, as well as the work performed by the team of lawyers, accountants and business people involved in preparing the registration statement and verifying the accuracy and adequacy of the information contained therein, vary during the three stages of the process.

Details regarding the rules governing offers and sales during the registration process are beyond the scope of this book. The SEC recently adopted rule changes aimed at modernizing the securities offering process. If your professor discusses these new rules you may need to delve deeper into the rules governing the offering process than is done in the book. Also beyond the scope of this book are details concerning what the registration statement and prospectus must disclose, and the manner in which the SEC's staff reviews the registration statement and declares it effective. These details are usually outside the scope of the basic business course but are usually covered in the course on Securities Regulation.

b.   What is the Liability for Failure to Comply?

Noncompliance with the registration provision of the 33 Act may result not only in criminal penalties and administrative sanctions, but also in civil liability for the company and various persons associated with the company. More specifically, § 11 imposes strict liability for any untrue statements or material omissions in the registration statement on the company (*i.e.*, the issuer), and on every person who signs the registration statement (the company's chief executive officer and chief financial officer are required to sign), every director, every person who provides an expert certification (such as the accountants who audit the financial statements in the registration statement), and the underwriters. See § 11(a).

Broadly speaking § 11 does away with the common law fraud requirements of scienter and reliance. It imposes strict liability on the company. The so-called individual defendants are liable unless they can meet the burden of showing that they exercised "due diligence." In general, due diligence requires that the individual defendants show that they made a reasonable investigation and that they were not negligent in failing to discover any material error or omission in the registration statement.

Section 12(a)(1) compliments § 11 by imposing liability for failure to register the securities or deliver a prospectus in accordance with the requirements of § 5.

In short, the 33 Act regulates the process of going public through a three-fold approach:

(1) Under § 5 the company cannot make any offers unless and until a registration statement has been filed with the SEC and it cannot make sales until the registration has been declared effective. If the company fails to comply—fails to register or deliver a prospectus as required—under § 12(1) the buyers have an absolute right of rescission (*i.e.*, get their money back).

(2) The 33 Act and rules adopted thereunder provide for a process of administrative review by the SEC but the statute clearly places ultimate responsibility for insuring the accuracy and adequacy of the registration statement on the issuer and certain others associated with the offering—*i.e.*, the potential defendants listed in § 11(a).

(3) Finally, if the offering documents are materially false or misleading the buyers have an absolute right of rescission under § 11. The issuer has no defenses. The other potential defendants named in § 11(a) must meet

the burden of showing that they acted with due diligence to escape liability.

3. EXEMPTIONS FROM REGISTRATION

a. When is Registration Required—In General

From reading § 5, it would appear that all offers and sales of securities, including ordinary trading transactions, would require registration. However, the apparent broad sweep of § 5 is tempered by a number of exemptions found in § 3 and § 4 and by the definitions found in § 2.

Because the 33 Act is structured this way, it creates a rebuttable presumption that registration is required. In other words, the burden is on the party claiming an exemption to establish his exemption.

The 33 Act and certain rules thereunder carve out a variety of exemptions from registration. The balance of this subsection considers some of the more common kinds of securities and transactions that for one reason or another are exempt from registration.

Trading transactions. Recall, we noted earlier that the most important distinction students in the basic business course need to understand in dealing with the 33 Act, is a distinction between so-called issuer transactions and so-called trading transactions. Ordinary trading transactions are exempt by § 4(1) which exempts transactions by any person other than an "issuer," "underwriter" or "dealer," all defined terms in § 2. The net effect of this broad exemption is to exempt all trading transactions from the registration requirement imposed by § 5. Stated differently, subject to the qualification noted in the footnote to this sentence, § 5 only requires registration of securities offered by the issuer.[3]

Security defined. Unless the thing being offered or sold is a "security," the 33 Act (as well as the 34 Act) does not apply, The term "security" is defined in § 2(1), which includes an extensive laundry list of all the things people normally think of as securities, including stocks, bonds, debentures, calls, puts, warrants, etc. Corporate stock is obviously a security, but sometimes, what constitutes a security, can be a close question.

What is an investment contract?

One of the phrases included in § 2(1) is the term **"investment contract**," a term which had no particular meaning in the investment community, prior to adoption of the 33 Act. The drafters included "investment contract" in the statute as a "catch-all." They probably thought that if they missed something in their broad definition of "security" in § 2(1), this phrase might pick it up. The drafters were right, investment contract has been broadly interpreted by the courts to include a number of novel types of interests that serve the same purpose as traditional securities.

The landmark case defining investment contract is *SEC v. W.J. Howey Co.* (1946), a case decided by the United States Supreme Court in 1946. The case involved the sale of specifically described tracts of orange trees in an orange grove in Florida. Under the test developed in

3. The strange and counterintuitive definition of "underwriter" in § 2(11) brings some sales of securities by persons in a control relationship with the issuer and some sales by persons who hold so-called "restricted securities" within the prohibitions of § 5. See § VIII.G.3.c– Resales by Affiliates and Holders of "Restricted Securities," *infra*.

Howey, as subsequently refined in later cases, the thing sold is an "investment contract" and thus a security, if a person (1) invests his money (2) in a common enterprise (3) with the expectation of profit (4) from the efforts of others. The *Howey* test has been applied in hundreds of cases and has brought many things, not generally associated with the world of stocks and bonds, such as scotch whiskey receipts, self improvement courses, cosmetics, earthworms, beavers, cemetery lots, animal feeding programs, pooled litigation funds and computer modules, within the definition of "security" and thus, within the scope of federal securities regulation.

Are partnership and LLC interests securities?

One of the most important applications of the *Howey* test in the basic business course is its application to the question of whether interests in partnerships and LLCs are securities.

In analyzing partnership interests, the first question should be—was it a general partnership or a limited partnership? In a traditional general partnership (including an LLP) all of the general partners have a right of management, unless they have contracted away that right. Thus, the presumption is that general partnership interests are not securities. The traditional general partnership fails the part of the *Howey* test that requires "reliance on the efforts of others."

Limited partnership interests, on the other hand, have generally been held to be securities. By law, the general partner has the exclusive authority to manage the enterprise and the limited partners are mere passive investors who rely on the efforts of the general partner to make them money. There have been a few exceptional cases where general partnership interests have been held to be securities. These cases generally involved situations where either under the terms of the partnership agreement or as a matter of practical reality, though the plaintiff was legally a general partner, she was in reality a passive investor relying on the efforts of others.

The applicability of the Federal Securities Laws to LLCs is not settled at this time. It seems likely that as the law of LLCs develops, the question of whether LLC interests are securities will be analyzed under reasoning analogous to that presently applied to partnerships.

An overview of various exemptions. We now turn to the exemptions in sections 3 and 4. Section 3(a) exempts certain securities from registration because of the nature of the securities. These include government securities, securities issued by banks and charitable institutions and short-term commercial paper. These exemptions are narrow and highly technical and their application is outside the scope of anything likely to be encountered in the basic business course.

Section 3(a)(11), as qualified and defined by Rule 147, provides the so-called **"intrastate exemption."** That exemption exempts securities offered and sold solely within the state in which the issuer is incorporated and does the principal amount of its business, provided that the distribution comes to rest in that state.

Section 3(b) is an enabling provision which gives the SEC power to create exemptions for offerings up to $10 million, which it believes are necessary or appropriate. An important exemption created under the authority of

§ 3(b) is the so-called **Reg. A exemption** found in Rules 252–263 under the 33 Act. While technically an exemption, Reg. A is actually a simplified type of registration available to issuers offering securities valued at less than $5 million. The exemptions under Rules 504 and 505 of Regulation D, discussed below, were also adopted under the enabling authority of § 3(b).

b. The private offering exemption and Regulation D

The exemption from registration most often relied on by issuers is some form of the so called "private offering" exemption found in § 4(2). Since private placements are by far the most important class of exemptions relied on by business associations seeking to raise money without registration, most professors, to one degree or another, cover the private offering exemption in the basic business association course.

As previously noted, the statutory authority for the "private offering exemption" is found in § 4(2) of the 33 Act. Section 4(2) exempts "**transactions by an issuer not involving a public offering.**" A lot of administrative and judicial gloss, as well as a lot of history, surrounds those nine words. While the gist of what § 4(2) intended to exempt is relatively simple a bit of history is necessary to understand the scope of the modern private offering exemption.

The private offering exemption permits issuers to issue securities without registration in certain **close corporation** situations. For example, a promoter starts a business which he intends to manage and raises the money to finance the venture by selling stock in his company to a small number of friends, relatives or business associates. There is clearly no reason to require registration in this situation. The investors are relying on a preexisting relationship and personal knowledge.

Another situation where the private offering exemption is clearly available is the so-called **institutional private placement**. For example, a company goes to a small group of knowledgeable investors such as insurance companies, venture capital firms or pension funds and sells them either equity or debt securities. These investors can get whatever information they need directly from the company. They have no need for a prospectus. These types of private placements are an important source of financing for both well established large companies and high tech startups.

No one has ever questioned the need or the desirability of having a private placement exemption. But for years there was a problem defining the **scope of the exemption**. All we basically knew (from an early SEC release) was that (1) **numbers** are important—an offering to few is more likely to be private than an offering to many and (2) **relationships** are also important—an offering limited to people with a pre-existing relationship is more likely to be private than an offering to strangers. This makes sense but it is too indefinite to give corporate planners the degree of certainty they desire.

The landmark decision on the scope of the § 4(2) private placement exemption, *SEC v. Ralston Purina* (1953), was handed down by the United States Supreme Court. But instead of giving us the certainty needed, *Ralston Purina* further muddied the waters.

The question in *Ralston Purina* was whether offers by Ralston Purina to certain "key" employees pursuant to an employee stock purchase plan without registration violated § 5. Ralston Purina claimed that the sales were exempt from registration as a "private offering" under § 4(2). The Supreme Court held that Ralston Purina had violated § 5 and the opinion attempted to lay down a test defining the scope of the private offering exemption.

The *Ralston Purina* Opinion established two overriding requirements, both of which had to be present, for an offering to be "private" as opposed to "public:"

(1)   "Do the offerees need the protection of the act or can they fend for themselves?" This has come to be known as the **Sophistication Requirement**.

(2)   "Do the offerees have access to the type of information that a registration statement would provide." This has come to be known as the **Access to Information Requirement**.

The tests of *Ralston Purina*—sophistication and access to information—make sense and they are still the law today. However, they are highly subjective standards which are hard to determine prospectively.

In addition, if any of the original purchasers turned around and sold the securities he bought in a private placement too soon, that might be considered "purchasing with a view to distribution." And that selling purchaser might be deemed a "statutory underwriter," as defined in § 2(11). That would destroy the exemption and subject the issuer to liability for failure to comply with the registration requirements of § 5. This requirement is necessary, because absent the requirement, the original purchasers could be used as conduits to effect a wider distribution.

This requirement, which added to the uncertainty surrounding the statutory private offering exemption, is still the rule today. Buyers in a private placement acquire so-called "restricted securities." This means resales of such securities are subject to restrictions. Resales of restricted securities and so called "control stock" are now governed by Rule 144, discussed in § VIII.G.3.c, *infra*.

Regulation D. Most of the problems, which existed in the vague world of *Ralston Purina*, have now been resolved under Reg. D, a series of eight rules (Rules 501–508) under the 33 Act. Reg. D, first adopted in 1982 and subsequently liberalized through amendment, provides an innovative scheme that provided the necessary certainty by combining exemptions adopted under the authority of two different statutory enabling provisions— § 4(2) and § 3(b).

Reg. D creates **safe harbors**. If you meet the requirements of Reg. D, you do not have to register. But the reverse is not true. If you fail to meet the requirements of Reg. D, it does not necessarily mean you have violated § 5 of the 33 Act. It does mean that you have to sustain the burden of proof that you come within the § 4(2) exemption as defined by *Ralston Purina*. In other words, the case law may still provide an exemption in the rare, but not unheard of, case where an issuer does not fully comply with all of the terms and conditions of Reg. D. Obviously, structuring a deal that meets one or more Reg. D safe harbors is a much safer legal option.

The Three Reg. D Exemptions. Reg. D provides three exemptions—Rules 504, 505 and 506. The exemptions are qualified by the other five rules in Reg. D. Even though the three exemptions co-exist within a single regulation and contain a number of common conditions, it is important to understand they are three separate exemptions, which rest on two separate statutory enabling provisions—§ 3(b) and § 4(2).

Rule 504. The gist of Rule 504, as amended, is simple. Essentially this exemption now says if you raise less than $1 million during a 12 month period, you are too small for the SEC to bother with. The SEC might come after you for fraud, but not for failure to register.

Rule 505 is an exemption which allows issuers to raise up to $5 million by selling securities to up to 35 nonaccredited investors plus an unlimited number of accredited investors (defined below). The statutory authority for Rule 505, like Rule 504, is § 3(b) under which the SEC has authority to grant exceptions for offerings up to $10 million, subject to whatever conditions the SEC wants to place on the exemption. In the case of Rule 505, the number of purchasers is limited and the dollar amount of the offering, though larger than Rule 504, is still limited.

Rule 506 is an exemption under which the number of purchasers permitted are the same as under 505—*i.e.*, 35 non-accredited investors plus any number of accredited investors. But there are two significant differences between Rules 505 and 506:

(1) **There is no dollar cap on the amount of money you can raise under 506.** You can raise $200 billion or more if you can find investors to buy that

quantity of your securities and still comply with the other requirements of the rule.

(2) **Under 506 the nonaccredited investors have to be sophisticated**. In other words, if you have non accredited investors in a 506 offering, you must make subjective judgements about sophistication and access to information under the tests of *Ralston Purina*.

The reason for the distinction between the 505 and 506 exemptions goes to the heart of understanding Reg. D. The statutory authority for Rule 506 is § 4(2) rather than § 3(b). Rule 506 is a definitional rule. It defines situations in which the § 4(2) private offering exemption is available. The SEC has broad rule making power under the 33 Act, but that power is not broad enough to allow the SEC to ignore decisions of the United States Supreme Court. *Ralston Purina* said sophistication is the test and so any rule grounded on § 4(2) has to meet that test.

Rule 506 is structured so that accredited investors are conclusively presumed to be sophisticated, although, as discussed below, this is a fiction. Many accredited investors are not, in fact, sophisticated.

Conditions and requirements of Reg. D. Reg. D has substituted a detailed set of regulations for a broad based common law test. The Rule 505 and 506 exemptions are subject to a number of definitions, qualifications, conditions and requirements, the most important of which will now be discussed.

Accredited investors. Accredited investor ("AI") is the most important definition in Reg. D. Rule 501(a) sets out in detail and with certainty the classes of persons that qualify as AIs. They include:

Institutional investors. Banks, insurance companies, broker/dealers, registered investment companies, savings and loan associations, and other institutional investors qualify as AIs.

Directors, executive officers or general partners of the issuer or a parent. High level people with the company or its parent qualify as AIs.

Net worth of $1 million or more. If the combined net worth of a husband and wife at the time of purchase exceeds $1 million, including their equity in their personal residence, they qualify as accredited investors.

An example will illustrate how far removed the accredited investor requirement of Reg. D is from the sophistication requirement of *Ralston Purina*. A widow, with her now deceased husband, in the 1960s bought a nice little house on an acre of land in a suburb near Los Angeles for 10% down and a $50,000 mortgage. Now the widow owns that house free and clear and it is worth $1.5 million. Even though that widow may not have another asset to her name and no business or investment experience at all she is an AI because she meets the definition in Rule 501(a). The point is: One does not have to be sophisticated to be an AI. She just has to meet the test of an AI under Rule 501(a).[4]

---

4. Not only is Reg. D more certain and more objective than *Ralston Purina*, it also has the effect of broadening the exemption. Many people who meet the 501(a) definition of "accredited investor" would not come close to meeting the "sophistication" requirement of *Ralston Purina*.

Income. A person who had an individual income in excess of $200,000 or a joint income with his/her spouse of $300,000 in each of the last two years and reasonably expects income at the same or higher levels during the current year qualifies as an AI.

These are the main categories of AIs and the name of the game under Reg. D is to find AIs. There is no limit on the number of accredited investors under either Rules 505 or 506.

Integration is another important concept under Reg. D, as well as certain other exemptions. The concept of integration is—if two or more offerings are part of a **single plan of financing**, they are treated as a single distribution, even if they are broken up into different offerings. The effect of integration may destroy the exemption, as illustrated by the following example.

Assume an oil company has a 640–acre development prospect under lease. The company wants to develop the property with a total of eight wells on the lease at a cost of $1 million per well—a total cost of $8 million. Can the company create 8 separate Limited Partnerships, raise $1 million in each and get a 504 exemption for each offering? The answer depends on whether the offerings are integrated—*i.e.*, considered a single plan of financing.

Prior to adoption of Reg. D it was often hard to determine what would trigger integration—an obviously fact-sensitive concept. The main factors considered are: (1) Were the sales part of a single plan of financing? (2) Did they involve the same class of securities? and (3) Were the sales made at about the same time, for the same consideration and for the same purpose?

It was hard to determine which of the factors might control and what mix might tip the balance in a given case. Reg. D provided certainty. **Today, if the offerings are more than six months apart, they will not be integrated**. The fact-sensitive pre-Reg. D integration tests now only apply if the offerings take place within 6 months of one another.

Information requirement. As previously stated, in addition to sophistication, *Ralston Purina* had a second requirement—access to information. The information requirement is carried forward into Reg. D.

Rules 505 and 506 have identical information requirements. The first is the issuer must prepare and deliver a disclosure document (usually called a "private placement memo") to all nonaccredited investors. No disclosure document is required for accredited investors. Thus, if a deal is limited to accredited investors no private placement memo is prepared; but if non-AIs are in the deal a private placement memo is usually prepared and copies are delivered to everyone.

Under Rule 502(b), the level of disclosure required depends on the amount of money the issuer is raising and whether or not the issuer is a 34 Act reporting company (*i.e.*, a company subject to the SEC's continuing disclosure requirements). Details regarding the type and level of disclosure required are outside the scope of this book. The important point to remember is that no disclosure document is necessary if the offering is limited to accredited investors.

The no general solicitation rule. The Rule 505 and 506 exemptions are subject to Rule 502(c), the so-called "no general solicitation rule." The no general solicitation rule clearly prohibits almost all forms of general solicitation of potential investors for a proposed offering of securities under Rules 505 or 506. Under the no general solicitation rule, neither the issuer nor anyone raising money on its behalf, can put ads in the paper, make cold calls or send direct mailings aimed at soliciting investors. Neither can the issuer or anyone associated with the issuer do an information seminar on its product, if a purpose of the seminar is to hype the stock as well as sell the product. Any of these acts will destroy the exemption.

An issuer who relies on a Rule 505 or 506 exemption may look for investors among: (1) people with whom it has a preexisting relationship and people referred by those people, through word of mouth contact and (2) venture capitalists or industry partners. Industry partners include customers, suppliers and other companies in the industry. That is about as far as an issuer can go without violating the no general solicitation rule.

c. Resales by Affiliates and Holders of Restricted Securities

As previously stated most offers and sales that require registration under the 33 Act are offers and sales by the issuer. However, because the term "Underwriter" is defined in § 2 (11) in a way that is much broader then the common meaning of the term, some offers and sales by persons other than the issuer may be deemed to be sales by an underwriter and thus violate § 5, unless registered.

Section 2 (11) of the 33 Act defines "underwriter" as:

"any person who has purchased from an issuer **with a view to** ... **distribution** ... [F]or the purpose of this definition, the term "issuer" is defined to **include any person who controls the issuer**."

Under this definition persons, other than those performing traditional investment banking functions, may become underwriters, and thus subject to the registration requirements of § 5.[5] Two examples are:

(1)   If one or more of the original purchasers in a private placement turn around and immediately resell the securities they acquired in the private placement, they become "statutory underwriters" and destroy the exemption.

(2)   If a person in a control relationship with the issuer (*i.e.* an "affiliate") sells, under the last sentence of the underwriter definition, any person who assists the affiliate in selling may become a statutory underwriter and destroy the exemption.

Several years ago the SEC adopted **Rule 144**, which regulates sales in both of the above situations. Rule 144 is a safeharbor rule which regulates the sale of securities by **affiliates** (a term defined in Rule 405) and **holders of restricted securities**. Rule 144 defines the circumstances under which holders of restricted securities (*i.e.,*

---

5. The 33 Act contains a wonderland of defined terms, but no definition in the Act is conceptually harder to understand than the definition of "underwriter." Rule 144 is a complex rule that deals with problems raised by this complex definition. These problems are largely outside the scope of the basic business course and are deferred to the course in securities regulation. However, some notion of how and when Rule 144 applies may be helpful in the basic business course because the concepts interact with other basic issues. Also, some professors cover Rule 144 in the basic business course.

securities acquired in a private offering) and affiliates (persons in a control relationship with the issuer) can sell their securities without destroying the exemption.

Sales of restricted securities under Rule 144. Rule 144's restrictions on the resale of **restricted securities** depend on how long one holds the restricted securities:

(1) Securities held for less than one year—cannot be resold.

(2) Securities held for more than two years—are freely saleable.

(3) Securities held between one and two years may be sold, subject to a number of requirements set out in Rule 144, as follows:

    a. The restricted securities must have been held for a least one year.

    b. Adequate current information about the issuer must be available. (144(c))

    c. The amount of restricted securities a holder can sell during any 3 month period is limited by 144(e) to the greater of: 1% of the issuers outstanding securities, or the average weekly trading volume of the security for the four weeks preceding the notice of sale.

    d. The securities must be sold in a brokers' transaction without any solicitation of buyers. (144(f)).

    e. A notice of sale must be filed with the SEC. (144(h)).

As stated above, after two years all of the detailed restrictions and limitations set forth in paragraph (3) above go away and the restricted securities become freely saleable.

Sales by affiliates under Rule 144. An "affiliate" can also sell securities under Rule 144 if he complies with all of the requirements set forth in paragraph (3) above **except the holding period**. The good news for the affiliate is that he does not have to wait a year before being able to sell any securities. He can sell, subject to the requirements and limitations of Rule 144, immediately. The bad news is that the **restrictions on sales by an affiliate do not go away after two years**. The control person has to comply with these restrictions as long as he remains in a control relationship with the issuer. The reason is under the governing definition, holding period is irrelevant in determining "affiliate" status.

4.   THE ANTIFRAUD REQUIREMENT

In addition to requiring issuers to register securities (or find an exemption from registration) the 33 Act also prohibits fraud in the sale of securities. As noted earlier, § 17 and § 12(a)(2), the antifraud provisions in the 33 Act, prohibit false or misleading statements or material omissions in any prospectus or oral communication used to sell the securities. We learned about fraud in the purchase or sale of securities in Chapter VII, when we discussed Rule 10b–5. In general, the same type of conduct is prohibited in connection with public offerings under the 33 Act. Two points should be kept in mind:

(1)   If the issuer commits fraud in connection with its sale of securities (*i.e.*, an "issuer transaction"), it is subject to strict liability. But if the fraud is committed in connection with the resale of outstanding securities (*i.e.*, a "trading transaction") there is no liability absent scienter.

(2)   While many sales of securities are exempt from the registration requirement of § 5, no sale of securities is exempt from the antifraud provisions of the 33 Act or Rule 10b–5 under the 34 Act.

CHAPTER IX

HOW DO THE OWNERS OF
A BUSINESS MAKE
MONEY?

Generally, the owners of a business, regardless of the form of business association, can make money in three ways: (1) by being paid a salary by the business, (2) by receiving distributions of all or part of the profits from the business or (3) by selling all or part of their interest in the business at a profit. Many of the answers to the issues discussed in this chapter are governed by areas of the law other than the law of business associations—*i.e.*, contract law, tax law, etc. However, the type of business association and the governing statutes often have an impact on how the owners of the business make money.

A. PARTNERSHIPS

How do the owners of a partnership make money?

1. SALARY

Partners' salaries are usually governed by the partnership agreement. If the partnership agreement does not contain a provision that governs an issue relating to salaries, the default provisions in the relevant partnership statute will govern.

Examples:

a.   Assume *A*, *B* and *C* are partners in the ABC Taco Stand, a partnership, governed by RUPA. *A* works at the partnership full time. *B* and *C* are investors and do not work at the partnership. In the absence of agreement is *A* entitled to receive a salary?

No. RUPA (§ 401(h)) provides that a partner is not entitled to remuneration for services performed for the partnership (except compensation for winding up the partnership's business). As we learned earlier, this is merely the default rule which the parties can alter by agreement. See, *e.g.*, RUPA § 103(a). For *A* to receive a salary, a majority of the partners must agree to pay him a salary. RUPA § 401(h).

b.   Assume the partnership agreement provides that *A* will receive an annual salary of $50,000. After a year *A* feels he is entitled to a raise to $60,000. Who is required to authorize the increase?

Since the increase in salary would effect a change in the partnership agreement, all of the partners must agree to the raise. RUPA § 401(j).

c.   Can the partnership pay *C* a salary even though she does not do any work for the partnership?

Yes. If the partners agree, the partnership can pay her a salary. However, the salary paid to *C* would reduce the distributions the other two partners could receive.

The above are random examples which illustrate the following basic points regarding partners' salaries: (1) contract law (*i.e.* the partnership agreement) usually controls matters relating to partners' salaries, (2) if a partner is to receive a salary the partnership agreement must so provide and (3) persons drafting partnership agreements must be aware of the default provisions in the governing statute so that they can draft around those default provisions that do not reflect their needs or desires.

2.   DISTRIBUTIONS AND PROFITS

"Profits" and "distributions" are not synonyms. There can be profits without distributions and distributions without profits. Profits are determined by accounting principles and distributions by vote of the partners. Partners' rights to profits and distributions, like partners' salaries, are usually governed by the partnership agreement. But, again, default provisions of the governing statute may control, if the parties do not contract around those provisions, as illustrated by the following examples.

Examples:

   a.   Assume *A*, *B* and *C* are partners in the ABC Taco Stand, a partnership governed by RUPA. *C* invests $75,000 in the partnership, *B* invests $25,000. *A* does not invest any money in the partnership but works full time for the partnership and draws a salary. The partnership makes a profit of $99,000 in 2004. How will the profits be shared among *A*, *B* and *C*?

   Each partner will get $33,000. Absent an agreement to the contrary each partner is entitled to an equal share of the profits. RUPA § 401(b).

   b.   Assume the partnership makes a profit of $99,000 in 2002 and the profits are allocated equally to each partner. *A* wants a distribution of substantially all of his

share of the partnership's profits, but *B* and *C* believe
that the partnership should make no distributions to
partners, but rather should use the $99,000 for capital
improvements and advertising. Who decides what distributions the partners will receive?

Assuming there is no provision in the partnership
agreement which controls, the decision as to distributions would be made by a majority of the partners (here
B and *C* could out vote *A*). See RUPA § 4.01(j).

RUPA § 4.01(a) should also be considered. This provision requires that each partner have a capital account
and defines the "**partner's capital account**" as an
amount that equals the partner's capital contributions
plus allocations of profit to the partner *minus* distributions to the partner and allocations of losses to the
partner.

The capital accounts of the various partners govern
how the assets of the partnership will be distributed
upon liquidation of the partnership. Distributions upon
liquidation are a matter you will learn about in the next
chapter.

3. SALES OF PARTNERSHIP INTERESTS AND DISTRIBUTIONS UPON WITHDRAWAL OF A PARTNER

You will learn about these matters in the next chapter
when I discuss the dissolution of partnerships. For now
you should focus on the fundamental fact that partnerships are readily terminable. And that upon termination
the withdrawing partner is generally entitled to receive
fair market value for her interest in the partnership.
This differs significantly from corporate law where termi-

nation of the corporate entity is usually not an option. This distinguishing attribute between partnership law and corporate law is often referred to as "exit rules," which were discussed in Chapter II and will be further discussed in Chapter X.

How much of the money made by the partnership do the partners (as opposed to the IRS) get to keep?

Under Subchapter K, partnerships and associations taxable as partnerships are not separate taxable entities, but rather are treated as conduits through which the tax consequences of their activities are passed through to their owners. As previously noted this tax scheme is generally referred to as "pass through taxation." The partnership prepares an informational tax return, but it pays no tax. Rather the tax is allocated to the partners, who receive Form K–1's and include their share of the income or loss generated by the partnership on their individual returns. The result is that taxable income is only taxed once—at the individual level. However, since the tax is on "profits" at the partnership level rather than on "distributions" to the partners, the partners may be required to pay taxes on income which they do not receive.

Under "check the box," an elective scheme of taxation adopted in 1997, except for publicly traded partnerships, the vast majority of partnerships (and other unincorporated business associations) can choose to be taxed either as partnerships or corporations on an elective basis simply by checking the appropriate box, the first time they file a tax return. As previously noted in Chapter II, generally partners get to keep a greater share of the money made by the business by electing to be taxed as partnerships and almost all partnerships so elect.

B. CORPORATIONS

In theory, owners of a corporation (*i.e.*, "shareholders") can make money the same way as partners. However, as a practical matter the way shareholders of a corporation make money will depend on whether they are shareholders of a **close corporation** or shareholders of a **public corporation**, a distinction that arises in many areas of corporate law. Recall you previously learned that the most important difference between close and public corporations is the presence of a market for shares of a public corporation compared to the absence of a market for shares of a close corporation. This distinction obviously has an impact on how the shareholders make money.

The typical shareholder of a public corporation hopes to make money from her investment either by receiving part of the corporation's profits through distributions called "dividends" or by selling her shares for more than she paid for them, called "capital gains" or a combination of the two called "total return." She faces business issues (*i.e.*, picking stocks that go up rather than down in value), deciding when to buy and when to sell (*i.e.*, buying low and selling high) and tax issues (*i.e.*, long term capital gains or ordinary income). But, the ordinary shareholder in a public corporation is strictly a passive investor, who hopes to make money from ownership of the stock, but has no expectation of making money directly from the operation of the business.

By contrast, shareholders of close corporations may face many legal issues which pertain to making money from the business. Basically shareholders of a corporation make money in the same way as partners in a partnership:

(1) profit from the sale of their interest in the business,

(2) distributions from the earnings of the business (*i.e.*, "dividends") and

(3) salary.

But the business considerations as well as the legal issues differ in a corporation.

1.   PROFITS FROM THE SALE OF THE BUSINESS

You will learn about selling the business in Chapter X. You learned about "going public" (which is the functional equivalent of selling a part of the business) in Chapter VIII. For now, reconsider the problem of the minority shareholder whose minority interest is likely unsaleable, due to the absence of a market. He does not have the ability to "exit" by forcing a dissolution or disassociation like a partner in a partnership can do (as we will discuss in the next chapter). For this reason, a buy-sell agreement (discussed in § V.B.3.c, *supra*) is often critical to minority shareholders of close corporations.

2.   DIVIDENDS

a.   Definitions and Concepts Related to Dividends

What is a dividend?

A "dividend" is a payment out of current or retained earnings made to shareholders in propor-

tion to the number of shares they own. Dividends are usually paid, periodically, at the discretion of directors.

Payments by a corporation to its shareholders other than those out of past or current earnings are called "capital distributions," "return of capital" or simply "distributions." Notice the definition of a dividend is based on an accounting concept—retained earnings. This is another example of a point made earlier that some knowledge of accounting is helpful in many areas of the law of business structures.

The tax laws recognize this distinction. Dividends are taxable to the shareholders as ordinary income (the maximum tax on dividends was recently reduced to 15%), while returns of capital are not taxed.

What is the effect of paying dividends?

The effect of a dividend payment, or for that matter any corporate distribution, is to transfer assets from the corporation to its shareholders.

Who might be harmed by the payment of dividends?

Creditors. Creditors might be counting on the assets paid out as dividends to satisfy their claims against the corporation. The creditors are concerned that the shareholders might exhaust the corporation's assets by paying dividends to themselves. For this reason, creditors often limit the amount of dividends a corporation may pay through contractual restrictions in loan agreements.

Minority shareholders. In close corporations, dividend policy may be used to skew the rewards of ownership in favor of majority shareholders at the expense of minority shareholders or to "freeze out" minority shareholders. The board of directors of closely held corporations are almost always the majority shareholders and/or persons under their control. As managers of the corporation the majority shareholders typically receive money from the corporation in the form of salary and benefits rather than dividends.

On the other hand, minority shareholders' (who are not employed by the corporation) main means of receiving money from the corporation is through dividends. Unlike partners, it is difficult for minority shareholders in a close corporation to force a dissolution in which they can cash out their interest in the business at fair market value. This is another example of why it is important for minority shareholders to establish an exit strategy contractually.

Tax consideration: dividends compared to salaries.

As previously noted, except in Subchapter S corporations, dividends are subject to double taxation (the corporation is taxed on its profits and shareholders are taxed on the portion of such profits distributed to them by way of dividends). On the other hand, salaries are deductible at the corporate level as ordinary and necessary business expenses.

Who decides when and in what amount dividends are to be paid?

Decisions on the payment of dividends are within the **discretion of the board of directors** and the board's discretion is protected under the business judgement rule. While the board's discretion in paying dividends is extremely broad it may be limited in three ways:

1. Contractual Limitations. Provisions in loan agreements, indentures or other contracts may limit the payment of dividends, usually to protect creditors.

2. Statutory Limitations. Provisions in the state corporate statute limit the payment of dividends by designating the sources out of which dividends can be paid.

3. Judicial Limitations. The courts require that the board does not abuse its discretion in paying dividends.

The first of the above limitations is governed by contract law and needs no further discussion. The second and third limitations are discussed in the next two subsections.

b. When *Can* Dividends be Paid? ("Permissive Dividends")

The statutes of every state establish tests for determining when dividends can be paid—permissive dividends. The state corporate statutes generally impose two tests: (1) a solvency test and (2) some version of what is generally referred to as a "balance sheet" test. The balance sheet test varies widely from state to state.

Consider, for example, MBCA § 6.40, which imposes the following requirements for payment of distributions, including permissive dividends:

1. Solvency Test. If, after giving effect to the distribution, the corporation is able to pay its debts as they come due in the ordinary course of business, it may pay dividends.

2. Balance Sheet Test. If, after giving effect to the distribution, the corporation's total assets are greater than the sum of its total liabilities and the amount necessary to satisfy any preferential liquidation rights, it may pay dividends.

Modern Approach. The MBCA merely requires that you look at the total assets (things the corporation owns, as reflected on the left side of the balance sheet) and total liabilities (what the corporation owes, as reflected on the right hand side of the balance sheet). And if the assets exceed the liabilities, dividends can be paid from any source available to the corporation, provided the solvency test is also met. This is tantamount to saying as long as paying a dividend does not render the corporation insolvent or unable to satisfy preferential rights, dividends may be paid.

Traditional approach. While some states have adopted the approach of MBCA § 6.40, most states still follow the so-called "traditional" approach which is more restrictive than the MBCA approach. In addition to a solvency requirement, a corporate statute based on the traditional approach also contains restrictions based upon the amount reflected in accounts shown on the balance sheet. The restrictions, which vary from state to state, are phrased in accounting terms applicable to the three accounts which comprise the "shareholders equity" of the balance sheet.

One such account is called "**retained earnings**" or "**earned surplus**," terms used to describe the total cumulative earnings of the corporation since its inception less the amount paid out as dividends or other distributions. In other words, **retained earnings** (or **earned surplus**), consist of value generated by the business and retained in the business (*i.e.*, net profits over the years less distributions over the years). All states permit dividends to be paid out of retained earnings. Some states limit dividend payments to the amount shown in the retained earnings account.

The other two components of the shareholders equity section of the balance sheet relate to capital raised by the corporation from the sale of its stock, as opposed to the sale of goods and services.

Stated capital (which also goes by several other names including "common stock" or "capital stock") is the number of shares outstanding times the par value per share (or the amount allocated to stated capital by the board of directors in the case of "no par" stock).

Capital surplus (sometimes called "paid in capital") is the dollar amount over par value (or the amount designated as capital in the case of no par stock) paid for shares of the corporation at the time of the original issuance.

Some states allow dividends to be paid out of capital surplus, as well as retained earnings, but none allow dividends to be paid from stated capital.

The traditional approach requires you to understand the three accounts discussed above and how the various state statutes define the restrictions. Under the modern approach, as typified by the MBCA, this becomes irrelevant, and the process is simplified. The modern approach reflects the decline in importance of the concept of par value.

c. When Must Dividends be Paid? (Mandatory Dividends)

Assuming a corporation has funds available for the payment of dividends under statutory tests discussed above, the board has broad discretion as to whether or not to pay dividends. Suits to compel payment of dividends are relatively rare and when they occur, they almost always occur in close corporations. They typically involve suits by minority shareholders against majority shareholders, who control the board (and thus the dividend policy).

Zidell v. Zidell, Inc. (Ore. 1977) is a good illustration of this type of law suit. The case involved a closely held corporation owned by various members of the Zidell family. Arnold, the plaintiff, owned ⅜ of the outstanding shares; his brother Emery owned ⅜ of the outstanding shares and Emery's son Jay owned the remaining ¼ of the outstanding shares. Until 1973 all three worked for the corporation and drew salaries. During the years prior to 1973 the corporation paid little or no dividends. In 1973, after Arnold's demand for a raise in salary from $30,000 to $50,000 per year was refused, Arnold resigned.

In his suit to compel the payment of dividends, Arnold presented evidence showing the corporation had sufficient retained earnings to pay greater dividends, that defendants were receiving substantial (though not excessive) compensation by way of salary and benefits and that there was hostility between Arnold and the other shareholders. Defendants' evidence, introduced to explain the board's conservative business policies, included tax considerations, plans for future possible expansion, needs to make future physical improvements, seasonal needs for cash to finance the purchase of inventory, etc.

The trial court ordered the corporation to pay larger dividends. It did not hold that Emery and Jay had acted in bad faith, but based its decision on grounds that larger dividends were necessary to give Arnold a reasonable return on his equity in the corporation.

The Oregon Supreme Court reversed the trial court and held that to compel the payment of dividends, plaintiff had to show "**bad faith**" on the part of the defendants. The fact that Arnold resigned his employment, rather than being fired, obviously hurt his case. This case illustrates that a plaintiff seeking to compel the payment of dividends faces an uphill battle because the directors' discretion as to payment of dividends is protected by the business judgment rule.

Occasionally, however, courts do order the board to pay dividends. The Supreme Court of Michigan ordered a corporation to pay dividends in one of the most famous cases in the annals of corporate law, *Dodge v. Ford Motor Co.* (Mich. 1919).

In 1916, when this case arose, the Ford Motor Company ("Ford") was an extremely successful closely held corporation. Ford had paid large dividends in prior years. At the time of suit, Ford had $112 million in surplus. Profits for the then current year were expected to exceed $60 million and cash on hand exceeded $54 million—all exceptionally large amounts in 1916.

The early investors in Ford (minority shareholders) had made a very good investment. Two of those early shareholders, the Dodge brothers, had used a good portion of the money they had received from Ford in dividends to start their own car company.

Henry Ford, the controlling shareholder and CEO of Ford, announced that Ford was canceling the payment of dividends. The Dodge brothers brought suit to compel the payment of dividends. Henry Ford probably sealed his own fate at the trial. Rather than speaking vaguely about future contingencies, the large capital needs of an automobile manufacturer, the need to expand to in order to maximize profits, etc., he was straightforward on the witness stand. Mr. Ford said he wanted to build a new plant and increase production so he could build more cars less expensively and drive down the price of cars.

Henry Ford testified he wanted to make as many cars as possible, as cheap as possible so that in Mr. Ford's words "any American with a decent job could afford one." Most people (apparently including the judges) thought that was dumb. Why not charge more for the cars? But Ford turned out to be right. He understood that in the long run the company could make far more money by making cars cheaper and selling more of them. Ford also paid its workers substantially more than the going wage. Most people thought that was also dumb, but it turned out to be smart. It gave Ford a stable work force in pre-union days. Today it is clear that Henry Ford's policies contributed greatly to the success of the Ford Motor Company.

These policies are part of what students learn from this case in business schools (schools some corporate lawyer refer to as "client schools") around the country. And the business students can relate Henry Fords policies to policies followed by many successful modern-day companies, such as: Wal Mart, Dell Computer and Southwest Airlines.

In law school, the case teaches us a different lesson. If Henry Ford had testified that he wanted to produce cars less expensively so he could increase Ford's profits, it is unlikely that the court would have overruled his decision to discontinue dividends and plow the money back into the business. But the Michigan Supreme Court found that Henry Ford's stated reasons were imprudent. That finding, coupled with the large cash surpluses and Ford's history of paying dividends, caused the court to order Ford to pay dividends.

But courts are reluctant to compel the payment of dividends. The *Ford* case is an anomaly. It is one of few cases, other than obvious attempts by the majority to freeze out the minority, where a company was ordered to pay dividends.

The reason is the business judgment rule. Judges are usually reluctant to substitute their business judgment for that of the board of directors. This case seems to support the wisdom of the business judgment rule. In hindsight, it is clear that Henry Ford's business judgement proved to be better than the court's. This famous case does not alter the general rule, that in the absence of clear evidence of **bad faith** or **conflict of interest**, the courts will rarely second guess the business judgment of the board on questions concerning the payment of dividends.

3. SALARY

The legal issues likely to arise with respect to the payment by a corporation of salary and other benefits also differ in publicly held and closely held corporations.

a. Publicly Held Corporations

In publicly held corporations, where ownership is separate from management, the board typically sets the compensation of the CEO and other senior executives by resolutions, usually adopted on an annual basis. The "compensation package" often consists of (1) salary, (2) bonuses, (3) deferred compensation, (4) stock options and (5) other benefits.

Obviously, the executives want to obtain the most generous compensation package they can and the board of directors has wide discretion in fixing executive compensation. Often senior corporate executives are also members of the board or have influence over the members of the board charged with fixing their compensation. This brings into play issues discussed earlier in conflict of interest situations and possible suits for violation of fiduciary duties. See § VI.A.3, *supra*.

Today, most publicly held companies have compensation committees, composed of outside directors (directors who are not employees of the company), which set the compensation of the corporation's top executives. Additionally, public corporations usually get shareholder approval of compensation plans through the proxy solicitation process.

The law does impose a standard of **reasonableness** on compensation and in cases where shareholders attack an executive's compensation as unreasonable, the courts may review the fairness of an executive's compensation. However, even in this post-Enron era, where excessive executive compensation has become a hot topic of discussion in the law reviews, full fledged judicial fairness review of executive compensation is relatively rare.

Courts are reluctant to review the fairness of executive salaries and have developed a rule for limited judicial review. When a majority of informed disinterested directors or shareholders approve the compensation of a senior executive, the compensation package will **not** be treated as a form of self dealing and will not be subject to **fairness review** by the courts. In other words, if disinterested approval is obtained, the courts will give decisions concerning executive compensation the same degree of deference under the business judgment rule as they give other types of operating decisions, such as whether to play day or night baseball. A plaintiff has to show that the executive's compensation had no relationship to the value of the services performed—a **waste** standard. But if disinterested approval is not obtained, courts may review the compensation package under a **fairness** standard.

b. Close Corporations

In the typical closely held corporation, most if not all of the shareholders are likely to be employees of the corporation. Often such employment and the accompanying salary is the shareholder's main reason for becoming a shareholder and several employment related issues may arise.

Reasonable salaries. Salaries are often utilized to counteract the impact of double taxation which is imposed under Subchapter C of the IRC. Recall the tax rule is that while reasonable salaries are deductible by the corporation as an ordinary and necessary business expenses, the same monies paid in the form of dividends are not deductible by the corporation. Thus, in closely held corporations (particularly where all of the shareholders are employed by the corporation) there is a strong incentive to set salaries as high as possible to avoid taxes at the corporate level. The IRS routinely reviews the reasonableness of salaries and often disallows the deduction for part of the salary, which they view as a dividend. A number of cases have litigated this issue.

Protecting future salary; exit strategy. Even larger issues relating to salary might arise in close corporations where some, but not all of the shareholders, are employed by the corporation. For example, assume that *A*, *B* and *C* are the founders and each owns ⅓ of the outstanding shares of ABC Tacos, Inc., a corporation. Each originally invested $25,000 in the business, each is employed full time in the business, and each depends on the business as the primary source of his livelihood. As is typical of close corporations, ABC Tacos, Inc. pays no dividends, but most of the company's current earnings are distributed to the owners through payment of salaries and benefits. Following several successful years of operation, there is a disagreement. *A* and *B* remove *C* from the board and then fire *C* as an employee. Following *C*'s termination of employment, *A* and *B* continue their policy of paying no dividends and distributing most of the company's earning to themselves through salaries and benefits.

These were essentially the facts of *Wilkes v. Springside Nursing Home, Inc.* (Mass. 1976), discussed in § VI.D, *supra,* in connection with our discussion of the stricter fiduciary duties that some, but not all, states impose on control shareholders of close corporations. Here we revisit the facts of *Wilkes* to discuss ways in which the problem could have been avoided. Lawyers who represent businesses work as "counselors" (planners to avoid litigation) as much, if not more, than they work as litigators resolving disputes. And many professors like to test students' ability to see planning issues.

How would you handle an exam question that requires you to focus on planning issues raised by the above example?

First, you look at the probable expectations of the parties to the deal. Continued employment by, and salary from, the business were probably a big part of C's reason for doing the deal. While C's shares in the corporation are, in theory freely transferable, seldom does anyone want to buy a minority interest in a close corporation. Further, a minority shareholder in a corporation, unlike a partner in a partnership, can not easily compel a dissolution in which his interest is bought out. Controlling shareholders may have some incentive to buy out minority shareholders because disgruntled minority shareholders can be a nuisance. But the price the controlling shareholders are willing to pay the minority shareholders of their interests is often inadequate.

Second, once you recognize the underlying economics, the solution should become relatively clear. The minority shareholder (*C* in our example) should realize the importance of an exit strategy going into the deal and provide for a potential exit. In earlier sections of the book we have discussed various devices through which *C*'s exit could be achieved, such as buy-sell agreements and employment contracts. Material covered earlier also raises the issue of whether the corporation is the best type of business association for the business in my example.

How much of the money made by a corporation do the shareholders (as opposed to the IRS) get to keep?

Subchapter C of the IRC provides that a corporation is a separate taxable entity, independent of its shareholders. As a result, corporations file tax returns and pay tax on whatever taxable income the corporation earns. If the corporation then distributes the income to shareholders, as dividends, the shareholders pay tax on the dividends they receive.

This is referred to as double taxation because the earnings of a C corporation are subject to federal income taxation at two different levels—first at the corporate level and second at the shareholder level, if the shareholder receives dividends from the corporation. The impact of double taxation may significantly reduce the amount of the company's earnings that the owners get to keep. For example, assume a situation in which the marginal tax rate is 35% for both the corporation and a shareholder. In that case every $100 of the corporation's pre-tax earnings becomes $42.25 when it is distributed as dividends, following taxation at both the corporate and personal levels [*i.e.,* \$100 x (1 − 0.35) x (1 − 0.35) = \$42.25]. The numbers in the above example merely illustrate the concept and effect of double taxation. They do not reflect the current tax rate, which was recently lowered to a maximum of 15% on dividends and capital gains.

In closely held corporations, double taxation does not necessarily mean that the corporation and its shareholders will wind up paying more taxes. The disadvantage of double taxation can sometimes be mitigated through a technique known as **"zeroing out income"** at the corporate level. Essentially this entails **not paying dividends**, but rather **accumulating cash** at the corporate level or paying out profits to shareholders in the form of **salaries** or **benefits.** As a practical matter, "zeroing" can only be done when there is significant identity of interest among the shareholders of the corporation. Unless you have a professor who emphasizes taxation, applications relating to zeroing out income are not likely to be tested in the basic business course.

Subchapter S permits closely held corporations that meet certain specified requirements to elect to be taxed in a way that avoids double taxation. Subchapter S taxation is generally similar to the way in which partnerships are taxed under Subchapter K, discussed earlier. A Subchapter S corporation has all of the basic corporate attributes of any other corporation. The only difference is the way it is taxed.

To be eligible for Subchapter S tax treatment, a corporation must meet the following requirements on the date of the election: (1) it must be a domestic corporation; (2)

with no more than 75 shareholders; (3) each shareholder must be an individual, a decedent's estate or a certain type of trust; (4) no shareholder may be a nonresident alien; and (5) the corporation may have only one class of stock outstanding. In general, the tax treatment under Subchapter S and Subchapter K are similar in that both provide **pass through taxation**, and thus eliminate the problem of double taxation. The details vary, in ways beyond your needs in the basic business course.

C.   LIMITED LIABILITY COMPANIES

The owners ("members") of a Limited Liability Company ("LLC") make money the same way as partners of a partnership or shareholders of a close corporation: by sharing in the earnings of the business, and by selling their ownership interests for more than they paid for them. Also, members employed by the LLC may receive salaries.

Most issues relating to an LLC's payments to its members are governed by the operating agreement. Recall most LLC statutes have adopted a policy of giving maximum effect to freedom of contract and the provisions of the operating agreement. See, *e.g.*, Del. LLCA § 18–1101(b).

The governing statutes do contain default rules which govern, if but only if, an issue is not covered in the operating agreement. Thus, the main point to keep in mind with respect to LLCs is a drafting point—anticipate the expectations and desires of the parties to the deal and draft an operating agreement that abrogates any default provisions in the governing statute that do not

346 MAKING MONEY Ch. IX

reflect those expectations and desires. Many professors emphasize drafting with respect to LLCs because the statutes are diverse and the LLC is so new that there is not yet much case law.

How much of the money made by the LLC do the members (as opposed to the IRS) get to keep?

Today, under the "check the box" regulations of IRS, almost all LLCs are taxed like partnerships under Subchapter K of IRC.

Until January 1, 1997, the IRS had a set of regulations, known as the "Kintner Rules," under which the IRS determined which unincorporated limited liability entities would be taxed as corporations under Subchapter C and which would be taxed as partnerships under Subchapter K. The basic test under the Kintner Rules was whether a particular business association had more corporate attributes (*i.e.,* limited liability, continuity of life, centralized management and free transferability of interests) or more noncorporate attributes. If the business entity had more than two of the corporate attributes listed above, it would be taxed as a corporation under Subchapter C. Consequently, many first generation LLC statutes had provisions intended to negate transferability and continuity of existence to facilitate pass through tax treatment. These were called "bullet proof" LLC statutes.

With the repeal of the Kintner Rules and adoption of "check the box," all of that is now history and many states have amended their LLC statutes to reflect this change in the tax laws. More importantly, with the elimination of the uncertainty as to their tax status under the arcane Kintner Rules, the LLC has emerged as the business association of choice for thousands of closely-held businesses throughout the United States.

CHAPTER X

HOW DO BUSINESS ASSOCIATIONS END?

Business associations have a life cycle. As is the case with most relationships, at some point in time most business associations end. Some business associations end very quickly; others last a very long time. The end games vary, as do the legal issues raised in connection with the end games. Most issues are outside the scope of the basic course in business associations (and this book). An advanced course, which deals with corporate end games called Mergers and Acquisitions ("M & A"), is offered by almost all law schools.

Most professors in the basic business associations course touch on the fundamental concepts of both **dissolutions** and **mergers and acquisitions**, the primary types of end games employed by partnerships and corporations. Your professor will likely expect you to understand the procedures employed in ending a business association.

There are many different options for achieving the same basic end game result and you should understand what these procedures have in common and how they differ.

A. PARTNERSHIPS

Recall some state partnership laws are based on the Uniform Partnership Act ("UPA"), while others are based on the Revised Uniform Partnership Act ("RUPA"). In general, partnership breakups usually involve "dissolutions" and/or "dissociations," two highly technical concepts defined in the UPA and RUPA.[1]

1. UPA DISSOLUTION COMPARED WITH RUPA DISSOCIATION

a. Dissolution under the UPA

Dissolution is a key UPA end game concept, which is defined in UPA § 29. Under §§ 29–32 of the UPA, "dissolution" of the partnership occurs every time a partner files for bankruptcy, dies, or otherwise withdraws from the partnership. This is consistent with the UPA's view of a partnership as an aggregate of its members. Under UPA, when a partner departs, the aggregate changes and the partnership is dissolved.

Under the UPA, a partner always has the power to withdraw and thus dissolve the partnership—regardless of what the partnership agreement might otherwise provide. If, for example, the partnership agreement provides for a ten year term and each partner promises that she will not withdraw from the partnership until the expiration of that term, a partner still has the legal power to withdraw and cause the dissolution of the partnership.

1. Dissolutions and dissociations are handled differently under UPA and RUPA. Since there are many state partnership statutes based on both model acts, I will discuss both.

However, a partner's exercise of this power may cause the partner to be liable for breach of contract.

Dissolution under the UPA does not necessarily mean that the business ends or is liquidated. The remaining partners can, and often do, decide to continue the business after dissolution, but the business is continued by a new legal partnership (technically a new business association).

Under UPA, the circumstances for continuing the business of a partnership after dissolution depend on (1) the partnership agreement's provisions on continuing the business after dissolution and (2) if there are no such provisions, the "default rules" of UPA. In the "real world," partnerships large enough to warrant hiring lawyers to deal with dissolution usually have written partnership agreements with provisions that govern continuing the business after dissolution. In law school classes, professors often teach and test the UPA or RUPA default rules.

Under the UPA default rules, if there is no term specified in the partnership agreement or if the term specified has expired, then the partnership business can be continued by the other partners only if all of the partners, including the partner who dissolved the partnership, agree that the business can be continued. If they agree to continue to the business, then the withdrawing partner is paid the value of her interest in the business as determined by § 42 of UPA.

If a partner leaves a partnership before the end of the term specified in the partnership agreement, then the business of the partnership can be continued if all of the partners other than the one who wrongfully dissolved the partnership so agree. If they decide to continue the business, the departing partner is again paid for the value of her interest. Again, look to § 42 of UPA to value that interest except (I) "goodwill" is not included in valuing the business and (ii) the payment to the departing partner is reduced by any damages caused by the premature dissolution.

If the partners do not decide to continue the business after UPA dissolution, the business is liquidated under UPA § 37 and § 40. The partnership is "wound up" under UPA § 37; the assets are sold and distributed to creditors and then to partners (including the departing partner) pursuant to UPA § 40. Regardless of whether the partnership business continues or is liquidated, dissolution raises creditors' rights issues. UPA §§ 33–36 governs the liability of partners on dissolution for partnership debts.

Think about the law school exam possibilities of UPA dissolution. Under the UPA, dissolution can always be triggered by the withdrawal of a partner. And under UPA, unless the partnership agreement otherwise provides, dissolution in essence triggers a liquidation right in each partner. If, for example, A, B, C, D and E are partners, and E withdraws, then A can prevent the continuation of the partnership business even though B, C and D favor continuation.

b. Dissociation Under RUPA

RUPA's end game default rules are significantly different from the UPA rules. While RUPA continues to use the terms "dissolution," "winding up," and "termination," (highly technical terms as defined in the statutes), RUPA adds a new term **"dissociation."**

Dissociation is about a partner's withdrawal from the partnership. Under RUPA, as under UPA, a partner always has the legal power to withdraw from a partnership, regardless of what the partnership agreement provides. RUPA, however, calls such withdrawal "dissociation," a term and concept not found in the UPA.

More important, under RUPA dissociation, does not always result in dissolution. First, RUPA § 103 states that a partnership agreement can provide that dissociation does not trigger dissolution. Second, RUPA § 801 provides that a partner's dissociation during a term partnership triggers dissolution only if at least half of the remaining partners so agree. Third, RUPA § 802 provides that partners can waive dissolution.

RUPA § 602 distinguishes between rightful and wrongful acts of dissociation. The major types of wrongful dissociation are (1) breaches of express provisions of the partnership agreement, (2) early withdrawal, (3) wrongful conduct that adversely affects the partnership business, and (4) willful breach of a duty of care, loyalty, good faith or fair dealing owed to the partnership under § 404. Unless the dissociation is expressly made wrongful, under the terms of § 602, the dissociation is considered rightful. A wrongful dissociation or a dissociation by death does not dissolve the partnership. Rather, it leads to a fork in the statutory road—either a wind up under Article 8 or a mandatory buyout under Article 7. Which fork is taken depends on the nature of the event of dissociation and how the remaining partners choose to treat the dissociation.

Again, think about the law school exam possibilities. *A*, *B*, *C*, *D*, *E* and *F* are partners, and their partnership agreement has a seven year term. After a year, *A* wants to withdraw. While she has the power to dissociate, her wrongful dissociation will not trigger dissolution of a RUPA partnership unless a majority of the partners so agree. If, however, their partnership agreement was at will, then *A*'s RUPA dissociation will result in RUPA dissolution unless, under § 802, all of the partners including the dissociating partner, waive the dissolution.

If a partner's dissociation is not followed by the partnership's dissolution, then the dissociating partner's interest in the partnership must be purchased pursuant to the buy out rules in Article 7 of RUPA. In statute talk, that means an Article 6 dissociation will always trigger either an Article 7 buy out or an Article 8 dissolution.

2. WINDING UP

The partnership's business does not end with dissolution under either statute. UPA § 30 and RUPA § 802 provide that dissolution does not terminate the partnership; instead, the partnership continues until the winding up process is complete. Winding up involves selling the partnership's assets and using the proceeds of the sale to pay the partnership's debts and settle the partners' accounts.

UPA § 37 and RUPA § 803 answer the question of which partners have wind up rights and responsibilities. Other provisions of the statutes answer questions about wind up payments. Under UPA § 40, "outside" debts, *i.e.*, debts owed to persons other than partners, are paid before "inside" debts, *i.e.*, debts owed to partners. RUPA § 807 eliminates this distinction. Under both UPA and RUPA, the partners have a contribution obligation. If the proceeds from the liquidation of partnership assets are not sufficient to pay creditors, the partners must contribute toward payment of the debt in the same proportion in which they share losses.

"Dissolution," "termination" and "winding up" are interrelated concepts that need to be understood. They are also "words of art" defined in the partnership statutes in a way that is different from the way these words are ordinarily used.

Dissolution is the point in time when the partners cease to carry on business together. **Termination** is the point in time when all the partnership's affairs have been wound up. **Winding up** is the period between dissolution and termination.

The following time line and example illustrates the process under the UPA.

Dissolution   ←Winding up→   Termination

●————————————————————●

(Six months in the following example)

Example: Assume that *A* and *B* form a partnership to operate a shoe store, which they call the AB Shoe Store. *A* is the financial partner who will supply the money. *B* is the "talent" who will run the shoe store. The partnership is governed by UPA. Since no term is specified for the partnership, the AB Shoe Store is a partnership which is terminable at will.

A and *B* begin business. They take a three year lease on a building, buy equipment and inventory and run a successful business for two and a half years. At that point *B*, the talent, who has managed to save over $20,000 from his share of the earnings of the shoe store decides he wants to go to law school. Six months before the lease expires, *B* notifies *A* that he wants to dissolve the partnership. *A*, the money, cannot find anyone else to run the shoe store so she agrees to dissolve and liquidate. At that point the **dissolution occurs** and the process of **winding up** begins.

During the wind up period the AB Shoe Store Partnership must continue to comply with all its contractual obligations, which include the lease on the building, contracts with suppliers and contracts between the partners—*i.e.,* the partnership agreement. It will doubtless quit buying inventory and try to liquidate the inventory it has on hand, probably through some sort of sale. It will reduce the assets of the partnership to cash, pay off the debts, and divide up what is left over. This is the **termination**.

In addition to a number of other differences, RUPA differs from UPA in the way it defines the concept of "dissolution." Under RUPA, all "dissociations" do not result in "dissolution." However, under RUPA, unlike under UPA, if there is a "dissolution" the result is always termination of the partnership business and liquidation of the partnership assets. Under RUPA, partners can agree to waive the dissolution, but absent a RUPA § 802 waiver, dissolution under RUPA results in winding up the partnership.

The winding up and termination process under Article 8 of RUPA is similar to the process described above under the UPA. The buyout process, on the other hand, is new to RUPA and is governed by Article 7 of RUPA.

3. PARTNERSHIP ACCOUNTS

Dissolution can trigger not only an obligation on the part of partners to share in operating losses by contributing to the payment of partnership debts, but also an obligation to share in investment losses by contributing to the settlement of the partnership accounts.

A partnership account is a bookkeeping device to keep track of how much a partner has invested in the partnership. Separate partnership accounts are kept for each partner.

When a partnership is dissolved, the partnership is obligated to pay each partner an amount measured by the balance in her partnership account. Both UPA § 40 and RUPA § 807 set out this default rule, obligating the partnership to repay partners' their capital contributions, after the partnership has paid its creditors. And, under both UPA § 40 and RUPA § 807, if, at dissolution, the sum of the balances of each the individual partner's partnership accounts exceeds the liquidation proceeds remaining after payment of creditors, then the partners will have to contribute additional funds to the partnership so that the losses from investments are shared appropriately.

Assume, for example, that *A*, *B* and *C* are partners. *A* made a $100,000 investment in the partnership. Although only *A* invested in the partnership, *A*, *B* and *C* agreed to share profits and losses equally. On dissolution, the liquidation proceeds are inadequate to pay creditors. Partnership debts exceed liquidation proceeds by $20,000. *A*'s partnership account has a $100,000 balance. The other partnership accounts have a zero (0) balance.

Obviously *A*, *B* and *C* are jointly and severally liable for the payment of the $20,000 to creditors. It should be equally obvious that the partnership also owes *A* $100,000 and this too becomes a liability of *B* and *C*. Remember *A*, *B* and *C* agree to share losses equally. Losses total $120,000 ($20,000 in operating losses plus 100,000 in investment losses). Under these facts, each of the three partners should bear $40,000 of the losses. If *A* and *B* both pay $40,000 to the partnership and the partnership pays $20,000 to the creditors and the other $60,000 to *A*, then each partner will lose $40,000.

The proceeds from dissolution of a partnership can exceed the partnership's obligations to creditors. If that happens, the excess goes first to satisfy partnership accounts. To illustrate, *A*, *B* and *C* are partners. *A* made a $100,000 investment. Although only *A* invested in the partnership, they agreed to share profits equally. On dissolution, the liquidation proceeds exceed the debts owed to creditors by $160,000. And *A*'s partnership account has a $100,000 balance. The other partnership accounts have a zero (0) balance. Under these facts, the first $100,000 of the surplus would go to *A* to pay the balance in his partnership account. *A*, *B* and *C* would then share equally in the remaining $60,000—each would be paid $20,000.

B. CORPORATIONS

1. DISSOLUTION

Dissolution is a possible "end game" for the corporation as well as the partnership. Dissolution, of course, means terminating the corporation's existence as an entity. This is in contrast to one or more stockholders of a corporation selling all of their stock in the corporation. For, example, if A and B, the sole owners of the AB Furniture Store, Inc. sell all of their stock in the AB Furniture Store, Inc. to X, who continues to operate the business, this is merely a change in ownership and not an end game for the corporation.

Dissolution is a much less common end game for corporations, then for partnerships, because perpetual existence and continuity of life are fundamental attributes of a corporation. However sometimes corporations are dissolved. Two types of dissolutions are authorized by the corporate statutes of all states—**voluntary dissolution** and **involuntary dissolution.** Other than sharing a common name, these two procedures have little else in common.

Voluntary Dissolution is a routine corporate procedure authorized by all state corporation statutes. Corporation statutes generally require that "voluntary dissolution" of the corporation be recommended by a majority of the directors and then approved by 2/3 of the shares entitled to vote. Cf. MBCA § 14.02. Ultimately, articles of dissolution are filed with the Secretary of State.

Involuntary Dissolution is a procedure under which dysfunctional shareholders who want a corporate divorce turn to the courts for relief. The state corporation statutes generally provide for judicial dissolution in a proceeding brought by a shareholder who establishes that "those in control of the corporation have acted ... in a manner that is illegal, oppressive, or fraudulent." Cf. MBCA § 14.30(2). Involuntary dissolutions (also called "judicial dissolutions") were previously discussed in § V.B.3.d.(2), *supra*.

In both voluntary and involuntary dissolution of a corporation, it is important to remember that: (1) the corporation continues after dissolution for the limited purpose of "winding up," (2) the creditors must be paid in full before the shareholders get anything from the dissolution and (3) the shareholders are not personally liable for the corporation's debts even if the corporation's creditors are not paid in full from the dissolution.

2. FRIENDLY ACQUISITIONS

Another possible end game for a corporation is some type of business combination. Business combinations can take a variety of forms. In fact, few corporate transactions provide the participants with so many different options for achieving the same basic economic end result as business combinations (also known as mergers and acquisitions). Most of the details regarding the various types of mergers and acquisitions are beyond the scope of the basic business course (and this book). However, you need to be aware of certain basics which are often covered in the basic course in business associations. Almost all law schools offer an advanced course on mergers and acquisitions. Students having an interest in practicing business law should consider taking that course.

First, you should be aware that business combinations take place in two different environments—**friendly acquisitions** and **hostile takeovers.** I will discuss certain concepts and legal issues that arse in friendly acquisitions in this subsection and will discuss certain concepts and legal issues that arise in hostile takeovers in the next subsection.

Friendly acquisitions are usually structured in one of three basic ways: (1) **Statutory Merger**, (2) **Purchase of Assets** or (3) **Purchase of Stock**. There are many variations on each of the three basic types of transactions and thus many hybrids, but for purposes of teaching and learning it is helpful to think in terms of these three basic types of transactions. The route taken in effecting a friendly acquisition can lead to different results, from a legal, tax or business prospective, although the basic bottom line result ends up pretty much the same.

a. Merger

In a merger, two or more business entities combine into one business entity. For example, assume Bubba's Burritos, Inc., a privately held chain of Mexican restaurants, merges into McDonald's Corporation, a large publicly held company.

In this example, McDonald's would be referred to as the "surviving corporation" and Bubba's Burritos would be referred to as the "disappearing corporation" because it would in fact, and in law, disappear. MBCA § 11.06, typical of state corporate statutes, provides: "When a merger takes effect ... the separate existence of every corporation except the surviving corporation ceases."

(1) Effects of a Merger

The merger agreement governs the effects of a merger on the shareholders of the disappearing corporation. The merger agreement can provide for the issuance of stock of the surviving corporation to the shareholders of the disappearing corporation. Alternatively, the shareholders of the disappearing corporation can be paid cash (called a "cash out merger") or they can be paid a combination of cash and stock. All this depends on the terms of the deal the parties negotiate.

The state corporate statutes govern the effects of a merger on the creditors of the disappearing corporation. Typically, the surviving corporation gets both the assets and the liabilities of the disappearing corporation. In other words, creditors of the disappearing corporation become creditors of the surviving corporation.

Think about the possible effects of a merger on the surviving corporation and its shareholders. New assets, new liabilities, possibly new shareholders. To control the effects of the merger on the surviving corporation, deals are sometimes structured as triangular mergers or as consolidations. These are examples of common variations (beyond the scope of this book) on the methods of acquisitions discussed.

(2) Shareholder Protection

Because of the effect of a merger on shareholders of both the surviving and disappearing corporations, shareholders of both corporations, both by statute and under the case law are given several different types of legal protection. The two most common are: (1) sue the directors who approved the merger alleging breach of the duty of care or duty of loyalty and (2) vote against the merger and assert dissenting shareholder's right of appraisal.

(a) Sue the Directors Who Approved the Merger for Breach of Duty of Care or of Duty of Loyalty

As required by the MBCA and other corporate statutes, the board of directors of each of the merging corporations must agree on a plan of merger. See MBCA § 11.02. As we have seen from our earlier consideration of cases such as *Smith v. Van Gorkom* (Del. 1985), discussed in § VI.A.2.a, *supra*, shareholders who are dissatisfied with what they receive in a merger sometimes sue the directors, who approved the merger, alleging they breached their duty of care in approving the merger.[2]

Shareholders may also sue directors for breach of the duty of loyalty when a director engages in self-dealing or is on both sides of the deal. We have previously considered *Weinberger v. UOP, Inc.* (Del. 1983), discussed *in* § VI.B.2.b, *supra*. Recall that case involved a cash out merger of UOP into its parent corporation Signal. The *Weinberger* case established the so called "intrinsic fairness" test which requires both "fair dealing" and "fair price" in cash out mergers and held that Signal failed to

---

2. Shareholders may also sue under Rule 10b–5 under the 34 Act, if they can show "deception" in connection with the merger. See § VII.B.2, *supra*.

meet either prong of the test in the UOP merger transaction.

(b) Vote Against the Merger and Assert Dissenting Shareholders' Right of Appraisal

Subject to limited exceptions, a merger requires not only approval by the board of directors of each of the merging companies, but also the approval of the shareholders. A single shareholder's vote against a merger will not prevent the merger from happening. While state corporation statutes vary as to what level of approval is required, no state requires unanimous approval of the shareholders for a merger. Instead of providing a veto to shareholders who oppose the merger, state corporations statutes provide shareholders with **"appraisal rights."** See, *e.g.*, Del. § 262.

A shareholder who opposes a merger and complies with the detailed statutory requirements in Del. § 262 (or MBCA chapter 13 or the relevant state corporation statute) has more than the right to have her shares "appraised" or valued. Rather, a shareholder who properly asserts her dissenting shareholder's right of appraisal can compel the corporation to pay her in cash the "fair value" of her shares as determined by the judicial appraisal process.

To illustrate, *S* is a 10% shareholder of T Co. which merges into A, Inc. No more T Co.; no more T Co. shares. The merger agreement values T Co. at $3 million and provides that T Co. shareholders will receive consideration that has a value of $3 million. This consideration can be A, Inc. stock, or other stock, or other property or cash. Cf. MBCA § 11.01. As a 10% shareholder, *S* would

get consideration with a value of $300,000. *S* instead
"complies with the detailed statutory requirements" and
properly asserts her dissenting shareholder's right of
appraisal. What if the court decides that the "fair value"
of T Co. was $5 million, not $3 million? Even though T
Co. only received consideration with a value of $3 mil-
lion, *S*, as a dissenting shareholder who "complies with
the detailed statutory requirements" has a right to be
paid $500,000 in cash from T Co. This will mean not only
more for *S* but less for T Co.'s other shareholders. T Co.
will only have consideration with a value of $2,500,0000
(not $2,700,000) to distribute to the other shareholders.

Note the limiting phrase in the preceding paragraph:
"Complies with the detailed statutory requirements."
The statutory appraisal rights commonly require shareholders wishing to assert appraisal rights to comply with
complex and exacting notice and procedural requirements. See, *e.g.* Del. § 262 and MBCA Chapter 13.

While detailed statutory provisions govern how shareholders must assert their right to be paid "fair value,"
there are virtually no statutory provisions governing how
a court determines what "fair value" is. There are,
however, a number of judicially developed standards for
determining the "fair value" of the dissenting shares.

b. Purchase of Assets

As an alternative to a statutory merger, one corporation can sell all of its assets to another corporation, in
consideration for cash, stock of the acquiring corporation
or a combination of the two. For example, assume that
instead of merging into McDonald's Corporation, Bub-

ba's Burritos sells all of its assets to McDonald's. The overall economic impact of the sale of assets transaction would be substantially the same as that of the merger transaction. However, if the transaction is a sale of assets rather than a statutory merger, the effect on shareholders and creditors is different.[3]

(1) Effect of Purchase of Assets on Shareholders

If Bubba's Burritos merges into McDonald's, then the shareholders of Bubba's Burritos receive McDonald's stock or cash from McDonald's. Similarly, if Bubba's Burritos sells all of its assets to McDonald's then Bubba's Burritos, Inc., will receive McDonald's stock or cash from McDonald's which can be distributed to its shareholders. The economic consequences to Bubba's Burritos' shareholders and McDonald's shareholders of a purchase of assets are substantially the same as the economic consequences of a merger.

The legal rights of Bubba's Burritos and McDonald's shareholders in a purchase of assets are, however, different from the legal rights of the shareholders in a merger. While state corporation statutes require a corporation to obtain the approval of its shareholders in order to sell all or substantially all of its assets, Delaware and most states do not provide appraisal rights for the shareholders of the selling corporation. More significantly, under most state corporate statutes, the shareholders of the acquiring corporation have neither appraisal rights nor the right to vote on their corporation's buying the assets.

3. There are also differences in the tax consequence, which are covered in the course on taxation of business entities.

(2) Effect of Purchase of Assets on the Creditors

There are also significant differences in the effect on the creditors of Bubba's Burritos, Inc., which depend on whether Bubba's Burritos merges into McDonald's or sells all its assets to McDonald's. Recall that if Bubba's Burritos, Inc. merges into McDonald's, the merger provisions of the relevant state corporate law makes the creditors of Bubba's Burritos, Inc. creditors of McDonald's.

There are no comparable statutory provisions making a buyer of the assets of a corporation liable to that corporation's creditors. And, the general common law rule is that the buyer of a corporation's assets is not liable for the selling corporation's debts. Accordingly, if Bubba's Burritos sold its assets to McDonald's, creditors of Bubba's Burritos could not collect from McDonald's. Rather, Bubba's Burritos creditors would be limited to collecting their claims from Bubba's Burritos.

There will still be a Bubba's Burritos, Inc. to collect from. By selling all of its assets, Bubba's Burritos, Inc. may be going out of the burrito business but it continues to exist as a legal entity. Saying the same thing differently—a corporation's sale of assets does not automatically terminate the legal existence of the corporate entity. Often, however, sale of all of a corporation's assets is followed by the corporation's dissolution—which does terminate its legal existence, as already discussed.

(3) The de facto merger doctrine

The de facto merger doctrine is a judge made doctrine that may come into play in a sale of assets transactions and impact the rights of both shareholders and creditors. The rationale behind the de facto merger doctrine is that since the end result of a sale of asset transaction is substantially the same as a merger, the impact on shareholders and creditors should be equivalent.—*i.e.* the law should treat the transaction like a statutory merger, with the effect that the purchasing corporation should automatically assume the debt of the acquired corporation and shareholders should have appraisal rights comparable to those in a statutory merger. The leading case applying the de facto merger approach is *Farris v. Glen Alden Corp.* (Pa. 1958). Subsequent cases have distinguished *Farris* and today the case is considered, at best, a minority rule.

c. Purchase of Stock

A third way to structure a friendly acquisition is for one corporation to buy all or most of another corporation's outstanding stock. In our example, McDonald's could buy a controlling block of Bubba's Burritos stock from some or all of Bubba's Burritos shareholders. As consideration for the purchase of such shares McDonald's could either issue the selling shareholders shares or McDonald's stock or pay such selling shareholders cash for the shares acquired.

McDonald's could then either operate Bubba's Burritos as subsidiary of McDonald's or liquidate the Bubba's Burritos, Inc. through either a parent-subsidiary merger or a dissolution.

Despite the similarity of outcome (McDonald's acquires ownership and control of Bubba's Burritos under all three types of transactions), you should notice an obvious, but critical difference between a purchase of stock and both a merger and a purchase of assets. Bubba's Burritos, Inc., as an entity, is not affected by the stock transaction. Only its ownership changes. Equally obvious, the purchase of stock does not require any agreement between the board of the purchasing company (McDonald's in our example) and the board of the company which is being acquired (Bubba's Burritos in our example). The deal is between McDonald's and the individual shareholders of Bubba's Burritos, whose stock McDonald's is buying. This means the acquisition can go forward even if the board of the corporation being acquired opposes the deal. This is why, as we will see in the next section, stock purchase is the vehicle used in hostile takeovers of publicly held companies.

Many factors—business, tax and legal considerations—may play a part in determining how to structure a friendly acquisition. Operating considerations may also be considered. For example, since Bubba's Burritos sells a different product than McDonald's (Mexican food rather than hamburgers) it might make operating sense to keep the entity alive and operate Bubba's Burritos as a subsidiary of McDonald's.

Finally, I will mention that some people refer to the three types of friendly acquisitions, discussed above, as *A*, *B* and *C* reorganizations (*A*—mergers; *B*—purchase of stock; and *C*—purchase of assets). This is a reference to subsections of section 368 of the IRC, which governs the tax consequences of mergers and acquisitions. This information may become relevant to you, if your professor is a tax expert. Tax lawyers have a tendency to communicate by citing sections of the IRC, which is a fact also worth knowing when you get out in practice and communicate with tax lawyers.

3. HOSTILE TAKEOVERS

The term "hostile takeover" is used to describe an attempt to gain control of a corporation over the objection of that corporation's management. In other words, if Alpha Corporation wants to acquire Beta Corporation and Alpha's management does not believe that Beta's management will be amenable to negotiating a friendly acquisition, Alpha may bypass Beta's management and make an offer directly to Beta's shareholders.

The acquiring company or individual is politely described as the "bidder." More colorfully, the acquiring company may be described as the "raider" or the "shark." The company whose stock is targeted for acquisition is called the "target company."

Sometimes control of a target company can be acquired by buying a controlling block of outstanding shares from a control person or members of a control group. Acquiring control by buying the interests of a control shareholders is a type of friendly acquisition. Hostile takeovers involve situations where the bidder is not able to acquire a sufficient number of shares of the target company to gain control from a single shareholder or an allied group. In these situations the bidder does not want to pay for any shares of the target company unless it is able to buy a sufficient number of shares to gain control of the target company.

If the target company is a public company, as is typically the case in hostile takeovers, the usual process for acquiring sufficient shares is a **"tender offer."** It is referred to as a tender offer because the existing shareholders are being asked to tender their shares for sale. In a tender offer, the bidder offers cash or securities of the bidder (or a package consisting of a combination of cash and securities) to the stockholders of the target company who tender their stock. The tender offer will almost always be conditioned on a sufficient number of the target's shares being tendered to ensure that the bidder gains control of the target company.

a. Defensive Measures and Fiduciary Duties

While taking over control of a company by acquiring a majority of that target company's outstanding stock does not require any action by the management of the target company's board of directors, it usually triggers defensive action by the management of the target company to prevent the takeover. Lawyers for companies that have been or are likely to be targets of hostile takeovers have been creative in developing (and naming) responses to takeover threats: "poison pills," "golden parachutes," "shark repellent bylaws," "white knights" and "pac-man defenses." All of these are colorful names for specific actions taken by management of the target company designed to prevent or repel a takeover. They are referred to as "defensive measures."

Defensive measures are simply maneuvers or transactions undertaken for the purpose of making it more difficult for the bidder to acquire control of the target company. When management uses defensive measures to prevent or repel a takeover, the action is often challenged on grounds that the officers and directors of the target company breached their fiduciary duties by using specific defensive measures to defend against the hostile takeover.

The courts, particularly the Delaware courts, have developed a body of case law which deals with the standard to apply in reviewing challenges to these defenses. These Delaware judicial opinions are based on specific facts and the facts tend to be extremely complex.

In broad overview, these cases raise conflict of interest problems similar to the conflict of interest problem we have already discussed in other contexts. Officers and directors of a target company who oppose a takeover of their company have an obvious conflict of interest. There is a high likelihood that they will lose their jobs if the takeover is successful. This is not, however, as clear cut a conflict of interest as when a director is doing business with the corporation or usurping a corporate opportunity. Management of the target company may be opposing the takeover for reasons they honestly and reasonably believe are in the best interests of the target company. On the other hand they may be opposing the takeover merely to protect their jobs.

This raises the question: **How far can management go in their defensive measures without violating their fiduciary duties**? The question is difficult, because the answer depends on the motives or subjective state of mind of the officers and directors. Often there are multiple motives. And all of this is complicated by the size of the deals, which are often large, and the complex nature of the facts usually encountered in these lawyer intensive take over battles.[4]

That having been said, while there are many factually sensitive variations and nuances, the foundation for the rules applied in cases involving the scope of defensive measures rests on tests developed by the Delaware Supreme Court in two famous cases, both decided in 1985:

> *Unocal Corp. v. Mesa Petroleum Co.* (Del. 1985) (the "Unocal case") in which Mesa Petroleum Co., which was controlled by T. Boone Pickens, attempted to acquire control of Unocal; and

> *Revlon, Inc. v. MacAndrews & Forbes Holdings, Inc.* (Del. 1985) (the "Revlon case") in which Ronald Perelman, through his holding company, MacAndrews & Forbes, acquired control of Revlon.

These two cases established two basic doctrines which have been applied in numerous subsequent cases involving litigation arising out of takeover attempts. Today these cases are part of the colorful jargon of takeover law. Lawyers often refer to companies "being in the Revlon Mode" or "invoking their Unocal Defenses."

The *Unocal* case speaks to the question of what defensive measures are proper.

The *Revlon* case speaks to the question of when management of the target company has to give up the fight—*i.e.*, when they can no longer engage in defensive measures.

4. The law of hostile takeovers is not as complex as most students perceive it to be, but students often have difficulty understanding the opinions because the opinions are usually fact specific and the facts tend to be extremely complex.

In the *Revlon* case, the management of Revlon, the target company, did not want Mr. Perelman to acquire control of Revlon. It was clear that if Mr. Perelman acquired control of Revlon he would terminate the senior managers of Revlon. Looking for a "white knight," Revlon gave Forsman Little & Co. an option to acquire two of Revlon's most desirable divisions (*i.e.*, "crown jewels" of Revlon) for over $100 million less than the appraised value of the two divisions. Presumably, the management of Revlon felt that if Revlon no longer owned these "crown jewels," Mr. Perelman would no longer want to acquire control of Revlon.

The Delaware Supreme Court invalidated the Forsman Little option and held that once a takeover becomes inevitable, the board must discontinue defensive measures and assume the role of an auctioneer. Their fiduciary duties required management to maximize shareholder values—*i.e.*, get the best offer possible for the target company or its assets.

Obviously, questions have arisen in subsequent cases as to: (1) what is the best offer and (2) when must a company discontinue defensive action (in the jargon of tender offer litigation—when is the company in the "Revlon Mode").

The factual variations are infinite and beyond the scope of this book. But two basic points can be made: (1) the highest price, though usually the most single important factor, does not necessarily equate to the best offer and (2) a company gets in the Revlon Mode when it becomes clear from the facts that the company will no longer remain independent in its present form.

The main consequences of the *Revlon* case are: (1) if the target company is in the "Revlon Mode," management has to give up the fight but (2) the converse is also true—until the company gets into the Revlon Mode it can use defensive measures— its management can fight to make it more difficult for the bidder to acquire their company.

The *Unocal* case sets the limits on the kind of defensive measures the target company's management can take prior to getting into the "Revlon Mode." Again, in the jargon of tender offer litigation, lawyers say that "until it gets in the Revlon Mode" a target company can invoke its "Unocal Defenses"—meaning assert defenses that meet the test laid down in the *Unocal* case.

The *Unocal* case sets forth a broad based test by which the courts determine whether or not the board of the target company went too far in their defensive actions. The test fashioned by the Delaware Supreme Court in *Unocal* puts the burden on management of the target company to prove that:

(1) they acted in good faith,

(2) based on reasonable investigation they felt there was a threat to their company, and

(3) the defensive measures they took bear a reasonable relationship to the threat that they perceived.

In general, this test requires management to show that it took defensive measures for the purpose of protecting the company's interests, rather than for the purpose of protecting managements' jobs or negotiating a better severance package.

b. Statutory regulations

While there are no court-imposed fiduciary duty limits to takeover efforts by the bidder company's board of directors (presumably because the bidder's board does not owe a fiduciary duty to the target company), there are federal and state statutory regulations. The details of both are outside the scope of this book and are not likely matters you need to be concerned with in the basic business associations course.

In 1968, Congress added sections 13 (d) and (e) and sections 14 (d), (e) and (f) to the 34 Act. These amendments, known as the Williams Act, regulate various aspects of tender offers and related matters. The Williams Act applies only to tender offers for companies registered under § 12 of the 34 Act (the same subset of companies subject to the proxy rules discussed in § V.B.4.b., *supra).* The Williams Act mainly requires disclosure by bidders or perspective bidders. It also contains substantive rules which prohibit a bidder from using certain tactics characterized as high-pressure or fraudulent.

In addition, many states have enacted statutes that make hostile takeovers more difficult, regardless of whether there has been compliance with the Williams Act.

4. BANKRUPTCY

For a number of corporations and other business associations, the end game is played in the bankruptcy courts. Chapter 11 and then sometimes Chapter 7.

That is another law school course. And, another nutshell.

*

INDEX

References are to Pages

————

—A—

—B—

—C—

—D—

EXEMPTIONS FROM REGISTRATION
See Federal Securities Laws; Registration of Securities—When Required

EXIT RULES, 30
Corporations, 358–69
Partnerships, 349–57

—F—

FEDERAL SECURITIES LAWS
Federal regulation of fraud, 220–25
Federal regulation of proxy solicitation, 147–51
Federal regulation of tender offers, 375
Overview of 33 and 34 Acts, 298–300
Private Placements, 309–18
Public offerings, 301–05
Sarbanes–Oxley Law, 18
See also Insider Trading; Proxy Rules; Regulation D; Rule 10b–5

FIDUCIARY, 160–61

FIDUCIARY DUTIES
Agents, 20
Close corporations, 194–99
Control shareholders, 183–93
Directors and officers, 161–182
Duty of care, 162–73
Duty of loyalty, 173–82
Freeze-out mergers, 186–89
Hostile takeovers, 370–74
LLCs, 199–202
Partners, 193–94

FINANCING, 277–81

FINANCIAL STATEMENTS
See Accounting

FORMATION
Corporations, 59–60
Limited liability companies, 72–74
Partnerships,
    General partnerships, 52–56
    Limited liability partnerships, 57–59
    Limited partnerships, 56–67